327
DOT

D0526147

Imperial Encounters

ROL'

U.W.E.

23 JUN 1999

Library Services

FR - 21962
LL

BORDERLINES

Imperial Encounters
The Politics of Representation in
North-South Relations

ROXANNE LYNN DOTY

U.W.E.

8 SEP 1999

Library Services

BORDERLINES, VOLUME 5

University of Minnesota Press

Minneapolis

London

Published with assistance from the Margaret S. Harding Memorial
Endowment honoring the first director of the University of Minnesota Press.

Copyright 1996 by the Regents of the University of Minnesota

A version of chapter 4 was published as "Foreign Policy as Social
Construction: A Post-Positivist Analysis of U.S. Counterinsurgency Policy
in the Philippines" in *International Studies Quarterly* 37, no. 3 (1993);
reprinted by permission.

All rights reserved. No part of this publication may be reproduced, stored
in a retrieval system, or transmitted, in any form or by any means, electronic,
mechanical, photocopying, recording, or otherwise, without the prior
written permission of the publisher.

Published by the University of Minnesota Press
111 Third Avenue South, Suite 290
Minneapolis, MN 55401-2520
Printed in the United States of America on acid-free paper
Second printing, 1997
Library of Congress Cataloging-in-Publication Data
Doty, Roxanne Lynn.
    Imperial encounters : the politics of representation in North–
South relations / Roxanne Lynn Doty.
        p.   cm. — (Borderlines ; v. 5)
    Includes bibliographical references and index.
    ISBN 0-8166-2762-2
    ISBN 0-8166-2763-0 (pbk.)
    1. International relations — Social aspects.   2. Developing
countries — Foreign relations — Social aspects.   3. Discourse
analysis.   4. Imperialism — Social aspects.   I. Title.   II. Series:
Borderlines (Minneapolis, Minn.) ; v. 5
JX1395.D645   1996
327 — dc20   95-46540

The University of Minnesota is an
equal-opportunity educator and employer.

Contents

Acknowledgments

There are numerous individuals whose direct or indirect influence was indispensable to this project. Most directly, I would like to thank Raymond Duvall and David Sylvan for their encouragement and confidence when I began this project at the University of Minnesota, and for their encouragement for me to see it through to completion. I am indebted to Pat McGowan for stimulating my initial interest in North/South relations and to Richard Ashley for his many critical writings. I would also like to thank the editors of this series, Michael Shapiro and David Campbell, and Lisa Freeman of the University of Minnesota Press, as well as Suresht Bald and one anonymous reviewer. This book is dedicated to Kristen Doty, who makes it all worthwhile; I hope she will grow up with a critical awareness of some of the more damaging representational strategies at work around her.

Introduction

While scholars and policy makers in the North have been preoccupied with events in post–cold war Eastern Europe and the former Soviet Union, the "third world" has by no means ceased to be of concern. North-South relations continue to be an important aspect of the post–cold war world.[1] To say this, however, presumes the a priori existence of the North and the South as unproblematic entities that encounter and interact with one another. North-South relations are then conceived as a realm of theory and practice concerned with these interactions. The issues encompassed by these interactions have included a wide range of topics including colonialism, imperialism, neoimperialism, cold war rivalries, concerns with the South's economic and political development, foreign aid, and the promotion of democracy and human rights. Most recently North-South relations have focused on international terrorism, the international drug trade, nuclear proliferation in the South, immigration and refugee movements from the South to the North, and international concerns with the spread of AIDS. Traditional, modernist orientations ranging from liberalism to neorealism to Marxist approaches would suggest that, while these issues are complex, they constitute the nature of North-South relations.[2]

To suggest that these issues exhaust the content of North-South relations, however, obscures the *productivity* of the practices that have been important aspects of these relations. In other words, the various issues that have been central to North-South relations have been characterized by practices that have been implicated in the production of meanings and identities. These meanings and identities cannot be separated from the relations that have developed between the North and the South. In contrast to traditional orientations, I suggest that North-South relations have been about a great deal more than these issues. While encounters between the North and the South have indeed been focused on these topics, the issues themselves have provided the contexts within which identities have been constructed and reconstructed. In the process of attempting to formulate policy, resolve problems, and come to terms with various issues, subjects and objects themselves have been constructed. This study conceives of the field of North-South relations, in all of its dimensions, as constitutive of the identities of these entities. Arguably one of the most consequential elements present in all of the encounters between the North and the South has been the practice(s) of *representation* by the North of the South. By representation I mean the ways in which the South has been discursively represented by policy makers, scholars, journalists, and others in the North. This does not refer to the "truth" and "knowledge" that the North has discovered and accumulated about the South, but rather to the ways in which regimes of "truth" and "knowledge" have been produced.[3] The contexts within which specific encounters have taken place and the issues relevant to these contexts have been occasions for the proliferation and circulation of various representations.

Thinking of North-South relations in terms of representation reorients and complicates the way we understand this particular aspect of global politics. North-South relations become more than an area of theory and practice in which various policies have been enacted and theories formulated; they become a realm of politics wherein the very identities of peoples, states, and regions are constructed through representational practices. Thinking in terms of representational practices calls our attention to an economy of abstract binary oppositions that we routinely draw upon and that frame our thinking. Developed/underdeveloped, "first world"/"third world," core/periphery, metropolis/satellite, advanced industrialized/less developed, modern/traditional, and real states/quasi states are just a few that readily come to mind. While there is nothing natural, inevitable, or arguably even useful about these divisions, they remain widely circulated and accepted as legitimate ways to categorize regions and peoples of the world. Thinking in terms of representational practices highlights the arbitrary, constructed, and political nature of these and many other oppositions through which we have come to "know" the world and its inhabitants and that have enabled and justified certain practices and policies.

Conceptualizing North-South relations in terms of representational practices, this study undertakes a *critical genealogy* of North-South relations. It is necessarily partial in that a complete genealogy would cover a great deal more terrain—spatially, temporally, and intellectually—than is possible in a single study. What I seek to do in this study is to isolate several specific historical encounters between the Anglo-European world and the imperialized countries. I refer to these as imperial encounters. While the term *encounter* implies the presence of two entities (i.e., the North and the South), the term *imperial encounters* is meant to convey the idea of asymmetrical encounters in which one entity has been able to construct "realities" that were taken seriously and acted upon and the other entity has been denied equal degrees or kinds of agency. The representations I focus on are predominantly those by the North. The Northern narratives that accompanied its encounters with various regions of the South are imbued with unquestioned presumptions regarding freedom, democracy, and self-determination as well as the identities of the subjects who are entitled to enjoy these things. These narratives serve as windows onto more global systems of representation. Within these specific encounters we can locate elements of both continuity and discontinuity over time, and of both repetition and variation across locales in the rhetoric that has discursively constructed what has come to be known as the "third world." Equally important, though, has been the simultaneous construction of the "first world." As Said pointed out in his seminal study, Orientalism "has less to do with the Orient than it does with 'our' world" (1979: 12). In a similar vein, the "third world" has also served as a site for the self-elaboration of the "first world" and the representational practices that have constructed one have simultaneously constructed the other. If, as Todorov (1984: 5) has suggested, the conquest of America heralded and established our present identity, subsequent imperial encounters have both destabilized and sustained the identities of the "first world" self and the "third world" other.

The importance of undertaking an empirical study that proceeds from this conceptualization is that analysis moves away from the conventional *why* questions to *how* questions. Analysis examines not only how social identities get constructed, but also what practices and policies are thereby made possible. Why questions generally take as unproblematic the *possibility* that particular policies and practices could happen. They presuppose the identities of social actors and a background of social meanings. In contrast, how questions examine how meanings are produced and attached to various social subjects and objects, thus constituting particular interpretive dispositions that create certain possibilities and preclude others.

How questions thus highlight an important aspect of *power* that why questions too often neglect: the way in which power works to constitute particular modes of subjectivity and interpretive dispositions. Indeed, the kind of how questions I address in this study are implicitly questions of power. This is not the kind of power that pre-existing social actors possess and use. Rather, it is a kind of power that produces meanings, subject identities, their interrelationships, and a range of imaginable conduct. *Power as productive* is central to the kind of how questions raised in this study.[4]

REPRESENTATION AND GLOBAL POLITICS

The question of representation has historically been excluded from the academic study of international relations.[5] This exclusion has, to an important degree, shaped the horizons of the discipline. This has been especially significant when it comes to North-South relations because in an important sense this whole subfield revolves around the differences between these two entities. Sometimes these differences are represented in primarily economic terms (e.g., levels of development), and sometimes in terms of military power differentials. Representations of economic and military power differences, however, take place within political and social circumstances in which other kinds of differences are explicitly or implicitly presumed. Because the question of representation has been excluded, the historical construction and consequences of these differences have not been considered legitimate realms of inquiry. This exclusion has in many instances resulted in the complicity of international relations scholarship with particular constructions of the South and of the "reality" of the South's place in international relations.

This study begins with the premise that representation is an inherent and important aspect of global political life and therefore a critical and legitimate area of inquiry. International relations are inextricably bound up with discursive practices that put into circulation representations that are taken as "truth." The goal of analyzing these practices is not to reveal essential truths that have been obscured, but rather to examine *how* certain representations underlie the production of knowledge and identities and how these representations make various courses of action possible. As Said (1979: 21) notes, there is no such thing as a delivered presence, but there is a *re-presence,* or representation. Such an assertion does not deny the existence of the material world, but rather suggests that material objects and subjects are constituted as such within discourse. So, for example, when U.S. troops march into Grenada, this is certainly "real," though the march of troops across a piece of geographic space is in itself singularly uninteresting and socially irrelevant outside of the representations that produce meaning. It is only when "American" is attached to the troops and "Grenada" to the geographic space that meaning is created. What the physical behavior itself *is,* though, is still far from certain until discursive practices constitute it as an "invasion," a "show of force," a "training exercise," a "rescue," and so on. What is "really" going on in such a situation is inextricably linked to the discourse within which it is located. To attempt a neat separation between discursive and nondiscursive practices, understanding the former as purely linguistic, assumes a series of dichotomies — thought/reality, appearance/essence, mind/matter, word/world, subjective/objective — that a critical genealogy calls into question. Against this, the perspective taken here affirms the material and performative character of discourse.[6]

In suggesting that global politics, and specifically the aspect that has to do with relations between the North and the South, is linked to representational practices I am suggesting that the issues and concerns that constitute these relations occur within a "reality" whose content has for the most part been defined by the representational practices of the "first world." Focusing on discursive practices enables one to examine how the processes that produce "truth" and "knowledge" work and how they are articulated with the exercise of political, military, and economic power.

Drawing especially upon the writings of Michel Foucault and Jacques Derrida, as well as extensions of their work by Laclau (1990), and Laclau and Mouffe (1990), I understand a discourse to be a structured, relational totality. A discourse delineates the terms of intelligibility whereby a particular "reality" can be known and acted upon. When we speak of a discourse we may be referring to a specific group of texts, but also importantly to the social practices to which those texts are inextricably linked. To refer to a discourse as a "structured totality" is not meant to suggest that it is closed, stable, and fixed once and for all. On the contrary, a discourse is inherently open-ended and incomplete. Its exterior limits are constituted by other discourses that are themselves also open, inherently unstable, and always in the process of being articulated. This understanding of discourse implies an overlapping quality to different discourses. Any fixing of a discourse and the identities that are constructed by it, then, can only ever be of a partial nature. It is the overflowing and incomplete nature of discourses that opens up spaces for change, discontinuity, and variation.

The partial fixity within a discourse enables one to make sense of things, enables one to "know" and to act upon what one "knows." This duality, that is, the impossibility of ultimate closure together with the fact of partial fixation, is of key importance.[7] Derrida's concept of differance, which suggests that meaning is at once differential and deferred, highlights this dual nature of discourse. Meaning is not simply the result of differentiation, but is also the result of deferral, that is, the putting off of encounter with the missing presence that the sign is presumed to be moving toward. The circulation of signs defers the moment in which we encounter the thing itself (Derrida 1982: 9). "Every concept is involved in a chain within which it refers to the other, to other concepts, by means of a *systematic play of differences*" (ibid.: 11).

This should not be taken to imply total contingency and the impossibility of any meaning at all. Rather, the play within language is both made possible and limited by a dominant signifier, the center of a discursive structure, the point where the substitution of signifiers is no longer possible (Derrida 1978: 279). The signifying chain stops. The task of a critical analysis is to deconstruct the center itself, to expose its arbitrariness and contingency and thereby call attention to the play of power in constructing all centers.

Just as Derrida suggests that "one could reconsider all the pairs of opposites on which philosophy is constructed and on which our discourse lives, not in order to see opposition erase itself but to see what indicates that each of the terms must appear as the differance of the other, as the other different and deferred in the economy of the same" (1982: 17), one could make a similar suggestion regarding the politics of North-South relations. We could reconsider all the pairs of opposites on which these relations have been constructed to see that each of the terms appears as the differance of the other: the "third world" as the different and deferred "first world," the periphery as the different and deferred core. This calls attention to the importance of the periphery in constructing the core itself. Discussing Said's work, Young (1990: 139) suggests that Orientalism articulated an internal dislocation within Western culture, which consistently fantasizes itself as constituting some kind of integral totality. The "essence" of this integral totality exists only vis-à-vis its different and deferred other.[8]

The discourses that have been instantiated in the various imperial encounters between North and South have been characterized by the active movement of different forces, which creates the possibility of meaning. The fact that particular meanings and identities have been widely taken to be fixed and true is indicative of the inextricable link between power and knowledge. This link, in effect, stops the signifying chain, at least temporarily, creates a center, and permits meanings and identities to become naturalized, taken for granted. The naturalization of meaning has had consequences ranging from the appropriation of land, labor, and resources to the subjugation and extermination of entire groups of people. It has also, however, always been incomplete, implying the possibility for transformation as well as the need for reinscribing the status quo. Such an understanding suggests the need for a critical examination of the coexistence of the seemingly opposed but inseparable forces by which a discourse is partially fixed but by which it also becomes impossible to institute total closure.

GLOBAL AUTHORITY AND HEGEMONY

The exclusion of the issue of representation from international relations has had important implications for the way we understand the concept of hegemony. Despite the widespread use and diverse understandings of this concept in international relations, the discursive aspect of hegemony remains relatively underexplored.[9] While understandings of hegemony range from narrow conceptions such as a preponderance of military resources to a broader Gramscian conceptualization, one can note that existing definitions contain an important a priori presumption of given categories of identity: for example, class, state elites, great powers. This a priori givenness both presumes the relevance of particular categories (and the irrelevance of others) and at the same time mystifies the discursive construction of the categories themselves.[10]

The perspective I take in this study suggests that the hegemonic dimension of global politics is inextricably linked to representational practices. The exercise of consent and coercion does not occur within a given society inhabited by given social actors. Rather, hegemony involves the very production of categories of identity and the society of which they are a part. Hegemonic practices are those practices that seek to create the fixedness of meaning that my earlier discussion suggested is ultimately impossible. The very possibility of hegemony then exists in the always open, always in process nature of discourse.[11] It thus makes sense to suggest that the hegemonic dimension of politics increases as it becomes more difficult to fix meanings in any stable way. Laclau (1990: 28) likens this difficulty to an *organic crisis* in which there is a proliferation of social elements that assume the character of *floating signifiers,* that is, signifiers whose meanings have not been fixed by virtue of being articulated into a particular dominant discursive formation. For an example, Laclau uses the signifier "democracy," which acquires particular meanings when it is articulated with other signifiers. When democracy is articulated with antifascism it takes on a different meaning than it does when it is articulated with anticommunism. Expanding on this, it can be suggested that the signifier democracy currently is being articulated with free enterprise and capitalist market principles in an attempt to constitute a hegemonic formation. Organic crises can accompany periods of change. Laclau and Mouffe suggest that the hegemonic form of politics becomes dominant only at the beginning of modern times, when the reproduction of the different social areas takes place in permanently changing conditions that constantly require the construction of new systems of differences.[12] This is particularly pertinent for this study. North-South relations have taken place within the context of expansions and (re)constructions of international society that have been characterized by permanently changing conditions, crises of identity and authority, and the continuous creation of new systems of differences. This is evident in the continuities and discontinuities found among colonial, counterinsurgency, and contemporary discourses.

Foucault's discussion (1972: chapter 2) of the unity of fields such as medicine and economics is pertinent to understanding the construction and reconstruction of hegemonic formations. He argues that unity in these fields is based on a *regularity in dispersion* rather than on (1) reference to the same object, (2) a style of statement, (3) the concepts involved, or (4) themes. These four items can also be rejected as the basis for the unity of something called the "third world" or the "first world." Since this study is suggesting that the "third world," as well as the "first world," is constituted and reconstituted through representational practices, any unity to be found would be not in the a priori existence of the objects but in the space or field of their emergence that discourses create. Nor is unity to be found in any consistent style of statement. There have been very diverse kinds of statements regarding the "third world." For example, statements made by missionary societies and anticolonial societies constitute a normative kind of statement, while statements of travel writers and historians are often, at least ostensibly, descriptive statements. Official government statements have been of both kinds as well as being prescriptive. Theoretical social science statements have consisted of a variety of kinds of statements including normative, prescriptive, and descriptive. The concepts involved in the field of study and practice of relations between the "first world" and the "third world" have similarly been multiple and varied. While certain themes have been prevalent in North-South relations, these also have been multiple, varied, and continually changing. Just note the wide variety of topics mentioned earlier that have been of concern to North-South relations.

Unity then is not to be found in a priori objects or a coherence among concepts and themes but rather in a regularity in the logic of the representational practices that have accompanied the North's many and varied encounters with the South. The goal of this study is to elucidate this regularity through an examination of multiple and varied representational practices.

REPRESENTATIONAL PRACTICES

Laclau and Mouffe (1985: 112) use the term *nodal points* to refer to privileged discursive points that fix meaning and establish positions that make predication possible. To hegemonize a content amounts to fixing its meaning around nodal points (Laclau 1990: 28). It is possible to locate representational practices in texts that work to establish these nodal points. These representational practices simultaneously construct the "other," which is often ostensibly the object of various practices, and also importantly construct the "self" vis-à-vis this "other." In this section I discuss some of the representational strategies I look for in the various texts used in this study.

One of the most important aspects of a discourse is its capacity to naturalize. Naturalization occurs through *presupposition,* which creates background knowledge that is taken to be true. This background knowledge entails an implicit theorization of how the world works and also an elaboration of the nature of its inhabitants. The North's encounters with the South have been accompanied by such implicit theorizations, however crude they have been. Naturalization can occur simply through statements of "fact," that is, ostensible descriptions of what simply "is," or through a process of substitution whereby one term in a pair of binary oppositions trades places with or merges with its counterpart from another pair. For example, the nature/culture and Oriental/European oppositions merge into new oppositions between the civilized European and the instinctual Oriental (Spurr 1993: 160).

Classification is an important rhetorical strategy that is closely linked with naturalization. The construction of classificatory schemes often serves to naturalize by placing human beings into the categories in which they "naturally" belong. Hierarchies are often established based upon the presumed essential character of various kinds of human beings. The "economy of the stereotype" is frequently at work in processes of classification. This permits a quick and easy image without the responsibility of specificity and accuracy (Morrison 1992: 67).

Foucault (1979) suggests that *surveillance* is an integral element in disciplinary practices. Procedures of observation and examination are important strategies by which human beings come to be "known," classified, and acted upon. Many of the encounters between the North and the South have been occasions for the North to gather "facts," define and monitor situations and problems, and subsequently enact policies deriving from those "facts" and definitions. Surveillance renders subjects knowable, visible objects of disciplinary power.

One significant consequence of the North's encounters with the South has been the denial of effective agency to the South. One way in which this denial occurs is through a process of *negation*. Negation has constructed various regions making up the "third world" as blank spaces waiting to be filled in by Western writing, as a "people without history," in the words of Eric Wolf (1982). Within these blank spaces the West may write such things as civilization, progress, modernization, and democracy. Imperial encounters become missions of deliverance and salvation rather than conquests and exploitations.

The rhetorical strategies found in discourses entail the *positioning* of subjects and objects vis-à-vis one another. What defines a particular kind of subject is, in large part, the relationships that subject is positioned in relative to other kinds of subjects. Naturalization, classification, surveillance, and negation, in addition to constructing subjects, establish various kinds of relationships between subjects and between subjects and objects. Some of the important kinds of relationships that position subjects are those of opposition, identity, similarity, and complementarity.

Underlying the positioning of subjects and objects are two ostensibly opposed logics that work together to simultaneously fix and subvert identities. These are the *logic of difference* and the *logic of equivalence*. The logic of difference attempts to fix the positions of social agents as stable, positive differences. Identities are presumed to be based upon foundational essences and are portrayed as being merely different from other identities. Different identities occupy specified places in a system of relations that constitute society (here international society).

The logic of equivalence reveals the contingent and unstable nature of systems of differences and subverts the positive identities created by differences. Foundational essences are revealed to be arbitrary constructions made possible by the power/knowledge nexus. Laclau and Mouffe (1985: 127) use the example of a colonized country to explain how these two opposed logics work. In such a situation the logic of difference is at work in constructing social agents occupying different positions within society. This logic works through differences in skin color, custom/culture, dress, and language. These are presumed to constitute the essence of colonial identities. The logic of equivalence is simultaneously at work, however, in that each of the contents of these differential elements is equivalent to the others in terms of their common differentiation between colonizer and colonized. The individual differences are canceled out insofar as they are used to express something identical underlying them. What that identical something is, however, is always deferred, permitting the reconstitution of relational identities through the construction of new differences. What we find, instead of positive foundational identities, is a continuous movement of differences and a continuous deferral of any transcendental signified that would enable us to identify the essence of difference.

As I will suggest throughout my analysis of specific cases, these representational strategies are intensified in times of crisis, when naturalized identities and the existing order are at risk of being called into question. This is consistent with the notion of hegemonizing practices intensifying during times of organic crisis when the North was confronted with the potential loss of control and authority.

CASES

Edward Said (1979: 16) has suggested that the act of beginning necessarily involves an act of delimitation by which something is cut out of a great mass of material. This book and the cases I have selected for it involves two important delimitations. One concerns the universe of possible cases. There have been all too many imperial encounters between the North and the South, which makes the universe of potential cases quite large. My selection, like all selections, is therefore somewhat arbitrary. Nevertheless, I believe my selections are good ones. The second delimitation is perhaps more serious and is one in which I must also plead guilty to engaging in an exclusionary practice. The representations that this study focuses on are for the most part representations of the South by the North. This study thus excludes many indigenous, local "third world" voices. This exclusion is not meant to suggest that any alternative representations that may be present in what I have excluded are unimportant. Nor do I mean to attribute passivity to those excluded voices. Rather, this study is intended to emphasize the fact that encounters between the North and the South were (and are) such that the North's representations of "reality" enabled practices of domination, exploitation, and brutality, practices that probably would have been considered unthinkable, reprehensible, and unjustifiable were an alternative "reality" taken seriously. Alternative representations did indeed exist, but they were either marginalized or systematically silenced. Indeed, ignoring alternative representations would seem to have been necessary in order for certain practices such as colonization to be made possible.

In Parts I and II I focus on two specific sets of relationships, or imperial encounters. These encounters occurred within the context of two exemplary themes in the relations between the North and the South: colonialism and counterinsurgency. The two sets of relationships are (1) the United States and the Philippines and (2) Britain and Kenya. While there have been all too many imperial encounters between the North and the South, Great Britain and the United States do seem to stand out as exemplars of the "first world." Their imperial encounters were numerous and varied, and in many respects their narratives exemplify the representational practices that continue to frame our understanding and knowledge of the "third world."

I have chosen to focus on two particular incidents within the context of the relationship between each of these hegemonic powers and one of its colonies or neocolonies. The two incidents illustrate the continuity and change, repetition and variation that occur within the politics of representation. These incidents were also accompanied by either a crisis of identity or a crisis of authority in which the naturalness of the existing order was in danger of unraveling. They are thus good illustrations of crisis, rupture, and hegemonic practices. It is at just such moments that rhetoric is intensified. These moments of crisis engendered discussion, debate, directives, and other forms of discourse that provide a source of "data" from which to examine the representational practices that attempt to reaffirm or reconstruct identities. While the focus is on these two specific cases, I make connections to the broader contexts within which these cases were located and the rhetorical practices found at this broader level. This enables me to suggest that the rhetoric in the specific instances was not idiosyncratic but rather part of a larger discursive economy through which global power and authority were exercised.

In Part III I cast my analytic net more broadly by engaging a number of contemporary discursive practices focused on North-South relations. Here I focus on the North's concern with democracy and human rights in the South. This concern has been linked with various issues such as foreign "assistance," military aid, and covert and overt intervention. I examine discourses beginning with the period when democracy in the South became a concern for United States policy makers in the mid-1960s to current discourses on the spread of democracy and increased international concern with human rights. I conclude with a chapter focusing on North American academic discourse on North-South relations.

OUTLINE OF CHAPTERS

Chapters 2 and 3 examine two different colonial discourses, one involving a decision to colonize and the other involving the issue of forced labor within a colonial context. Chapter 2 examines the representational practices present in the debates and discussions surrounding the United States' decision to annex the Philippine Islands in 1899 and the subsequent debates over what to do with the Philippines once they had been annexed. In that colonialism was in conflict with many of the principles the United States professed to cherish, this event was rife with debate. In addition, very little was known at the time about the Philippine Islands and their inhabitants, so much narrative was devoted to "describing" and coming to "know" this place and its peoples. The sources for this chapter were nearly infinite. Discussions and debates took place in scholarly journals; scholarly lectures and addresses; popular publications; newspapers; books written by travel writers, politicians, and humanitarians; and official government circles. The most prolonged and arguably the most impassioned discussions were the congressional debates. This arena of discourse was important because the annexation decision was dependent upon Senate approval. Thus, a large amount of textual data for this chapter was obtained from congressional records. These debates did not, of course, take place in a vacuum, and considerable overlap in the various arenas is evident.

Chapter 3 examines the representational practices found within the context of a "labor crisis" that occurred around the time that Kenya was formally declared a British colony. In contrast to the United States' annexation of the Philippines, British assumption of control over Kenya was not rife with discussion, commentary, and debate. The British business of colonialism was politics as usual, not a crisis that called into question honor, integrity, and self-identity. Rather, the "crisis" involved the extreme shortage of black African labor available to work on white European farms and the question of whether the British government should be involved in the use of force to obtain such labor. Occurring against the background of questions regarding the conditions to be imposed upon the nations that accepted mandates for the territories taken from Germany in World War I, then being assigned to different European powers under the provisions of the Covenant of the League of Nations, this "crisis" called into question the very foundations of Britain's imperial system. Questions had arisen concerning the purposes for which the mandatory power would be allowed to impose regulations upon the "native." Imposing forced labor in Britain's "own territory" thus had implications that went beyond East Africa. This issue was considered of "high imperial importance"; it involved principles that affected "the very foundations of our Imperial System and the methods we intend to employ in the conduct of that system in the years to come" (Lord Islington, House of Lords Debates, July 14, 1920).

Chapters 4 and 5 move away from the colonial context to a later period. Counterinsurgency provides the background for the cases I examine in these two chapters. Counterinsurgency has been one of the major contexts within which North-South encounters have occurred. While counterinsurgency operations generally are associated with superpower confrontation and its shift to "third world" locales or what has been termed "proxy wars," they have not always taken place within the context of superpower confrontation. British counterinsurgency operations in Kenya in the 1950s, the topic of chapter 5, provide a good example of this. It highlights the fact that the discourse of counterinsurgency draws upon several elements. It can consist of an articulation of colonial discourse with cold war discourse, but this is not always the case. Insurgency revolving around liberationist claims in Kenya was not framed within a cold war discursive context.

Chapter 4 examines U.S. counterinsurgency policy in the Philippines during the Huk rebellion, circa 1950–55. Counterinsurgency policies were a major element of post–World War II U.S. foreign policy toward the group of countries collectively referred to as the "third world." Such policies were considered essential within the context of a world divided along the geopolitical lines of East versus West with each side seeking to win the hearts and minds of those not yet fully committed to one camp. Many "conversations" have taken place and documents have been generated within the context of specific counterinsurgency operations.

Counterinsurgency occurs within the context of profound material power differentials. The hierarchy of military and economic power that exists between the United States and the "third world" is for the most part indisputable. What has not been previously examined, however, is the way in which language works to construct a kind of hierarchy that may or may not coincide with military and economic hierarchies. When these hierarchies do coincide, important implications follow for the kinds of practices that are made possible.

One of the earliest and most paradigmatic instances of U.S. counterinsurgency policy occurred in the Philippines during the Huk rebellion. After independence, the Philippines became a symbol of U.S. benevolence regarding its position as a former colonial power. Philippine independence was proof that the United States had benign intentions when it annexed the islands and had been successful in its "civilizing mission." The Philippines were thus an important source of both prestige and identity for the United States. The Huk rebellion, therefore, presented the United States with a dilemma. On the one hand, overt intervention would call into question the sovereignty and independence of the Philippines, which in turn would call into question the success of the U.S. effort to "civilize" a people and cultivate a democracy. On the other hand, the "loss" of the Philippines to communism would also mean a failure on the part of the United States. The discourse instantiated in response to this dilemma worked to construct identities and simultaneously positioned the subjects that were so constructed. We can note elements of continuity and discontinuity with earlier colonial discourses.

In Chapter 5 I examine the debates and discussions surrounding British counterinsurgency policy in what became known as the Mau Mau rebellion in Kenya in the 1950s.[13] This event has been described as precipitating "what was probably the gravest crisis in the history of Britain's African colonies" and the first struggle between black Africans and white minority rule in modern Africa (Edgerton 1989: vii). Its significance for the future of British colonialism as well as for nonwhite people more generally is illustrated in the words of Sir Leslie Plummer, a member of the British Parliament: "We cannot hide Mau Mau-ism. We cannot hide the causes of Mau Mau-ism. In cold water flats in Harlem and in the hot, tropical parts of the British possessions, coloured people, coloured races, colonial peoples are discussing what is going on in Kenya today" (House of Commons, November 7, 1952: 520).

The rebellion was thus an important event from the perspective of British colonial history, African history, and liberation struggles more generally. It occurred against the background of massive "third world" upheavals following the Second World War, when the European empires were being dismantled, for example, by Nehru in India, Nasser in Egypt, and Sukarno in Indonesia. Despite the proclamation of a senior British colonial official in 1939 that "in Africa we can be sure that we have unlimited time in which to work," this revolutionary wave exploded in Africa as well (Stavrianos 1981: 665). Ghana (formerly the Gold Coast), Sierra Leone, and Gambia in British West Africa and Senegal, the Ivory Coast, and Niger in French Africa were just a few of the scenes of struggles going on at this time.

The Mau Mau rebellion and British policy toward it engendered a large amount of commentary, debate, and discussion: official reports, books written by those who had "knowledge" of and experience in Kenya, and media coverage, as well as fictional accounts such as Robert Ruark's well-known *Something of Value*, which became a major motion picture starring Rock Hudson and Sidney Poitier. Discussions surrounding this event encompassed the nature of the "African" in general and the Kikuyu in particular, the nature of the British and other white settlers, as well as notions of what constituted legitimate protest or nationalist liberation movements. Mau Mau was also the occasion for numerous discussions of Kenya's problems and possible solutions. More significant for this study, it was the occasion for a variety of representational practices by which particular identities were constructed and relationships perpetuated as well as subverted.

Chapters 6 and 7 move on to more contemporary discourses. While it may be tempting to feel smugly self-confident that the representational practices examined in the earlier chapters are a thing of the past, we should refrain from such self-congratulatory inclinations. In Chapter 6 I focus on several discourses revolving around the concern with democracy and human rights in the South. The time period covered in this chapter ranges from the mid-1960s, when this became a relevant foreign policy issue in the United States, to the current international concern with the spread of democracy and human rights practices. These more contemporary discourses give us glimpses of both continuities and discontinuities with previous representational practices.

In Chapter 7, I examine contemporary North American social science discourses on North-South relations. Though I have included academic discourse at several points in the earlier chapters, here I focus exclusively on academic discourses dealing with the field of North-South relations. These are what Foucault refers to as discourses of the "community of experts." Social science is a "doubtful science" in the Foucauldian sense. Foucault refers to the social sciences as those that have not crossed the threshold of scientificity or the threshold of epistemologization, as have disciplines such as physics (Foucault 1980c; Dreyfus and Rabinow 1983: 117). The relationship between power and knowledge can more readily be discerned in the doubtful sciences than in the natural sciences. Examining these discourses prompts the question of what role they play in the larger context. This leads us to more general questions about power and its relationship to knowledge. We substitute the internal intelligibility (of social science discourses on North-South relations) for a different intelligibility, that is, their place within a larger discursive formation. I examine these discourses in light of the larger discursive formations analyzed in the previous chapters.

The conclusion brings together the analyses of the six empirical chapters. I discuss the discontinuities, the breaks in representational practices over time as well as the elements of continuity, the traces.

I reflect upon the consequences of excluding the issue of representation from international relations scholarship and urge a broadened understanding of power and its implication in the construction of meaning and identities.

I

Colonialism(s)

Introduction to Part I

Two centuries later, the Enlightenment returns: but not at all as a way for the West to take cognizance of its present possibilities and of the liberties to which it can have access, but as a way of interrogating it on its limits and on the powers which it has abused.

MICHEL FOUCAULT
"GEORGES CANGUILHEM: PHILOSOPHER OF ERROR"

Foucault refers here (1980: 54) to the questioning, begun at the close of the colonial era, that challenged the entitlement of Western culture, Western science, and Western rationality itself to claim universal validity. As Said (1993) notes, however, there has been relatively little attention to the imperial experience in challenging this priority of the West. Nowhere has this lack of critical attention been more evident than in the discipline of international relations, which has systematically built a wall of silence around challenges to Western expertise and knowledge, especially regarding the non-Western "other." International relations has claimed for itself the exclusive representational authority to define and analyze the "essential" agents, structures, and processes of global life and to relegate to the margins the nonessentials. This authority and the knowledge it facilitates has been based upon the experiences and the power of the relatively small portion of the world referred to as the West and the even smaller portion within that realm referred to as the major powers. In the process, international relations has taken as a given the identity of the West and its subjects/agents, ignoring the historical experiences and encounters with "others" against which the identities of these subjects/agents have been constituted.

This study aims to be a corrective to this silence. As such, it can be located within the general concern with interrogating the relationship between various claims drawing upon Enlightenment and humanist values and the economic and political domination of European and American colonialism (see Young 1990). It constitutes an effort to contribute to our understanding and questioning of how various forms of Western power and knowledge have been mutually implicated in practices of domination and hegemony and how, in the course of these practices, international identities have been constructed.

Colonialism(s) represents this collusion between power and knowledge and Enlightment and humanist values at its extreme. This is not to suggest that these values have been used in a simplistically instrumental fashion to enable the expansion of Western power and control. What is important is not so much the intentions and calculations of the individuals who bear some of the responsibility for the advance of Western power. Rather, it is the taken-for-granted assumptions and the naturalized categories of knowledge embedded in and produced within the context of the promotion of Western values that are of primary concern here.

Humanist values can be found in all of the discourses examined in this study. Sometimes they are quite explicitly expressed, while at other times they are more implicit. What remains constant is their presence alongside practices that would seem to be in direct contradiction to these values. As the Bible has often accompanied the flag and the rifle, Enlightenment values have often accompanied practices of domination and exploitation. In the two encounters I examine in chapters 3 and 4, humanist values explicitly animate and inform the narratives and debates — and domination and exploitation are obvious. Understanding how this uneasy coexistence has been made possible and understanding its consequences require an analysis of the representational practices and the accompanying forms of knowledge that have made specific historical happenings possible.

It should be clear from my discussion of discourse in chapter 1 that I am not implying a simple relationship of causality between discursive practices and the various behaviors that have been part of colonialism. To reiterate, behavior has no meaning at all outside of discourse. The issue then becomes not determining the cause(s) of behavior but rather deconstructing the meanings that have been given to, and by virtue of being so given have made possible, the various practices that have been present in imperial encounters.

As Young (1990: 18) points out, the deconstruction of the center and its relation to the margin examined by Derrida (1978) can operate geographically as well as conceptually. In the encounters examined here, both conceptual and geographic centers and margins were mutually constructed, and humanist values justified and made possible imperial practices of violence, domination, and exploitation.

2

To Be or Not to Be a Colonial Power

Take up the White Man's burden
Send forth the best ye breed
Go bind your sons to exile
To serve your captives' need;
To wait in heavy harness
On fluttered fold and wild
Your new-caught sullen peoples,
Half devil and half child.
Take up the White Man's burden
And reap his old reward
The blame of those ye better
The hate of those ye guard
The cry of hosts ye humor
(Ah slowly!) toward the light:
"Why brought ye us from bondage,
Our beloved Egyptian night?"
                RUDYARD KIPLING, "THE WHITE MAN'S BURDEN"[1]

As the nineteenth century drew to a close, United States policy makers knew virtually nothing about the Philippine Islands or the human beings who lived there. Recreating the scene at President McKinley's cabinet meeting as word of Commodore Dewey's victory in Manila Bay arrived, Mark Twain satirically suggested that two questions arose:

(1) What is Manila? A town, continent, archipelago, or what? This was found difficult. Some members believed it was one of these things, some another. The President reserved his opinion.

(2) Where was it? Some members thought it was somewhere, some thought it was elsewhere, others thought not. Again, the President declined to commit himself.[2]

This piece of geography that was somewhere or elsewhere and the people inhabiting it came to occupy a central place in the concerns of U.S. policy makers and those whose "knowledge" influenced them. The Philippines were to become the site for debates over America's role in the world, the exportability of democracy and other American institutions, and the meaning of the "American experiment" (Brands 1992: vi). At a more fundamental level, the Philippines were to become a site for the self-elaboration of the identity of the United States—the occasion for "lamenting the passing of a country that never was" (Drinnon 1980: 312).

Occurring against the background of various issues that called into question the identity of the United States as a unique power, debates over whether or not to annex the Philippines provided the occasion for a reaffirmation of what the United States *was*. This reaffirmation took place, to a large extent, vis-à-vis the construction of the Philippine/Filipino other. Despite the United States' relative lack of experience with formal colonization as well as its ignorance regarding the Philippines and the Filipinos, it had ample experience with "others": blacks, Mexicans, and "Red Indians." This experience was drawn upon in coming to "know" the Filipinos and in justifying U.S. practices and policies. Significantly, the discourse instantiated in this imperial encounter exemplified the representational practices that were at work more globally in constructing the West and its colonial other(s).

BACKGROUND

The United States encountered the Philippines in an overall atmosphere of domestic decline that threatened to call into question the "American exceptionalism" that differentiated the United States from European powers. During the months prior to Senate ratification of the Paris Peace Treaty, which marked the formal conclusion of the Spanish-American War and the official annexation of the Philippines, there were ominous indications that the United States was at war with itself in the domestic realm. On the economic front, it was experiencing its most serious crisis ever. The public was increasingly aware of disparities in wealth. The country was experiencing the worst labor violence in its history, often leading to bloodshed. In the context of the end of Reconstruction, de facto apartheid, and decreased protection of Indian lands, the United States was becoming increasingly obsessed with the issue of race. Increased immigration of "Old Worlders" who did not look like "Americans" or share the same Protestant faith (Jews and Catholics, for example) also raised questions about America's future and contributed to a growing nativist trend.[3]

The possibility that the United States would become a colonial power would remove one of the few remaining distinctions between it and Europe. The victory at Manila Bay threatened to cause the United States to "forget what we are and for what we stand" (Jordan 1901: 41). The chart of the "noble and gallant ship of state had been torn into tatters and the craft was drifting on a wild and unknown sea" (Turner, January 19, 1899). This, then, was a time of crisis, a rupture in the existing order that called into question identities and the naturalness of this order. As I suggested in chapter 1, rhetoric is intensified in times of crisis, when naturalized identities are at risk of coming undone, when authority is being questioned, and when the reproduction of identities takes place in different and permanently changing arenas. Annexation and the subsequent war between the United States and the Philippines presented one more arena for the reproduction of the identity of the United States. This reproduction took place in debates and discussions regarding the policies the United States should pursue in the Philippines.

Annexation was by no means a foregone conclusion. Nor was it the only available course of action. Other options included returning the Philippines to Spain, keeping them as an American protectorate, or arranging an international agreement for their neutralization, as had been done with Belgium (Welch 1979: 6; Brands 1992: 25). Perhaps the most logical alternative was simply to recognize the Philippines as a sovereign, independent nation. After all, when Commodore Dewey sailed into Manila in 1898, the Spaniards had for all intents and purposes already been defeated by the Filipinos themselves (Kalaw 1916; *Congressional Record*, 56th Congress, 2d session, 1900–1901: 3353–83). Filipino leaders had been promised independence and demanded that this promise be kept.[4] Yet, despite the arguments made by Filipino leaders, this option came to be regarded as the least desirable or rational course of action for the United States to follow. Independence became unthinkable, even though formal colonization ran counter to many of the United States' professed principles. "There was nothing left to do but take them all and educate the Filipinos and uplift and civilize them," President McKinley said in an interview in November 1899 (Brands 1992: 25).

The discursive process by which this "white man's burden" option came to be regarded as the only viable course of action is an exemplar in the politics of representation. Instantiated in U.S. Senate debates and reports, academic writings, the press, journals, and magazines, the discourse surrounding this event worked to construct a "reality" wherein independence for the Philippines was not within the range of imaginable possibilities. This discourse contained a double bind whereby even those opposed to annexation and imperialism contributed to an articulation of "truth" and "knowledge" with economic and political power that produced a particular representation of the United States and its other(s) that not only justified annexation but set the stage for future relationships and practices.

SELF-AFFIRMATION: CONSTRUCTING AMERICAN MANHOOD

Much of the identity construction that took place focused on "American manhood." The construction of the United States as a particular kind of subject was simultaneously the construction of "American manhood." At issue was whether the United States was to continue to be a place "where a man can stand up by virtue of his manhood and say I am a man" or whether it was to be "so effeminate that we are incompetent to colonize, to develop, and to govern territorial possessions" (Hoar, January 9, 1899: 496; Nelson, January 20, 1899: 834). American manhood was a nodal point to which both opponents and proponents of annexation referred. It functioned as a privileged signifier in fixing the meanings of other signifiers.

Professor Dean C. Worcester of the University of Michigan, whose four years in the Philippines collecting zoological specimens uniquely qualified him to write about "the Philippine Islands and their people," was called upon by President McKinley to be a member of the First Philippine Commission in January 1899.[5] Worcester strongly opposed withdrawal from the islands, suggesting that "to do so would stultify ourselves in the eyes of the world" (Drinnon 1980: 281). Stultification was implicitly linked with effeminate ineffectiveness. Worcester suggested that when the Spanish had arrived in the Philippines they had made progress in "subduing" the "tribes," but then had slowed down and "seemed to have lost much of their virility." Americans, on the other hand, had grown more virile in subduing all the tribes across a vast continent (Worcester 1921: 423–24).[6]

The competence to colonize and govern were not the only signifieds attached to this privileged signifier. American manhood was also linked to democracy. This link served to construct a distinctly American version of masculinity that was part and parcel of American exceptionalism. Opponents of acquisition and conquest of the Philippines, such as Stanford University president David Starr Jordan, drew upon and reinscribed this linkage. Jordan gained national attention with his widely distributed speeches denouncing the military and diplomatic policies of the McKinley administration. Jordan had three reasons for his opposition to imperialism. First, dominion was brute force: "The extension of dominion rests on the strength of arms. Men who cannot hold town meetings must obey through brute force" (Jordan 1901: 31). Second, dependent nations were slave nations. The use of brute force and the possession of slave nations was not consistent with democracy.

The third reason for Jordan's objection to imperialist policies was his belief that the making of men was of greater importance than the making of empires: "That government is best which makes the best men. In the training of manhood lies the certain pledge of better government in the future" (ibid.: 33). Jordan explicitly differentiated the United States from England, which had endured with a strong and good government despite its imperialist practices. But England was an oligarchy and an admiralty, not a democracy. The business of democracy was not to make government good but to make men strong: "The glory of the American Republic is that it is the embodiment of American manhood" (ibid.: 42). American manhood was inextricably linked to the glory of the American republic. The republic was both the manifestation of American manhood and the vehicle for the construction of a new kind of Anglo-Saxon man.

As Worcester differentiated the United States from Spain, Jordan contrasted the United States to England and Europe. Democracy, and therefore American manhood, was threatened by territorial expansion into the Philippines because it would not expand democracy or democratic institutions: "The proposed colonies are incapable of civilized self-government" (ibid.: 44).

The issue of American manhood also permeated the congressional debates about annexation:

> I believe that we shall have the wisdom, the self-restraint, and the ability to restore peace and order in those islands and give to their people an opportunity for self-government and for freedom under the protecting shield of the United States until the time shall come when they are able to stand alone, if such a thing be possible, and if they do not themselves desire to remain under our protection. This is a great, a difficult, and a noble task. I believe that American civilization is entirely capable of fulfilling it, and I should not have that profound a faith which I now cherish in American manhood if I did not think so. (Nelson, U.S. Senator, January 24, 1899: 834)

To congressional opponents of annexation, American manhood was threatened by the possibility of becoming more like the colonizing powers of Europe, giving way to the lust for imperial splendor and corrupting the integrity of the United States. An additional danger was that, if annexed, the Philippines might eventually be admitted into the union as a state. This would constitute "a degeneration and degradation of the homogeneous, continental Republic of our pride, too preposterous for the contemplation of serious and intelligent men" (Reid 1900: 14), it would "do such violence to our blood, to the history and traditions of our race, and would leave such frightful results in mongrelizing our citizenship" (Turner, January 19, 1899: 785).

Like Worcester, senators who favored annexation invoked the importance of American manhood. In fact, it was American manhood that would enable the United States to colonize the Philippines and still retain its integrity, honor, and benevolence. Because the United States was the kind of subject that shunned involvement in power politics, and because it was "God's best representative of law and order and justice on earth" (Spooner, *Congressional Record,* 55th Congress, 3d session, February 2, 1899: 1386), it had a duty to annex the Philippines so as to prevent their becoming the "spoil of other nations." Because the United States possessed wisdom and self-restraint, it could take on this noble task without subjecting the

Filipinos to the harsh and repressive colonial methods of Europe. American civilization and American manhood were up to this task (Lodge 1899: 959). American manhood could exercise self-restraint and control the lust that led to European colonialism, and at the same time protect colonial subjects.

Democracy, American manhood, and the glory of the United States were linked together in a complementary relationship. A threat to one was a threat to the others. While we can note differences regarding what constituted the threat and what American manhood demanded (that is, to colonize or not to colonize), American manhood itself occupied the center. But what was American manhood? What did it ultimately refer to? What gave American manhood its positivity? To attempt to answer this, we must turn to the signifying chain, the series of signifiers this term was linked to.

THE WESTERN BOND

Derrida (1978: 279) suggests that the dominant signifier that occupies the center of a discursive structure both makes the structure itself possible and limits its "play," that is, the "play" or movement of differences off one another. The logic of difference in the representational practices surrounding this imperial encounter drew upon and reinscribed several sets of oppositions. As I suggested earlier, England, Spain, and the rest of Europe were to a certain degree the U.S. "other(s)." It was vis-à-vis these Old World powers that the identity of the United States was constructed—an identity that shunned struggles over the balance of power and repressive imperial methods, and that was dedicated to the principles of human liberty (Spooner 1899: 1386; Money, February 3). When the United States and its European others were juxtaposed to the Filipinos, "the yellow Buddhists, Mohammedans, and Confucians" who would "do violence to our blood, to the history and traditions of our race and would leave such frightful results in mongrelizing our citizenship," however, they were reconfigured in a relation of similarity.[7]

What was being constructed here was a "Western bond" somewhat analogous to the masculine bonding examined by Jeffords (1989). The differences between European powers and the United States could be overcome by this "Western bond," which accentuated the differences between the West and the non-West.[8] This is clearly evident in British travel writer John Foreman's *The Philippine Islands*, published in 1899. Much of what United States policy makers came to "know" about the Philippine Islands and the Filipinos derived from British sources, especially travel writers. Foreman was allegedly the Englishman most "knowledgeable" about the Philippines at the time. His work was widely read and influenced President McKinley and others (Welch 1979: 102). Foreman's book was the only source cited by Worcester, the "expert" on the Philippine Islands (Drinnon 1980: 283). Foreman had also been summoned to Paris as an expert on the Philippines by the Paris Peace Commissioner (Storey 1901: 102). Foreman's work was drawn upon considerably in a February 15, 1901, Senate document (S. Doc 218) on the Philippines.

Foreman constructed a series of oppositions by which Spanish colonial rule could be distinguished from the kind of colonial rule the United States would impose:

> 1. Had the Spaniards followed their discoveries by social enlight- enment, by encouragement to commerce, and by the development of the new resources under their sway, they would—perhaps even to this day—have preserved the loyalty of those who yearned for and obtained freer institutions.
>
> 2. Conquest is admissible when it is exercised for the advance- ment of civilization and the conqueror takes upon himself the moral obligation to improve the conditions of the subjected peoples and render them happier.
>
> 3. An apology for conquest cannot, however, be found in the de- sire to spread any particular religion, especially Christianity, whose be- nign radiance was overshadowed by that debasing institution the Inqui- sition, which sought out the brightest intellects only to destroy them.
>
> 4. The repeated struggles for liberty, generation after generation, in all its colonies, tend to show that Spain's sovereignty was main- tained through the inspiration of fear rather than love and sympa- thy, and that Spain entirely failed to render colonial subjects happier than they were before.

That America's conception of the moral duties attaching to con- quest would be very different can hardly be a subject of doubt.

While the oppositions created here establish the benevolence and superiority of the United States as a conquering power, the common- alities between Spain and the United States are equally significant, if not more so. The most fundamental and consequential constitu- tive element of the Western bond is the right of conquest. While the basis of this right can vary—the divine right of conquest for the purpose of spreading a particular religion, the advancement of civilization and improvement of the subjected peoples—the right itself established a fundamental bond between powers possessing this right and a divide between these powers and their subjects/victims. Of particular importance was the naturalization of conquest itself. Conquest was a natural phenomenon, though the basis for it must continually be reconstructed at different times and places. Halle (1985: 35) noted this distinction between "rationalized imperialism," a sober, responsible, and unselfish kind of domination, and wanton exploitation. In the former, the conquerors were seen to have an obligation to advance the conquered along the paths of civilization. What cannot be questioned is the right of conquest itself, which must be presumed prior to any other arguments or specifications.

The Philippines and the Filipinos are represented alternatively as the prize of conquest, the object to be discovered, the subject without agency to be protected, improved, and rendered happy. The representation of the Philippines as Spain's "discovery" is a rhetorical strategy of negation implying a blank slate to be written on by Western power and knowledge. This representation of the Philippines and Filipinos is explored more fully later.

Others participated in the construction of this Western bond. Charles Denby, former U.S. minister to China and a member of the Philippine Commission, advocated seizing the Philippines as a stepping stone to the China market:

> We have the right as conquerors to hold the Philippines. We have the right to hold them as part of payment of a war indemnity. This policy may be characterized as unjust to Spain; but it is the result of the fortunes of war. All nations recognize that the conqueror may dictate the terms of peace. (Denby 1898: 280)

Again we find the naturalization of conquest among Western powers: "We are stretching out our hands for what nature meant should be ours" (ibid.: 281). The Philippines, the object of rivalry among such powers, can be won, traded, exchanged, acquired, managed, and controlled. "Injustice" applies to the nation that loses its object (Spain) rather than to the object itself (the Philippines).

The western bond was also written outside of the United States. For example, on December 12, 1898, the *Times* of London asserted:

It would be untrue to our faith in the healthy vigor and the practical capacities of the Anglo-Saxon stock to doubt that the necessities involved in the unexpected annexation of strange dependencies will call forth the governing faculty that has never been found wanting among the Englishmen, Scotchmen, and Irishmen who have built up the fabric of the British Empire. But our kinsmen on the other side of the Atlantic must not be tempted by their lack of experience in ruling subject races to imagine that their work has been accomplished when the Spanish flag has been hauled down and the Stars and Stripes hoisted in its place.

One the same day, the London *Daily Telegraph* proclaimed that with the formal signing of the Treaty of Peace by the United States and Spain, "the civilized world is free from the scourge of war." These articles and others were transmitted to the U.S. secretary of state, John Hay, from Henry White at the American Embassy in London. In a December 14, 1898, letter accompanying the articles, White conveyed to Hay England's satisfaction "at the fact that the Philippines have passed under our sway."

READING THE PHILIPPINES

We at least know that the Philippines are tenanted by a very peculiar mass, a heterogeneous compound of inefficient humanity.
U.S. SENATOR STEPHEN M. WHITE, JANUARY 23, 1899

The enabling condition for the Western bond was an "other" against which this identity defined itself. The "othering" of the subjects/objects of Western conquest took place along several axes. Chapter 11 of John Foreman's book, "Domesticated Natives — Origins — Character" was an attempt to "correctly depict the Philippine native character" and an exemplary work in the construction of the "other." This text, however, did not exist in a vacuum. Rather, it was situated within a complex and mutually reinforcing textual network, an intertext of representations that participated in the construction of a hierarchy of international identities. I will examine this intertext, the subject identities it constructed, and the practices that were thereby made possible.

Knowing the "Natives"

The imperial gaze of the West produced a Philippine identity that was visible, knowable, and ultimately in need of United States authority and control. "Descriptions" of the inhabitants of the Philippines served as implicit authorizations for the U.S. colonial project. These "descriptions" were driven by a logic of difference that established the identities and relative positions of the United States and its other(s) as fixed and natural. They were also points where power, "writing," and knowledge came together. Through detailed observation by travel writers such as John Foreman and academics such as Dean Worcester, as well as the work of the Philippine Commission, "knowledge" of the Filipino "native" was produced, disseminated, and put to use to justify U.S. conquest, violence, and subsequent control.

As I noted in chapter 1, classificatory schemes often serve to naturalize and hierarchize by placing human beings into stereotypical categories presumably designated by nature. Classification occurred at various levels, from Worcester's table of Filipino "tribes," which bore a strong resemblance to his table of birds of the Philippines, to more general classifications that differentiated Anglo-Europeans from their "others."[9] Worcester ranked Filipinos hierarchically from the Negritos, the lowest both physically and mentally, to the Indonesians of Mindaneo, the highest. This classificatory scheme, this rhetorical supplement to colonialism's divide and rule strategy, permitted the assertion that the Filipinos did not constitute "a people" or a "nation." It permitted the denial of homogeneity and the representation of the inhabitants of the Philippines as "a jumble of savage tribes."[10] U.S. colonizers could thus be represented as builders of nations and peoples rather than destroyers and exterminators.

Filipinos were also classified in less formal, less "scientific" ways. A distinction was made between the nationalist Katipunan, who dominated Philippine society through fear, terror, and compulsion, and the masses, who were "densely, almost inconceivably ignorant." The Katipunan appealed to the native ignorance and racial prejudice (Kennon 1901).[11] This representation of the good but ignorant (only slightly removed from savagery, according to Kennon) Filipino and the bad Filipino complemented the earlier representation and permitted the denial of any collective sense of revolutionary nationalism. The primitiveness of the good Filipinos prevented them from truly understanding and desiring freedom: "The writer has yet to meet a Filipino who understands what liberty is, as we know and understand liberty in America" (ibid.: 220). Such a representation functioned to dismiss the "insurgents'" rebellion as a movement that represented the masses. "Insurgent" leaders were terrorists, only nominally working for liberty. It thus fell to the United States to protect the good but densely ignorant masses from the tyrannical leaders and to instill in the masses a collective sense of identity and an appreciation of liberty, freedom, and democracy.

One can note an important contradiction here that U.S. foreign policy discourse worked to erase. The very use of the term *Filipino* implies some homogeneity. This term repeatedly entered U.S. discourse even while representational practices worked to deny homogeneity or "peoplehood" to the inhabitants of the Philippine Islands and then later took credit for creating a unified identity.

At a broader level, classification took place between Anglo-European peoples and non-Anglo Europeans. In this specific case it was the "Asiatic" or "Oriental" that was most often contrasted with the Anglo-European. These identity categories were linked in a relation of similarity to the "Chinese," the "Indian," and the "Negro." To varying degrees, all were problems to be solved: "Industrial training and industrial pride make a man of the Negro. Industrial interests may even make a man of the Chinaman, and the Indian disappears as our civilization touches him" (Jordan 1901: 32). Differentiation between Anglo-Europeans and their "others" revolved around reasoning processes and intellectual capabilities.[12] Foreman wrote:

> The reasoning of a native and European differs so largely, that the mental impulse of the two races is ever clashing. With the majority, no number of years of genial intercourse, without material profit, will arouse in the native breast a perceptible sympathy for the white race.
>
> The Filipino, like most Orientals, is a good imitator, but having no initiative genius, he is not efficient in anything. He has no attachment for any occupation in particular. Today he will be at the plough tomorrow a coachman, a collector of accounts, a valet, a sailor, and so on; or he will suddenly renounce social trammels in pursuit of lawless vagabondage.
>
> The native never looks ahead; he is never anxious about the future; but if left to himself, he will do all sorts of imprudent things, from sheer want of reflection on the consequences, when as he puts it, "his head is hot" from excitement due to any cause. (1899: 181, 182, 187)

These characteristics, through a widespread and prolonged process of repetition, endowed the Filipino with a particular kind of identity that moved in an unsteady fashion between two poles, both closer to nature than the rational adult. More benignly portrayed, Filipinos were childlike, lacking the rationality generally attributed to adults. They were impulsive, unreflective, imitative, and unaware of consequences. Less benignly portrayed, they were given an identity that was in many ways more animal than human. Foreman again:

> So long as he gets his good and fair treatment, and his stipulated wages paid in advance, he is content to act as a general utility man. If not pressed too hard, he will follow his superior like a faithful dog.

> Even over mud and swamp, a native is almost as sure-footed as a goat on the brink of a quarry. I have frequently been carried for miles in a hammock by four natives and relays through morassy districts too dangerous to travel on horseback. They are great adepts at climbing wherever it is possible for a human being to scale a height; like monkeys, they hold as much with their feet as with their hands; they ride any horse barebacked without fear; they are utterly careless about jumping into the sea among the sharks, which sometimes they will intentionally attack with knives, and I never knew a native who could not swim. (1899: 187, 188–89)

The animal analogy was not confined to travel writers. Senator Henry Cabot Lodge, an expansionist who argued in favor of annexation and the subsequent suppression of the Philippine insurrection, suggested that "a native family feeds; it does not breakfast or dine, it feeds. A wooden bowl of rice with perhaps a little meat stewed in with it, is put on the floor; the entire family squats around it; the fingers are used to convey the food into the mouth. I have never seen any Filipino eat otherwise" (March 7, 1900: 2632). Filipinos were positioned in a relation of similarity to dogs, monkeys, and other animals that "feed" rather than "dine." They were rendered specimens subject to observation, analysis, and judgment by the commanding gaze of the West.

Such representations rendered the Filipinos incapable of self-government and in need of guidance, tutoring, and uplifting. The unstable representation that alternatively shifted from that of child to animal made possible a wide range of practices. The child, while denied a fully developed identity and the agency that presumably goes with it, is nonetheless valued as a human being. The animal, while useful in terms of physical strength and the labor it can perform or even perhaps the loyalty it offers its master, is still a creature whose life is less valuable than a human being's.[13]

Todorov (1984: 42) describes this same process of "othering" as it pertained to Columbus's encounter with the inhabitants of the "New World." In one instance the "other" is represented as a human being potentially identical to one self. This is reflected in policies of conversion and assimilation. However, this "other" is always fixed as a partial presence of the self. Bhabha (1984) refers to this as "colonial mimicry," the desire for a reformed and recognizable other as a subject of difference that is almost but not quite the same. In another instance the "other" is seen as different from one self, and this difference is translated into terms of permanent superiority and inferiority. This results in practices ranging from enslavement and other forms of oppression to policies of annihilation. Hunt (1987: 69) also notes the prevalence of these two representations whereby the "other" might be regarded as holding some promise of improving its position in the hierarchy of race and alternatively as subhuman yet capable of great conquests.

Subduing the "Natives"

"Knowledge" of the "natives" not only enabled the U.S. colonial project as such but also justified in advance practices and policies at odds with the presumed benevolent and liberty-loving nature of the United States: the water torture and massacre of Filipinos.[14] Foreman wrote:

> In common with many other non-European races, an act of generosity or a voluntary concession of justice is regarded as a sign of weakness. Hence it is, that the experienced European is often compelled to be more harsh than his own nature dictates. (1899: 179)

Here it is established that the European is by nature not harsh but is often forced to be so as a result of the "fact" that non-European races regard generosity and justice as signs of weakness. This argument was echoed in the Senate debates. Senator Bacon of Georgia opposed annexation because it would constitute an enslavement of the Filipino people: "These alien people, the Mohammedans, these people accustomed to revolution, and to blood and to disorder" would compel the United States to use cruelty. "Nothing but the strong hand, nothing but cruelty, nothing but the iron rule will enable us to maintain that dominion" (Bacon, January 18, 1899: 738). John Barrett, U.S. minister to Siam, suggested that "the Asiatic appears to best advantage in lands which are dependent on some strong European government. Although civilization may not always seem to help him, it does far better by him when dispensed through forceful foreign hands than when caught in a haphazard way through his own agency" (Barrett 1899a: 919).

This justification for the control of "others" and the use of force and violence enjoyed more widespread representational currency. Even an anti-imperialist such as Andrew Carnegie could defend British practices in India while arguing against imperialism in general and particularly United States imperialism: "India has been subject to British rule for nearly two hundred years, and yet not one piece of artillery can yet be entrusted to native troops. The people still have to be held down as in the beginning" (Carnegie 1899: 371). Bacon also defended the British while arguing against annexation. Reading from an account of the practices of the British in India, Bacon argued thus:

> But only with the sword and gun can millions of the semicivilized be kept in subjection. The very best that can be said, and what is proper to be said, is that it was necessary that the English should perpetuate this cruelty, this butchery, if they would maintain their dominion in India. I have read it to illustrate the fact that in order to maintain dominion over such people only such desperate remedies can be applied. (Bacon 1899: 738)

Such representations made unremarkable, defensible, and even necessary otherwise reprehensible practices while at the same time constructing the identities of the subjects who engaged in these practices as well as those who were subjected to them. Britain, for example, could remain a "civilized" country while engaging in barbaric practices only through the continual deferral of the signifier "civilized" itself and the linking of its opposite, "uncivilized," to Filipinos and other non-Western peoples. It was this construction of the "other" through a logic of difference that enabled the deferral of the encounter with the thing (that is, civilized) itself. It was the nature of the Filipino, the Indian, "such people," that precipitated these practices: "There is nothing they delight in more than pillage, destruction, and bloodshed, and when once they become masters of the situation in an affray, there is no limit to their greed and savage cruelty" (Foreman 1899: 187).

Humanist values could be invoked and at the same time violated through the hierarchical classification of human beings that implied different standards of treatment for different kinds of subjects. The use of physical force and violence were justified even though the professed motives for U.S. "expansion" were to uplift and civilize. This should not be taken to suggest that there are "real" motives that are hidden by "professed" motives. This may or may not be the case. The more important point to be made is that the ethical prescriptions implied by Enlightenment values applied to some kinds of subjects, but not to others. As I noted in chapter 1, the division of humanity into different types has at least implicitly, and often explicitly, suggested different standards of "fairness": "If treated with kindness, according to European notions, he is lost" (Foreman 1899: 187). Humanist values have been defined and put into practice within the context of representational practices that have constructed a hierarchy of identities.

"Race," Agency, and the "Native"

We pray Thee that those who prefer to remain in darkness, and are even willing to fight in order to do so, may whether willingly or unwillingly, be brought into the light.
A UNIVERSITY OF PENNSYLVANIA FACULTY MEMBER[15]

"Race" functioned as a nodal point around which identities were fixed, "knowledge" was produced, and subjects were positioned vis-à-vis one another. The colonial intertext examined here is a manifestation of racism in its colonial moment.[16] The racialized categories produced through representational practices enabled the construction of self and other, American manhood and its racial other, and the formation of a Western bond.[17] As with questions of imperialism more generally, the question of U.S. policy regarding the Philippines carried forward the binary oppositions of advanced/superior and backward/inferior races. This was true of both those who advocated and those who opposed the acquisition of the Philippines. Anti-imperialist Andrew Carnegie believed that "contact of the superior race with the inferior demoralizes both" (Carnegie 1899). Anti-imperialist David Starr Jordan echoed this sentiment:

Wherever we have inferior and dependent races within our borders today, we have a political problem—the Negro problem, the Chinese problem, the Indian problem. These problems we slowly solve. Industrial training and industrial pride make a man of the Negro. Industrial interests may even make a man of the Chinaman, and the Indian disappears as our civilization touches him." (Jordan 1901: 32)

Filipinos were linked to the "Negro" and "the Chinaman and the Indian" in a relation of similarity. All were considered "alien races" that were "incapable of civilized self-government" (Jordan 1901: 44). The "Latin republics" were also part and parcel of this alien category. Jordan predicted that, although they were already independent, they would "fail for reasons inherent in the nature of the people."

The term *Oriental* was frequently used, along with *Asiatic, Asiatic mind,* and *Mohammedan.* These terms were never explicitly defined. Rather, they brought with them "unspoken truths"—a whole array of images and truths that were presumed to be already known. This was accomplished through linking together in relations of similarity and complementarity these terms and descriptions such as "lower element of humanity," "fatal and insidious element," "spotted people," "uncivilized," and "inferior races."

Equally significant, the racial classification served to constitute the white, Anglo-Saxon, superior peoples. As Said (1979: 227) notes, being a white man was both an idea and a reality. It involved a relation of superior to inferior and was a form of power and authority over nonwhites. It was a way of distinguishing self from other. The racial classifications carried with them the implicit identification of the "lower" races with suborders of "man" as well as with animals. This was clearly evident in the analogies made between Filipino natives and dogs, goats, and monkeys. Perhaps less obvious—but no less significant—was the practice, both rhetorical and nonrhetorical, of "domesticating the native," which carried with it the connotation of rendering an animal tame, unthreatening, and suitable for a harmless house pet.

These classifications rendered the Filipino incapable of exercising agency. As a University of Pennsylvania faculty member suggested, they were to be "willingly or unwillingly brought into the light." The United States had an obligation, not to honor its promise of independence, but rather "to do for the Filipinos more and bet-

ter than the mass of people can ask or think" (Wilcox 1900: 346).
In suggesting that the Filipinos were incapable of exercising agency,
I do not mean to replicate the representational practices examined
in this colonial discourse. Of course, Filipinos did in fact exercise
agency, as demonstrated in their demands for independence and their
willingness to risk and lose lives to fight for that goal. What I am
suggesting here is that the regime of truth constructed by this colonial discourse denied the Filipino capacity to exercise agency. This
regime of truth framed U.S. policy decisions and subsequent practices. Any exercise of agency on the part of Filipinos could be ignored, silenced, or brutally suppressed.[18] As Foucault (1982) points
out, power is only power (rather than solely physical force and violence) when it is addressed to individuals who are free to act in one
way or another. Power presupposes the capacity for agency rather
than denying it. In other words (and ironically), the very denial of
agency to the Filipinos in United States colonial discourse presupposed their capacity for agency.

Perhaps the most significant indication of the absence of agency
was the denial of that transcendental international signifier, sovereignty. Attributes that were attached to human beings to construct
particular identities were also attached to those abstract entities
and the bounded geographical space they embodied — that is, nation-states. In the case of the Philippines, this resulted in a nonsovereign identity. The sovereign/nonsovereign opposition created two
kinds of international identities. The United States, Britain, and the
rest of Europe were all sovereign subjects who could possess, dominate, control, and trade among themselves "other" kinds of subjects.
This "other" kind of subject was the nonsovereign subject who
could be possessed, dominated, controlled, and passed as an object
among sovereign subjects.

Complementing this binary opposition was a civilized/uncivilized
opposition. Civilized subjects could be either enlightened or despotic.
Both of these kinds of subjects were sovereign. The despotic possessed and controlled based on imperialistic motives; they were represented as tyrants who employed force. Spain was cast as this kind
of subject. Britain is at times cast as this kind of subject and at other
times as benevolent and kind.[19] The other kind of sovereign subject
was enlightened, moral, and free from any imperialist designs. This
type of subject engaged not in conquest but in "expansion." The

motives for "expansion" were to uplift and civilize, not through the use of physical force but by example and the reconstruction of other nonsovereign subjects in one's own image. The use of physical force and violence were not ruled out, but if they were required, it would be because of the nature of the victim, the recipient of the acts of force and violence. The United States was cast as this kind of subject.

The regime of truth created the possibility for certain practices. On the one hand, the Philippines were made annexable or colonizable. Even those who opposed annexation participated in a construction of the Filipino that made such a course of action possible. The use of physical force was made possible, and indeed was justified in advance. The same representational practices concomitantly created certain impossibilities. The Philippines would not be left alone to handle their own affairs, command their own resources, or engage in diplomatic relations with other countries. On the world stage, the Philippines were not international actors. In contrast to an approach that takes the identities of sovereign international actors as given, this analysis illustrates how, through the politics of representation, sovereignty became linked with other attributes to constitute different and unequal kinds of international subjects. These representational practices were part of a larger discursive economy that framed North-South relations at the turn of the century.

While this chapter has focused on the Philippines and the United States, evidence suggests that the representational practices described here were global in scope. This is clearly evident in the "Western bond" that constructed the "North." In a similar fashion, the Philippines, India, Cuba, Haiti, and the "American Indian" were constructed as like kinds of subjects. They were all "colonizable," though this did not mean that it was inevitable that they would in fact be colonized.[20]

DUALITY OF DISCOURSE: EQUIVALENCE, DEFERRAL, AND INSTABILITY

As I noted in chapter 1, there is a dual nature to discourse that consists of the impossibility of ultimate closure and the fact of partial fixation or partial closure. It is this partial closure that creates "reality," the identities of subjects, and that fixes meaning so as to make certain practices seem logical, rational, and natural. The representational practices discussed thus far have focused mainly on the fixed nature of this particular colonial discourse. This partial closure was accomplished through a logic of difference whereby self and other were represented as positive identities based upon foundational essences. At work simultaneously, however, was a logic of equivalence.

A chain of equivalences was created between the terms *civilized, rationality, reason,* and *sovereign,* on the one hand, and *uncivilized, instinctual,* and *dependent* on the other hand. These systematic ensembles of differences resulted in a unity by which different kinds of international identities were constituted. The linking together of various signifiers was necessary to constitute a particular identity, a "totality" of attributes separate and distinct from what lay beyond, that is, from other identities.

The logic of equivalence also had a destabilizing effect, however, revealing the contingent nature of all identities. The logic of equivalence subverts the specificity of each differential position insofar as the differences express something identical underlying them all. In other words, the positivity of terms such as *civilized* and *uncivilized* is subverted in that the difference expresses something identical to the reason/instinct difference, the superior/inferior difference, the sovereign/dependent difference. This identical something is merely the differentiation betweeen colonizer and colonized. The differential elements on either side of the sets of oppositions referred back to one another in an endless signifying chain. To be civilized was to be superior, which was to be rational, which was to be civilized, and so on. To be uncivilized was to be inferior, which was to be ruled by instinct and passion. We have a circle of signifiers with no positive content.

To be civilized was, of course, presumed to have some positive content, as were the other terms. Indeed, the power of representational practices depends on the unspoken assumption that signifiers have some positive content. Yet when we search for this positive content it always eludes us. We cannot find an intrinsic meaning or empirical referent for the term *civilized.* Indeed, colonial practices erased or called into question the differences between *civilized* and *uncivilized,* thereby denying any positivity to these terms. One could argue that *civilized* pointed to or referred to subjects who were "lovers of liberty," as these texts implied. But "lovers of liberty" itself had no intrinsic meaning that would permit it to unproblematically and naturally characterize certain subjects. Certainly, the Filipinos considered themselves lovers of liberty. We could try to point to an "empirical" state of affairs that would be indicative of subjects who were lovers of liberty, perhaps the absence of slavery. This, however, would mean that the United States was not civilized until 1865. Even if we could reach agreement on this, there would remain the problem that *slavery* itself has no intrinsic meaning. We could say that *slavery* refers to the absence of freedom, but then what does *freedom* refer to? After annexation, the Philippines certainly were not free. Are we to assume that by implication this meant that the United States was not civilized, since the United States was the reason the Philippines were not free? We could go on indefinitely with this example. My point, however, is that the terms in this example, as well as the other terms examined in this study, acquired their "positivity" only in relation to other terms.

The individual differences presumed by the various sets of oppositions found in this discourse were canceled out insofar as all of them were quite mobile and interchangeable. They could stand in for one another. They could refer to one thing one day and to another the next day. Spurr (1993: 168) points out that the mobility of a concept increases its practical value and enables it to function consistently in the service of power. Terms such as *civilized, benevolent,* and *rational* exhibited a mobility that enabled humanistic values to be invoked in justification of practices of subjugation, torture, and oppression. The term *civilized* could be attached to subjects who adhered to humanist values one day and the next day engaged in reprehensible antihumanist practices. This mobility deferred encounter with the presence that signifiers such as *civilized* are presumed to be moving toward. This colonial discourse was not about empirical referents grounded in some transcendental "reality." Identities were not preexisting, objective, and homogeneous points of unity. Rather, this discourse was an economy of representation by which "reality" and identities were created.

But meaning was in fact fixed, at least temporarily. How was this accomplished? Each of the oppositions depended upon a point of differentiation—a point where, for example, *civilized* became differentiated from *uncivilized*. This differentiation was made possible by a dominant signifier. The dominant signifier can be thought of as the center of the discursive structure: it both makes the structure itself possible and limits its play. It is the point where the substitution of signifiers is no longer possible (Derrida 1978: 279). The signifying chain stops. I would suggest that a distinctly "American" version of "white man" was the dominant signifier in these texts. The terms *civilized, enlightened, lovers of liberty, benevolent,* and so on became fused and came to rest with "white man" while the opposites came to rest with nonwhite races. "White man" was the reference point in relation to which the oppositional distinctions could be posited, the center that while governing the structure escaped structurality. "White man" was given transcendental status, implicitly understood to exist outside of the discursive system instead of itself being constructed by that system. A deconstructive reading of these texts reveals the contestations and rhetorical strategies that call this status into question. This analysis suggests that "white man" was itself a discursive construction with no positive content, a construction whose meaning depended on the construction of its "other." "White man" was never absolutely present outside a system of differences.[21]

In one sense the "findings" of this study are quite unremarkable. It is not surprising to find that U.S. foreign policy discourse at the turn of the century was racist. An important aspect of a critical analysis, however, is to make the unremarkable remarkable, to explore not only the "deep structure" of a discourse, but also the way in which foundations are undermined.[22] It is only by doing so that one can examine the processes by which "reality" and the identities of the world's subjects come to be taken as nonarbitrary, noncontingent, and natural. Equally important, though, is the exploration of the instabilities, the fragile nature of "fixed" identities and "reality." The "reality" instantiated in this discourse facilitated practices that led to the death of more than a million Filipinos and the subsequent denial of their right to self-government. This analysis suggests that representational practices were not epiphenomenal, as many orthodox approaches to international relations would suggest. Rather, they were central to making the practices of this particular foreign policy possible. This case was not about an encounter between two preexisting international subjects with fixed identities. Rather, it was about the production of "truth" and "knowledge" and their capacity to be widely circulated and accepted and to frame policy decisions.

This reorients and complicates our understanding of this particular incident and, by implication, North/South relations as well as international relations more generally. Discourses are embedded in practices and institutions that dominate Western encounters with the "Third World." While the categories and specific elements present in this turn-of-the-century discourse may not constitute our current "reality," it is possible that the underlying logic, by which the "other" is constructed as the different and deferred "self," is similar. Chapters 3 through 7 explore other imperial encounters and the discursive logic(s) at work in them.

3

Getting the "Natives" to Work

Powerfully built, they are capable of great feats of strength and endurance. Individuals will carry a load of 100 lbs. on their heads.

LORD FREDERICK LUGARD

It is not enough to say that economic inducements alone will bring the native to see the advantages of work and of raising his standard of living. BRITISH UNDERSECRETARY AMERY

In the interests of the natives themselves all over Africa we have to teach them to work. The progress of the native in civilization will not be secured until he has been convinced of the necessity and dignity of labor. Therefore I think that anything we reasonably can do to induce the native to labor is a desirable thing.

COLONIAL SECRETARY JOSEPH CHAMBERLAIN

Said (1978: 92) has suggested that for imperialists such as Balfour as well as for anti-imperialists like J. A. Hobson, the Oriental, like the African, is a member of a subject race and not exclusively an inhabitant of a geographical area. The same can be said of the "native." The colonial "native" was an operative category that functioned to classify human beings, though not necessarily according to geography or place of origin. The United States had its "natives" in the Philippines. The British had their "natives" in Africa and elsewhere. The specific referent of this term varied but almost always signified some kind of inferiority that coincided with an implicit racial hierarchy. "Natives" were a type of human being found in numerous geographical locales.

During the early twentieth century, Britain's "natives" in the East African Protectorate (the colony of Kenya after 1920) became inextricably bound up with the issue of labor. To speak of the "native" inevitably invoked images of either physical abilities as suggested by Lord Lugard or images of idleness and laziness, vices to be corrected by good colonial administration. Against the background of the post–World War I League of Nations mandate system and questions regarding the conditions that ought to be imposed on the nations who accepted mandates for the territories taken from Germany during the war, Britain encountered a "native labor problem" in Kenya that threatened to call into question the honor, integrity, and self-identity of Britain as a colonial power. As noted by Louis (1984), the Permanent Mandate Commission set standards for the entire colonial world as well as for the specific mandated territories. In addition, the Second Pan-African Congress had met in Paris in 1919 and called for greater responsibility on the part of colonial powers for the African peoples (Legum 1965: 151–52). The principle of trusteeship for the welfare of the "natives" thus became elevated in international discourse and had to be acknowledged by colonial powers. The tension between the exploitation of African labor and the protection and development implied by the notion of trusteeship animated the debates and discussions surrounding the "native labor crisis" circa 1920.

The crisis involved the extreme shortage of black African labor available to work on white European farms and the question of whether the British government should engage in a policy of forced labor. Questions had arisen in the League of Nations concerning the purposes for which the mandatory powers would be allowed to impose regulations upon the "native." Imposing forced labor in Britain's "own territory" (Kenya) thus had implications that went beyond East Africa. The "native labor problem" was considered of "high imperial importance," involving principles that affected "the very foundations of our Imperial System and the methods we intend to employ in the conduct of that system in the years to come" (Lord Islington, House of Lords, 1920). Viscount Bryce addressed the House of Lords on July 14, 1920:

We have been taking the line that every possible provision ought to be imposed in a Mandate for the benefit of the population in the territories to be administered under it. How can we effectively make that demand and continue to press it through our representatives in the League of Nations, unless we set a good example ourselves?

The relevance of this issue thus extended beyond the bounds of Kenya. One contemporary noted that "British East Africa is a test case for European imperialism in Africa" (*New Statesman,* April 10, 1920).

In the discourses surrounding this dilemma, we can locate many of the same rhetorical strategies discussed in Chapter 2. This lends support to the suggestion that the representational practices surrounding U.S. colonization of the Philippines were global in nature, though each imperial encounter is also unique, exhibiting its own fissures, contradictions, and points of instability. This chapter, then, should not be read solely as a repetition of that discourse in a different locale. The texts examined in this chapter, which include official government acts and ordinances, give us a glimpse into the basis through which British rule was exercised and filtered down to the African people. These policies (and policy documents) were the basis for the exercise of British colonial power. A deconstructive reading of them illuminates the presuppositions, the classifications of humanity, the discursive strategies that accompanied and enabled this rule.

Like the imperial encounter examined in chapter 2, what became known as the "native labor problem" in colonial Kenya was an occasion for representational practices that constructed particular kinds of identities for international subjects. While the labor problem is the animating issue for this chapter, other government policies — the alienation of land, the system of "native" reserves, "native" registration — were inextricably linked with labor and are thus an important part of this analysis.[1]

BACKGROUND

From the beginning of white settlement in Kenya, the creation of an expanding African labor force was a central feature of the economic history of the country (Rosberg and Nottingham 1966: 21). Swainson (1980: 7) notes that one of the chief functions of the colonial administration from the early period of European settlement had been to ensure a labor supply to the white estates. In the words of one of the European settlers, "Labour is the most important factor in this country's progress" (*East African Standard,* July 16, 1919). Although land policy had shaped the economy, the labor system was responsible for the greatest number of "evils" (Wylie 1977: 428). Some have even argued that Kenya's basic economic problem was not land but labor (Cell 1976: 6). Land and labor were, however, inextricably linked. The control of land was essential to the creation of an African labor force. In the words of Lord Delamere, one of Kenya's most prominent white settlers, "If the Africans had enough land, and therefore stock and produce for sale, they would not be obliged to go out and labor for others" (quoted in Maughan-Brown 1985: 25). This sentiment was echoed in a 1919 Economic Commission recommendation that "the natives should be concentrated in areas sufficient, but no more than sufficient, for their requirements" (ibid.).[2]

Complementing the colonial government's policy of land alienation, a system of tribal reserves developed. These reserves were ostensibly for the purpose of providing Africans with security and safety from "prosecution from their former enemies" (Proceedings of the Legislative Council of East Africa, 1920, 2d session, May 3–July 6). The Crown Lands Ordinance of 1902 had given the protectorate government jurisdiction over all lands subject to the right of occupation by Africans. African ownership was not recognized, only occupation and use of land. Land actually being used, "in actual occupation," by Africans could not be sold or leased to settlers, but the ordinance did not clearly define the meaning of "actual occupation." This was left to the administration, with the result that large tracts of land were alienated despite the fact that Africans were in occupancy and claimed rights to the land. Many of those who lost their land became squatters on the new European farms (Rosberg and Nottingham 1966: 153). The Crown Lands Ordinance of 1915 gave legal recognition to "native" reserves and also formally recognized that Africans had no inherent or legal rights to land. The official position was that "the theory of individual ownership of land as understood in English is absolutely foreign to the mind of any African until he has begun to absorb the ideas of an alien civilization" (ibid.: 154).[3]

Control of land was thus achieved through colonial legislation, leaving the control of labor an issue of major importance to both the white settler community and the British government, not to mention the African whose labor power was the object of colonial exploitation. Prior to World War I the boundaries between what was permissible and what was not were not clearly defined (Tignor 1976: 152). Van Zwanenburg (1975: 130) points out that part of the British colonial tradition had been to articulate public policy so that interpretation was left to the "man on the spot." This was most assuredly the case when it came to labor recruiting. The legislation that was put into place as a result of the postwar labor crisis made explicit and formalized practices that had always existed. This is what led to debate and discussion.

While labor shortages had been a permanent problem since the initiation of white settlement and demands for forced labor were a constant refrain from the white settlers, the situation reached a peak in 1919–21. As one contemporary pointed out, "In the years 1919 to 1921 the subjugation of the natives of East Africa was probably more complete than it ever will be again" (McGregor Ross 1927: 103). After 1918 the shortage of black African labor became acute and affected nearly all European employers.[4] As a result of the labor shortage, the Europeans placed increasing pressure on the colonial government to find a solution. The solution advanced by the settlers involved direct government action in recruiting African labor. On October 23, 1919, John Ainsworth, chief native commissioner, acting on instructions from Governor Edward Northey, issued a labor circular outlining a new government policy regarding the recruitment of labor. Its purpose was to convey to provincial and district commissioners the government's desire to increase the supply of labor to the white settlers and to outline some instructions for recruiting. With the issuance of this circular, the government of the East African Protectorate formally assumed responsibility for maintaining an adequate supply of labor (Gregory 1962: 28). This was the first time there had been an "administrative liability to provide labour for private interests" (Lord Islington, House of Lords, July 14, 1920: 125).

Commissioners were instructed to convey in strong terms to the native chiefs that they must assist in encouraging unemployed young men to go out and work on the plantations and not be "idle" in the reserves. Records were to be kept of the names of the chiefs who were helpful and those who were not. The circular warned that "should the labour difficulties continue it may be necessary to bring in other and special measures to meet the case" (7); the special measures that might have to be employed were left unspecified.

The first opposition to the labor circular came in the form of a memorandum published on November 8, 1919, in the *East African Standard,* the leading newspaper of Kenya. The memorandum, written by the bishops of the Church of England in East Africa and Uganda and by the senior representatives of the Church of Scotland Mission, became known as the "Bishops' Memorandum." The bishops' main objection to the labor circular was that while the terms "forced labor" and "compulsory labor" were carefully avoided throughout, that was sure to be the result. Thus ensued a series of debates, discussions, amendments to existing ordinances, and additional labor circulars.

In an effort to assuage the fears of the bishops, Ainsworth issued a second labor circular on February 20, 1920. He stressed that there was no intention that officers and chiefs should become recruiters or that men should be directed or ordered work. This circular was intended to silence criticism in East Africa, but criticism was beginning to mount in England. Members of the House of Commons had obtained a copy of the Bishops' Memorandum, though not the labor circular itself.[5] British undersecretary of state for the colonies Amery had obtained an unofficial copy of the circular and had spoken with Governor Northey. On April 20, 1920, a debate took place in the House of Commons regarding the labor circular. Amery defended the circular, saying that there was nothing in it that "necessarily involves anything beyond advice or encouragement to work or discouragement to be idle" (House of Commons Debates, April 20, 1920: 954).

On July 14, 1920, Northey issued a third circular at the direction of the colonial office (Tignor 1976: 17). It emphasized that it was the responsibility of administrative officers to see that native chiefs did not abuse their authority by engaging in oppression or favoritism in their efforts to encourage Africans to work. The circular stressed that "it is in the interests of the natives themselves for the young men to become wage earners and not remain idle in their Reserves for a large part of the year" (Cmd. 873, 1920: 7).[6] The circular also emphasized that government officials must ensure that the provisions of the Masters and Servants Amendment of 1919 be strictly enforced.[7] On the same day, a debate took place in the House of Lords on the government's policy regarding native labor. Much opposition to the labor circulars was voiced during this debate, and Lord Milner, secretary of state for the colonies, was asked to make a statement on native labor in British East Africa.

DISCIPLINARY TECHNOLOGY AND THE PRODUCTION OF AFRICAN IDENTITY

In his discussion of discipline, Foucault (1979: 198–203) draws upon two images: the leper and the plague. The image of the leper gave rise to rituals of exile, rejection, exclusion, and enclosure. The political dream underlying this image was that of a pure community, the dangerous and contaminated separated from the "real" population. The image of the plague, in contrast, gave rise to practices of observation, surveillance, correct training, and order. The leper was marked; the plague was analyzed. The political dream underlying the image of the plague is the dream of a disciplined society. The image of the leper underlies projects of exclusion, while the image of the plague underlies projects of discipline. As Foucault points out, however, the two images and the political projects they give rise to are not incompatible. Rather, they came together in the nineteenth century when techniques of discipline were applied to spaces of exclusion: "On the one hand, the lepers are treated as plague victims; the tactics of individualizing disciplines are imposed on the excluded; and, on the other hand, the universality of disciplinary control makes it possible to brand the 'leper' and to bring into play against him the dualistic mechanisms of exclusion" (ibid.: 199).

Colonial Kenya exemplifies the political dream of a pure community coming together with the political dream of a disciplined society. The dream of pure community took the form of an urge to create a new "white man's country." This was one of the central themes in Kenya's colonial history (Rosberg and Nottingham 1966: 19). The exemplar of this dream was the "White Highlands" of the Rift Valley, of which the creation of tribal reserves and alienation of African land was an important part. The White Highlands contained the most fertile, richest soil of Kenya, and it was where the impact of European settlement was most manifest (Furedi 1989: 8). Practices of exclusion in the form of reserves thus formed an important aspect of colonial administration. The dream of pure community was ultimately impossible, however, because of the white settlers' overwhelming dependence on African labor. The African "native" could not be made analogous to the leper. The "native" body was needed to supply the labor without which the dream of a pure white community could never be realized. This created a dilemma: how to reject and exclude the African as a human being equal to the European but simultaneously make the African body available for work. The perfectly governed, disciplined society became the political dream that would facilitate this. Practices of exclusion were joined with practices of discipline and inscribed on the body of the African "native."

British colonial administration in Kenya was thus based on a project of both exclusion and discipline, arguably making it rival Bentham's panopticon as an exemplar of disciplinary technology.[8] Hammond and Jablow (1977: 74–91) note the importance of colonial administration (as opposed to trade, education, and Christianity) for improving the African. While trade, education, and Christianity remained essential, the end of the nineteenth century witnessed a shift in focus to good administration and sound government as the means of ensuring the protection and progress of colonial subjects as well as the prosperity of the empire. Proper administration would alleviate the need to resort to force and would also enable Africans to fulfull an economic role while remaining separate from the "real" population—the white settlers.

Enclosures of "Native" Space

An important aspect of discipline is the spatial distribution and classification of a population. The lands ordinances and the system of tribal reserves are illustrative of Britain's focus on efficient administration and exemplify disciplinary technology in a colonial setting. The creation of tribal reserves facilitated the organization of bodies for the purpose of discipline, control, and security. While it was linked with land alienation and the promotion of capitalist agriculture, the creation of tribal reserves cannot be reduced solely to a single-minded calculation by capitalist interests. Ostensibly the primary aim of the reserves was to foster African security by regulating non-African entry into the reserve areas (Rosberg and Nottingham 1963: 154). Many missionary and humanitarian lobbies initially supported the establishment of reserves for this reason (Kennedy 1987: 147). Also of significance, the reserves were designed to mitigate "the dark mood of anxiety that pervaded the settler mentality" (ibid.: 149). The concern with settler security was evident in the recommendation of a 1905 Kenya Land Commission Committee that "reserves made for natives should be few in number but of large extent and far removed from European centers." This is certainly reminiscent of Foucault's suggestion that the control of space facilitated the "reduction of dangerous multitudes or wandering vagabonds to fixed and docile individuals" (Dreyfus and Rabinow 1983: 154). Again in 1919 the government's Land Settlement Commission recommended that a scheme be devised "for concentrating the natives in a number of areas distributed as widely as possible throughout the Reserves, sufficient, but not more than sufficient, for their requirements, leaving the interspersed tracts not needed for native occupation as available for white settlement" (Rosberg and Nottingham 1963: 43).

The separation of Africans and white settlers was also important in producing and maintaining the respective identities of these subjects, especially the latter. Kennedy (1987: 4) points to the importance of maintaining rigid lines of distinction in the social sphere in white settler colonies containing large indigenous populations upon whom settlers were dependent for labor. Indeed, one of the central themes in the relations between black and white was the resolution to the dilemma created by the white dependence upon black in the economic realm and the desire for disassociation in the social realm.[9] The control of space was thus a significant element of a disciplinary technology that, as Foucault points out *makes* individuals, "regards individuals both as objects and as instruments of its exercize" (1979: 170). Inherent in this process is the constitution and maintenance of social identities. The term *space* should not, however, be interpreted too narrowly or too literally. The physical separation of black and white was important, but it could not always be maintained because of the need for African labor. The control of discursive space was an important supplement to (and arguably a prerequisite for) the control of physical space. Acts such as the Masters and Servants Ordinance of 1910, while regulating relations between employers and servants, was also at pains to define the identities of the subjects who could occupy these hierarchical positions: "The word 'servant' means any Arab or Native employed for hire.... The word 'Native' means a native of Africa not being of European or Asiatic

race or origin" (13). Other less official, but no less powerful, practices of naming included European practices of giving derogatory
nicknames "monkey," "damn-fool" to domestics (Kennedy 1987:
155). These practices of exclusion, marking, and naming not only
produced the African colonial identity but also functioned to reproduce a particular identity for the white settlers. The fragility of these
identities is revealed by the fact that these practices of naming were
given such importance both officially and unofficially.

The lands ordinances and the system of tribal reserves both reflected and enabled the linking of African identity to the material
value of the body as labor supply. The right of individual ownership
of property presumed an individual identity that, through rhetorical
strategies of negation, the African was deemed to be lacking. Beyond the physical usefulness of the body as a disciplined and productive object, the African was a blank and uninteresting slate. Western contact was the key to the production and progress of the African
as an individual and as a human being. The words of Charles Eliot,
former governor of East Africa are illustrative:

> But there can be no doubt of the immense progress made in render-
> ing the civilization of the African at least possible, and it is a progress
> which need occasion no regrets, for we are not destroying any old or
> interesting system, but simply introducing order into blank, uninter-
> esting, brutal barbarism. (quoted in Cell 1976: 181–82)

The suggestion of blankness prior to European contact is, of course,
not unique to this case. It resonates with the U.S. denial of the existence of a Philippine "people" noted in chapter 2. Said (1993: 183)
also notes the French claim that an Algerian nation never existed. It is
implicit in all narratives of "discovery" that imply a prior emptiness.

Registering "Native" Identity

The control of space was accompanied by a system of surveillance
that was both totalizing and individualizing. In 1915, based on recommendations of the 1912 Native Labour Commission of East Africa, the Legislative Council passed the Native Registration Ordinance. This ordinance outlined a system that would identify natives
in the event of desertion from their employers.[10] The ordinance was
not put into practice until after the war, when the Kenyan Convention
of Associations decried the "appalling insecurity of native labour"

(McGregor Ross 1927: 188) and employers suggested that "the native is absolutely out of control" (Maxon 1980: 355). Registration was considered necessary in order to organize and control native labor: "Any of us who have had the handling of large numbers of natives know that unless natives are properly registered and can be identified by an efficient pass system, no one can control or depend on labour" (*East African Standard,* July 16, 1919).

In 1920 an amendment put the 1915 ordinance into effect. Under this system, every male African over the age of sixteen was required to register with a district officer and to carry a registration paper. This paper, carried inside a metal container, contained fingerprints and various other information regarding the "native's" employment, including the name and address of his last employer, the date he began work, the date he left it, and the rate of wages paid. Fingerprinting was considered essential because, in the words of Governor Northey, "when dealing with so vast a number of illiterate persons whose distinguishing characteristics were not readily discernible by Europeans the only reliable method was the fingerprint system" (Van Zwanenburg 1975: 187). When a man left his reserve, he was obliged to carry this metal container, known as a *kipande,* with him (Buell 1928: 357; McGregor Ross 1927: 189; Van Zwanenburg 1975: 187).

The intention behind this system was to identify deserters so that penalties could be enacted against them. This would also serve to discourage desertion. In a word, the system was a means of disciplining labor. As Governor Northey pointed out in an interview with the leading East African newspaper, there had been a "deterioration in discipline" and a "general relaxation in the manners and industry of the native" (*East African Standard,* August 7, 1919). Registration provided a visibility open to the gaze of the European employer and the British colonial authorities. The registration system was also individuating in that each "native" could be known, placed under surveillance, and disciplined if necessary.

The registration system was extremely popular with the employers and the government. It was considered beneficial to the "natives" themselves, giving them greater job security and preventing employers from cheating them on their wages. Beyond that, and perhaps of greater significance, it was seen as providing the African with an "identity" that was lacking prior to the registration system, a partial writing on the blank slate that was the African. Note the following assertions in the *East African Standard,* the leading Kenyan newspaper of the time:

> Prior to registration an innocent native could be wrongly accused, because one native is more or less like hundreds or thousands of others.... Now however he possesses an individuality that is indisputable, a signature on each finger tip.

> Prior to the introduction of this measure ... the names employed by natives among themselves have always been unreliable, variable and restricted in numbers. Many natives have the same name: the vast majority was and is illiterate ... (but the system) had encouraged each native to acquire self-reliance; it has taught him that as an individual he has both duties and privileges. (quoted in Van Zwanenburg 1975: 188–89)

One of the telling things about the registration system was the relative lack of debate and discussion it elicited, especially in comparison to the labor circulars. It was accepted as natural that this was an unobjectionable and appropriate policy. That "natives" lacked identity and could acquire self-identity and individuality through the issuance of a *kipande* was unremarkable and elicited little debate.

This discussion suggests that the kind of disciplinary power examined by Foucault was operative in societies outside of the European center. Indeed, the ultimate in panopticism may, in fact, have been in the colonies. As Kennedy (1987: 149) notes, the very fabric of African lives was shaped by statutory constraints such as reserves, master and servant ordinances, and registration requirements. This, of course, is not to deny or minimize the existence of brutal and repressive sovereign power that was always present in colonial relationships. It is, however, to suggest that this was perhaps only the most obvious manifestation of imperial power. The sovereign power of the imperial center and the disciplinary techniques of colonial administration were mutually enabling. Both entailed representational practices through which the African "native" was defined, individuated, and incorporated into Western knowledge and power.

"I WORK THEREFORE I AM": THE DANGERS OF IDLENESS

"Idleness" functioned as a privileged signifier enabling a resolution to the apparent contradiction between labor exploitation and the dictates of trusteeship. The privileged position of this signifier presumed that the locus of "native" being was in the physical body and the efficient uses to which it could be put. Putting the "natives" to work thus became an important aspect of their development and thereby part of the sacred trust itself. The "natives" should be "saved from dangerous idleness" (London *Times*, August 11, 1920). Putting the natives to work was not only necessary for the development of the country's resources but also essential for the development of the African. The day before the first labor circular was issued, Governor Northey declared:

> The white man must be paramount.... For the good of the country and for his own welfare he (the native) must be brought out to work.... Our policy, then, I believe, should be to encourage voluntary work in the first place but to provide power by legislation to prevent idleness. (quoted in Buell 1928: 333)

The labor circular itself stated that

> The necessity for an increased supply of labour cannot be brought too frequently before the various native authorities, nor can they be too often reminded that it is in their own interests to see that their young men become wage earners and do not remain idle for the greater part of the year.

And Undersecretary Amery echoed the necessity of encouraging the native to work:

> We have to face a very difficult problem in dealing with education and development of the natives. It is not enough to say that economic inducements alone will bring the native to see the advantages of work and of raising his standard of living. There are some native races, the American Red Indians, for instance, or many of the splendid tribes in Polynesia, who have shown no inclination to take any interests in any form of economic development, and who for this very reason, have tended to die out. (1920: 955)

Amery linked "natives" in Africa with "natives" in other geographical locations. The identity of all of these different "natives" revolved around the need to work. All implicitly had an inherent propensity to idleness that had to be overcome in order for them to progress and develop. This complements the notion that the locus of African identity was in the body, the physical. Development of the African "native" centered on the body and its usefulness, on overcoming idleness, not on the intellect.

The Bishops' Memorandum called into question the labor circular's opposition between idleler and wage earner by pointing out that there were different kinds of idleness. The bishops added a layer of complexity to the term *idleness*:

> No one who had lived in a native reserve will deny that there are days or months of practical idleness; but no one who has lived in a reserve and had the opportunity of closely watching native life but will realise that the native has also his months of strenuous work, cultivating and planting, harvesting, building, etc. (9)

The British texts equated idleness with laziness and elided what might be called practical idleness. The bishops' text left a space for the concept that Africans might be idle simply because it was not planting or harvesting season and all building and other work had been completed. The African "native" constructed in the bishops' text, however, was still "other" than the kind of subject that attached moral qualities to work. While in the bishops' text we find the recognition that not being a wage earner did not constitute idleness, we still find the construction of a kind of subject that had a potential for idleness. This is reflected in the bishops' accordance with the main purpose of the labor circular: "With the main purpose of that memorandum, the prevention of idleness, and the meeting, by all legitimate means, of the demand for necessary labour, we are in entire accord" (8).

The bishops agreed that preventing idleness on the part of the African must be a goal of the British. If the African had been an inherently moral kind of subject that attached moral qualities to work, the issue of idleness would not have arisen in the first place. But the African "native" had a tendency to "live a miserable life of idleness, drunkenness, and vice" (Governor Northey, quoted approvingly by Milner, House of Lords, July 14, 1920: 156). The bishops' concern with potential idleness on the part of the African indicates a basic, albeit more subtly articulated, agreement with Northey's statement.

This was also evident in the discourse of J. H. Oldham, a renowned church and missionary leader, who during the labor crisis was editor of the influential *International Review of Missions* and was about to assume the post of secretary of the International Missionary Council (Tignor 1976: 171). In August of 1920 Oldham had called all leading missionary representatives, including the bishops

of Mombasa, Uganda, and Zanzibar, to London for a special conference, at which they called for withdrawal of the labor circulars and
for the substitution of a policy in accord with the principle of trusteeship (Gregory 1962: 32). A memo was drafted and circulated among
members of the various missionary organizations, other humanitarians, and members of the House of Commons and the House of
Lords. On December 14, 1920, the memorandum was presented to
the Colonial Office and to the secretary of state for the colonies, who
promised that the subject would be given careful attention (ibid.).
The secretary subsequently retired and was replaced by Winston
Churchill. Though disheartened, Oldham renewed his campaign. After some revisions, the memorandum was forwarded to Edward F.
L. Wood, Churchill's parliamentary undersecretary of state, on May
24, 1921. I was unable to obtain a copy of the memorandum, but
in a related article published in the *International Review of Missions*
Oldham writes:

> There is no doubt that there is a good deal of idleness among the na-
> tives of East Africa, though inquiry seems to show that many of the
> statements on this subject are exaggerated. There is no question that
> the encouragement of habits of industry is a legitimate aim of the
> Government. But it by no means follows that the only method of
> doing this is to force the natives to seek work on European planta-
> tions. Habits of industry may equally be encouraged by a policy of
> education within the reserves, by the demonstration of improved
> methods of agriculture and by the development of native industries.
> The objection to any system of compulsion is that it creates a dis-
> taste for labour and so defeats its own end. (Oldham 1921: 191–92)

While he was opposed to forced labor, Oldham, like the bishops,
was nonetheless in agreement with those who thought that "natives"
must have habits of industry instilled in them. He agreed that this
was a legitimate goal of the government. This, of course, presupposed
that "natives" did not have or would not develop on their own sufficient "habits of industry." This construction of the "native" was
not limited to this particular case. The "native" as lazy or unappre-
ciative of the value of work was a major theme in British colonial
discourse. In the words of colonial secretary Joseph Chamberlain:

> In the interests of the natives themselves all over Africa we have to
> teach them to work. The progress of the native in civilization will
> not be secured until he has been convinced of the necessity and dig-

nity of labor. Therefore I think that anything we reasonably can do to induce the native to labor is a desirable thing. (quoted in Hinden 1949: 105)

The presumption that "natives" had a natural propensity to idleness is part of a much more encompassing discourse, both spatially and temporally. Spurr (1993: 157) notes that the Asiatic or non-European has been constructed as wholly content with idleness all the way back to Rousseau and that this persists into current times. Rousseau wrote, "Nature does so much for people there [Asia] that they have almost nothing to do. Provided that an Asiatic has women and repose, he is content" (quoted in Spurr 1993: 157). This representation expanded to West Africa, "where the myth of tropical exuberance encouraged the European to think that the Africans had no need to work" (Curtin 1964: 224). It also expanded to East Africa, where European protection was substituted for tropical exuberance in rendering the African idle.[11] In East Africa the Europeans suggested the following:

> We protected him [the African] from tribal warfare, with its sufferings on the part of weak tribes, of murder and pillage. The natives have no longer to live in fear by night, nor do they have to build forts nor hide their huts in forests and hills. The most important circumstance of the new regime is that bodies of fighting men no longer have to be maintained to defend the homes and lands of their tribes. Thus young and able-bodied men are idle. (*East African Standard*, December 4, 1920)

This construction implicitly places the "native" in a position much closer to nature than the European. Like nature, the "native" body becomes objectified; it is an object to be conquered, controlled, and mastered.[12] The humanity of the "native" is denied. His being is reduced to the materiality of his body.

Idleness and its taken-for-granted link with the African native not only resolved the contradiction between labor exploitation and trusteeship but also served as an enabling presupposition for colonial land alienation policies. Maughan-Brown (1985: 83–85) notes the mutually reinforcing myths of Kikuyu agricultural inefficiency and African idleness. Such representations supported policies that would give land to those who would use it productively (the white settlers) and take it away from those whose "primitive methods of African soil cultivation leads to soil erosion and very low productivity" (Elspeth Huxley, quoted in Maughan-Brown 1985: 83). These myths' lack of veracity made them no less powerful. Kennedy (1987: 28–29) points out that African agriculture in the early 1900s was much more efficient and successful than European agriculture. Local trade was dominated by African peasants. Indeed, this fact is in part responsible for the perpetual shortage of African labor to work on European farms. Swainson (1980: 7) points out that in 1913 products of black African origin furnished about three-quarters of the country's export earnings. Maughan-Brown (1985: 84) quotes from a 1917 annual report from the district commissioner for Naivasha: "Agriculture has made little progress except at the hands of native squatters." Despite these counterfacts, the myths persisted well into the 1950s, as evidenced in the words of one of the writers on "Mau Mau": "the African is so averse to labour, and the land he possesses so quickly degenerates into eroded soil, into fields untilled and undeveloped" (Leigh 1954: 210).

AUTHORIZING AUTHORITY: THE DOUBLE BIND OF OPPOSITIONAL DISCOURSE

Torgovnick (1990: 146) observes of Conrad's *Heart of Darkness* that it is both a "criticism of imperialism and yet [a] lavish, even loving repetition of primitivist tropes." She suggests that we need to talk about what the novella refuses to discuss. Similar suggestions have been made with respect to Rudyard Kipling's *Kim* (Said 1993). The double bind present in Conrad and Kipling is not limited to fictional literature but can also be found in narratives and debates surrounding "real" policy issues. This is especially notable in the bishops' discourse as well as that of others who objected to and interpreted the labor circulars as suggesting the use of forced labor.

The bishops' main objection to the labor circular was that while the terms "forced labour" and "compulsory labour" were carefully avoided throughout, this was sure to be the result. Africans were incapable of comprehending the subtleties involved in making the distinction between wishes and commands, influence and force, hints and orders: "To the native mind a hint and an order on the part of the Government are indistinguishable" (Bishops' Memorandum: 8). It was not, however, the idea of using influence that mainly troubled the bishops, but *who* would be using the influence:

But if the work of thus influencing potential labourers were confined to British officials, little harm might be done. It is when the
further step is taken, and native chiefs are charged with the business
of recruiting labour, that the door is flung wide open to almost any
abuse. (ibid.)

The bishops objected not to compulsion per se, but rather to the
way in which it would come about according to the policy outlined
in the labor circular:

Compulsory labour is not in itself an evil, and we would favor some
form of compulsion, at any rate for work of national importance
and provided that: It is frankly recognized as compulsion and legal-
ized as such, not veiled under such terms as advice, wishes, encouragement. The native understands a definite order; he does not understand Government wishes as distinct from commands. (ibid.)

Compulsion should be exercised "under the proper conditions,
guaranteed by the Government, and secured by regular inspection
and visitation" (ibid.: 11). The bishops expressed empathy with the
settlers and the government and stated that the missions welcomed
the king's general policy regarding labor:

We realise the difficulty in which both the Government and the Settlers are placed. We have no wish to add to that difficulty. We do
not believe that there is the least intention, on either side, of exploit-
ing natives for private ends; but experience has shown that it is
highly dangerous to place in the hands of Native Chiefs and Headmen vague and undefined powers and still more dangerous to expose to these powers not only men but women and children.

Some form, however, of compulsory service we believe, in present conditions, to be a necessity. It remains to find the best form in
which the compulsion may be exercised. We believe that the straight-
est road is the best; that the work will be best done directly, by Europeans, rather than indirectly through the native headman; and
legally, by definite enactment, under which each man knows his obligations and their limits rather than by incessant appeals and demands,
which leave the natives in a state of bewildered irritation, and will
we believe, fail to reach the desired end.

The Missions welcome His Excellency's general policy, as expressed in his recent memorandum, and recognize, in his labour proposals, the earnest effort to meet by all possible constitutional means
a great and pressing need. We believe, however, that it places far too

great a power in the hands of native chiefs and headmen, and we therefore desire to see it modified on the lines suggested above. (ibid.)

The effect of these representational practices was to naturalize a structure of authority centered on the ability or lack of ability to handle power and authority without abusing it. The African "native" was constructed as a subject who was incapable of handling power and authority without abuse. In contrast, British officials were unlikely to do harm.

This construction of the African "native" was simultaneously an assertion or reaffirmation of British identity. Indeed, the ability of Britain, as a colonial power, to exercise power and authority without abusing it was called into question by this whole issue of recruiting "native" labor. In a larger sense, this was an important element of trusteeship. Nor were the rhetorical strategies that reaffirmed British and colonial identities limited to this particular case. The opposition between those capable of managing others and those who were not was echoed in the text of Lord Frederick Lugard's *The Dual Mandate in British Tropical Africa,* regarded as "the most influential book on colonial affairs in the whole inter-war period" (Hetherington 1978: 4) and the "staple diet of reading in colonial administration for young cadet officers (Lee 1967: 43). In a section entitled "Description of the African," Lugard wrote: "The African negro is not naturally cruel, though his own insensibility to pain, and his disregard for life—whether his own or another's—cause him to appear callous to suffering.... He loves the display of power, but fails to appreciate its responsibility" (1922: 69).

One of the most fundamental presuppositions that undergirded the entire discourse surrounding the labor issue was the presumption that the white settlers' demand for labor was legitimate and necessary. Behind this presupposition was the presumption that it was unremarkable that white settlers were in Kenya in the first place, possessing the land that necessitated "native" labor. Even the bishops took this state of affairs for granted, thus contributing to the normalization of colonial conquest and the domination of black by white as well as the dispossession of "native" lands.

One of the most outspoken critics of British colonial policy in East Africa was Norman Leys. A former member of the colonial service who became highly critical of imperialism in general and in

East Africa in particular, Leys called into question the naturalization of European conquest. Leys was active with East African mis-
sionaries and during the "native labor crisis" carried on extensive
correspondence with the bishops and other missionary leaders, including J. H. Oldham. In a letter to W. E. Owen, archdeacon of
Kavironda, in Kenya, Leys suggested that "if the settlers' demands
are to be regarded as 'requirements' then our solution to the problem is impossible" (Cell 1976: 153). Here, Leys called into question
what was to be regarded as a "requirement." He also suggested
that attention be given to "what chiefs, what educated natives, what
ordinary natives desire in policy" (ibid.: 16).

In an important sense, Leys moved toward the outer perimeter
of the dominant rhetorical practices that made up this colonial discourse, but he was also caught in a double bind that repeated some
of the most important assumptions of colonial rule. This is illustrated in a 1918 letter that Leys wrote to the secretary of state for
the colonies describing the realities of colonial rule and outlining
what was considered a revolutionary program of reform for East
Africa. In this letter Leys made the following statements:

> The aim of governments in Eastern Africa must be one of acclimati-
> zation, of adaptation to feelings and beliefs widely different from
> those natural to a governing race or caste. Governments must do
> more than take directly upon themselves the duty of sharing the
> knowledge and the arts and the instruments of civilised life accord-
> ing to the measure of the capacity of their subjects. All that they
> must certainly undertake. But in addition the spirit of government
> must be African, not in the sense that Imperial problems have an
> African aspect but in the sense that there must be as instant and inti-
> mate a response to the states of mind of the governed as in the case
> of governments by the governed themselves. If governments cannot
> be by the people they must be with and in the people. We must leave
> it to them to set the problems, even if it is we who must decide
> them. (115)

> Whenever the members of a civilised race have opportunity of mak-
> ing profit out of the labour of a barbarous one, especially if it be to-
> tally void of political rights, enslavement is inevitable. (123)

Despite what was considered the revolutionary character of Leys's
discourse, it left intact the center of colonial discourse — the notion
that humanity was divided into civilized and barbarous, governing

and subject races. While admirably seeking to give a voice to the Africans themselves, Leys still considered the African to be a subject whose capacity for self-determination was not obvious: "The African may or may not prove to be capable, in the phrase of the day, of self-determination" (quoted in Cell 1976: 135).

CONCLUSION

We can note several resonances between this discourse and the U.S. discourse on the Philippines: the lack of responsibility on the part of the "native," the inherent tendency for "natives" to exercise power without appreciation of its ends, which makes it dangerous to place power in their hands, their lack of capacity to exercise self-determination. We can also note a similar subject positioning for Africans and Filipinos that implies qualities closer to animals than human beings. This is evident in Lugard's comment on the insensibility to pain of the "African negroes" and in chapter 2 in Foreman's use of analogies to the goat and the monkey in "describing" the Filipino "native." In both cases the physical body and its capabilities were an important constitutive feature of "native" identity. Intellectual activity, reflective reasoning, and creativity were not core elements of their identity.

As in the U.S. discourse, colonial representations of the "native" made thinkable and justified inequality and the use of force. The paternalistic rhetoric of trusteeship overlapped and indeed presupposed the truth of the discourse on power and authority. This created a discursive space that made possible a wide range of practices ranging from relatively (and I emphasize *relatively*) "benign" ones such as education and missionary work to the use of force and the institutionalization of policies based upon a "reality" made up of different and unequal human beings. A British colonial report issued in 1924 stated that "it is extremely difficult to bring forward a primitive people on the basis of equality" (Ormsby-Gore 1925: 45).

We also find an inherent instability and fragility in the identities and the "reality" constructed in this discourse. The realization of the dream of a pure community of white settlers in Kenya was of necessity contingent upon contamination of that white purity by black African labor and the physical proximity it entailed. The impossibility of total physical exile of the African "native" made disciplinary and representational practices that much more significant in producing the often tenuous boundary between white settler and black African "native" identities. The amount of work, in the form of both official government acts and ordinances and settler practices such as derogatory nicknames and special clothing to set their servants apart from themselves, that went into the creation of white and black identities itself attests to the rather fragile nature of these identities and thus the constant need to reinscribe them.

To suggest that the identities constructed by colonial practices of representation were fragile is not, however, to deny their power and durability. On the contrary, it is repetition and dissemination that give representations their power, not an inherent stability and closure. Highlighting the instability and incompleteness of a discourse alerts us to the necessity to examine the practices by which the "reality" inscribed in a discourse is made to seem natural, complete, and fixed. This, in turn, opens up a conceptual/analytic space for conceiving not of a kind of power that operates within the context of a given reality or is possessed and used by a priori, given identities, but rather of a power that *creates* "reality" and identities.

I am arguing that the representational practices examined in chapters 2 and 3 were practices of power that were fundamental in creating the late-nineteenth/early-twentieth-century "reality" that made possible an important aspect of international relations. Indeed, it is hard to imagine that the phenomenon of imperialism would have been possible in the absence of these kinds of representations. Said (1993: 3, 26) expresses uncertainty about whether the past is really past or continues in different forms. In Parts II and III I explore more recent encounters between North and South and the ways in which nineteenth-century imperial encounters continue to be implicated in the representational practices by which boundaries are drawn and international identities are constructed.

II

Insurgencies and Counterinsurgencies

Introduction to Part II

Counterinsurgency policies have been a major element of post–World War II foreign policy toward the countries collectively referred to as the "third world." Such policies were considered essential within the context of a world divided along the geopolitical lines of East versus West with each side seeking to win those not yet fully committed to either camp. Counterinsurgency has thus taken on a meaning that generally presumes the context of a communist-led, -supported, or -influenced insurgency. To so limit our understanding of this phenomenon, however, obscures the diverse and scattered elements that came together to give meaning and currency to the concept and practice of counterinsurgency.

Those elements can be found in the many and varied colonial responses to resistance on the part of colonized peoples. Neither these resistances nor the colonial responses to them are solely a post–World War II phenomenon. Rather, they span the horizon of colonialism itself. Nor are the contexts confined to concern with the spread of communism. Britian's counterinsurgency policy in Kenya during the 1950s, which is the subject of chapter 5, demonstrates this only too well. Mockaitis (1990: 13) points out, regarding British counterinsurgency, that its roots go back much further than post–World War II concerns with communism and suggests that Britain's first experience with counterinsurgency came with the Easter Rising of 1916 in Ireland. Bello (Klare and Kornbluh 1988: 158) notes that the Philippine insurrection of 1899–1902 allowed the United States Army free rein to develop and test a variety of counterinsurgency tactics that are still emulated today.

Much has been written about this topic from the point of view of those concerned with tactics of warfare and conflict and forms of intervention and those concerned with understanding and explaining how foreign policy is made (e.g., Blaufarb 1977; Klare and Kornbluh 1988; Shafer 1988). Counterinsurgency is generally understood as a response to an insurgency, which in turn is conceived of as a form of nontraditional conflict involving "subversion, guerrilla warfare, and terrorism" (Mockaitis 1990: 3). Counterinsurgency has thus gone way beyond the use of force and traditional methods of conflict, extending into the social, economic, and even psychological realms. Two important and related aspects of counterinsurgency that have received little or no attention are of utmost relevance in this study. The first involves an understanding of counterinsurgency as an exemplary site wherein the power/knowledge nexus operates. Counterinsurgency is not only a strategy or a set of tactics for putting down "internal" struggles; it also involves the power to define what is to be considered legitimate dissent, legitimate means of struggle, and the legitimate ends to which struggle is directed. Winning adherents involves the presumption of a domestic population who are at risk of corruption by an external force. Ironically, though, the very existence of an insurgent group that is considered a threat denies the legitimacy of an established order and calls into question just who the people are who are to be won. Counterinsurgency can thus be conceived of as a site and a practice wherein and whereby identities are constructed and boundaries are drawn so that threats to the existing order are attributed to the dangerous "Other(s)."

The second aspect of counterinsurgency that is important to this study involves the representational practices that have accompanied and enabled the reaffirmations of authority that are at the heart of counterinsurgency. Insurgencies are aimed at delegitimizing the authority of the existing order. Counterinsurgency thus aims to reaffirm that legitimacy. In many (most) instances the authority of the existing order has coincided, at least indirectly, with the authority of the West. Counterinsurgency thus involves representational practices by which the authority and values of the West are reaffirmed.

Considering these two aspects together, counterinsurgency can perhaps best be understood as a response to resistances that reveals the contingency and fragility of imperial and neoimperial authority. Insurgency itself reveals the failure of imperial authority to completely naturalize a particular way of being. Following Bhabha, Spurr (1993: 124) suggests that once authority begins to be asserted, a split opens between assertion and authority itself, in which the latter is revealed as conditional and contingent on its representation. Affirmations of authority can thus be seen as strategic devices necessary for the maintenance of that authority rather than as simple manifestations of an unquestioned presence. Counterinsurgency aims to restore (or in many cases to create) the status quo, to naturalize the authority of a particular social order, and to make deviant and illegitimate those who seek to disrupt it. At the same time, however, counterinsurgency reveals the contingent and incomplete nature of the representational practices that construct and naturalize social identities and positions of authority. In chapters 4 and 5 I examine two different instances of counterinsurgency, one within a cold war context and one that had little connection to the cold war. In contrast to most of those who have written about counterinsurgency, I do not seek to explain successes or failures in policy, nor to examine how foreign policy decisions were made. The focus here is on the discourse(s) surrounding these policies and the continuities and discontinuities in the representational practices examined in chapters 2 and 3.

4

Precocious Children, Adolescent Nations

We of the United States feel that we are merely entering into a new partnership with the Philippines — a partnership of two free and sovereign nations working in harmony and understanding. The United States and its partner of the Pacific, the Philippine Republic, have already chartered a pattern of relationships for all the world to study. Together, in the future, our two countries must prove the soundness and the wisdom of this great experiment in Pacific democracy.

PRESIDENT HARRY TRUMAN[1]

The two short-run crisis problems of (1) security and (2) the budget result largely from lack of sufficient but realizable development of her [the Philippines'] economic potential, of her political and social institutions, and fundamentally of the intellectual and moral characteristics of her people.

OFFICER IN CHARGE OF ECONOMIC AFFAIRS[2]

An understanding of the Philippine people is essential, and their shortcomings must be appraised against their historic background. A useful analogy is to regard them as precocious children without minimizing their potential as future world citizens.

U.S. EMBASSY MEMO[3]

On July 4, 1946, for the first time in history, an imperial nation voluntarily relinquished possession of its colonial conquest (Karnow 1989: 323). As the United States granted independence to the Philippines, the new relationship between the two was widely heralded as one of partnership and equality.[4] Discourses surrounding this event reflected certain discontinuities with the earlier colonial discourses. The Philippines were re-presented as a sovereign nation-state, inhabited by "a people" who replaced the "heterogeneous mass" of colonial times. The relationship between the United States and the Philippines was announced as a partnership. Though the Philippines had been confronted with many problems, they had year after year demonstrated a capacity for democratic self-government. They had earned the right of independence and as an infant republic stood at the threshold of an adventure in the society of other nations (MacArthur 1946). The emergence of the Philippines as a sovereign nation stood as proof conclusive that the United States stood for fair play, for aid to the weak, for liberty and freedom, for progress, and for prosperity for other peoples (McDonough 1946). The Philippines stood as a "monument to American unselfishness and helpfulness" (Villamin 1946).

Despite this optimistic beginning, the United States was soon to embark on an interventionist course that displayed little respect for Philippine sovereignty. Amid all the profession of sovereign equality, the postcolonial U.S.-Philippine relationship came to be constructed in such a manner that the United States was licensed to diagnose and judge the internal situation of the Philippines, and counterinsurgency came to be regarded as the only reasonable course of action. The rosy picture of an adolescent nation freed from its parental chains and ready to become a mature member of international society was soon to fade and give way to images of instability, corruption, and imminent danger. The re-presentation of the Philippines as a sovereign and independent state merged with earlier colonial representations, thereby constituting particular spaces of possibilities and impossibilities. The Philippines came to be represented as a realm of danger, susceptible to ominous threats to internal stability and order. The threat extended to the external stability of the region as a whole and to the prestige of the United States in that region and indeed in the world. The manifestation of this threat was found in the Hukbalahap. The prescription was counterinsurgency.

BACKGROUND

The Hukbalahap (Hukbong Bayan Labal Sa Hapon), or People's Army against the Japanese, originated in the early days of the war against Japan as a guerrilla fighting force, though its foundations were the peasant organizations that had emerged during the 1930s. It was the largest and most active organization in central Luzon. Widespread peasant unrest developed into rebellion between 1946 and the early 1950s. The rebellion reached its peak during 1951 and then began to fade between late 1951 and the first half of 1952. During this period, the countries of Asia and the Pacific figured prominently in U.S. foreign policy discourse. After the end of World War II, several things worked to shift the primary focus of U.S. attention away from Europe and toward the "third world" generally and Southeast Asia more specifically. The United States displayed an increasing desire to master developments in this part of the world.[5] The U.S. concern with the Philippines, while containing an economic and symbolic element, also stemmed from the perceived "communist threat," as manifested in the Huk rebellion.

During World War II, a large number of Filipinos joined guerrilla groups to resist Japanese occupation. One such group, the USAFFE, was led by U.S. officers who had evaded capture or by members of the Filipino elite who refused to cooperate with the Japanese. There were also autonomous resistance movements, not under the control of USAFFE. The most significant of these developed in central Luzon, which had been an area of intense peasant unrest even before the war. In March 1942, left-wing labor and peasant leaders and intellectuals established the People's Anti-Japanese Army, the Hukbalahap, which grew to about 10,000 members. In 1945, when U.S. troops entered central Luzon, the Huks assisted in the fight against the Japanese. After the Japanese were defeated, the Americans ordered the Huks to disband. In the words of one U.S. Army commander, "Avoid making them [the Hukbalahap] feel discriminated against. But disarm them as their areas of activity come within our sphere of control" (Kerkvliet 1977: 111). At the same time, the USAFFE forces were allowed to keep their arms. Unlike the USAFFE, the Hukbalahap was a popular-based guerrilla movement with political organizations in the villages. The USAFFE opposed the Huks for creating these extragovernmental units, portraying the Huks to the U.S. Army as "subversive, a radical organization. Its major operations and activities of carnage, revenge, banditry, and highjacking never have been equaled in any page of history of the Philippines" (quoted in ibid.: 115).

The Huks were also disliked by the landlords and political elites. The interests of the peasants were represented by the Huks, many of whom were peasants themselves. These interests were at odds with the status quo of elitist politics, which permitted a minimum of nonelite participation. The economic interests of the landed elite were also at odds with the economic interests of the peasants. Rarely could tenants go from one harvest to the next without running short of rice to eat, so the peasant/tenant had to borrow from the landlord. These "ration loans" were ended by the landlords in the early 1930s: "Haciendas had to be put on a more sound economic footing. You see, the landlord-tenant relationship is a business partnership, not a family. The landlord has invested capital in the land, and the tenants give their labor" (ibid.: 14). In addition, rents (the portion of the peasant's crop that had to be given to the landlord) went from 30 percent to 50 percent. At the same time, there was a land shortage caused by the commercialization of agriculture and rising population. Many small freeholders lost their land, and peasant incomes fell to subsistence levels or lower. These were some of the grievances that fueled the peasants' support of the rebellion.

This situation was significant for the United States. After independence the Philippines became a symbol of U.S. benevolence regarding its position as a colonial power. They were an important source of both prestige and identity for the United States. Philippine independence was proof that the United States had benign intentions when it annexed the islands and that it had been successful in its "civilizing mission": "When the United States relinquished sovereignty over the Philippines in 1946 it was the culmination of a half century of effort to cultivate an independent democratic state in the Orient," the U.S. ambassador to the Philippines, Myron Cowen, said (*New York Times,* June 11, 1950). The Huk rebellion therefore presented a dilemma. On the one hand, overt U.S. intervention would call into question the sovereignty and independence of the Philippines, which in turn would call into question the success of the U.S. effort to "civilize" a people and cultivate a democracy. On the other hand, losing the Philippines to communism would also mean a U.S. failure.

Within this context various documents, correspondence, and reports on the Philippine situation came into being and were circulated among various government officials. All of these texts did not necessarily refer directly to the Huk rebellion; U.S. interest in the Huks was part of a larger concern with communism in the Far East that became inextricably linked with the issue of economic and political development and perhaps most significantly with U.S. international identity.

GLOBAL PURPOSE AND WORLD GOVERNANCE

U.S. identity in 1950 was that of an exemplary world citizen, the living model of sovereign identity, stability, freedom, democracy, and material progress. Effecting global social purpose was its international mission.[6] This entailed fixing political identities and linking these identities with a particular social purpose, which was itself not in need of articulation, justification, or legitimation simply because it was "natural." Alternatives could not be considered. Counterinsurgency can be understood as a formalized practice whose goal is the production of social purpose. Ironically, however, it simultaneously reveals the failure of any collectively recognized purpose within a society, either a domestic society or an international society. While insurgency and counterinsurgency ostensibly refer to a particular domestic society, they have been inextricably linked with international politics, as this case demonstrates only too well.

Counterinsurgency politicizes the production of social purpose. The legitimation of particular social relationships and the need to silence alternatives expose the absence of any self-evident way of being. The result of a "successful" counterinsurgency program would be the production of international subjects (world citizens) who, while free to choose their own form of government, were nonetheless committed to a particular way of being and acting, and who saw certain goals and objectives as natural and worthy of pursuit. This was embodied in the concept of "total diplomacy": "The times call for a total diplomacy equal to the task of defense against Soviet expansion and to the task of building the kind of world in which our way of life can flourish" (Acheson 1950).

The "white man's burden" of the colonial period shifted from civilizing the uncivilized to global governance, the production of a world in which the U.S. way of life could flourish. While this bore traces of the earlier colonial mission, the project was now more complicated, more open-ended, and subject to more disruptions and contradictions. The kind of world in which the U.S. way of life could flourish was based on a fundamental tension that had to be constantly managed but could never be fully resolved. Indeed, it was this tension that animated U.S. policies in the postindependent "third world." This tension consisted of two elements.

The kind of world in which the U.S. way of life could flourish and that the United States thus strove to create was liberal, open, democratic, and pluralist. This implied the promotion of sovereignty and independence for its former colonies such as the Philippines, as well as for European colonies. The Philippines were particularly important to the United States in this regard: "[Philippine] independence and progress are daily reminders to other Asians of the value of Western democratic systems and concrete evidence of the U.S. attitude toward progress from colonial status to self-determination" (NSC policy statement on the Philippines, NSC5413/1: 1). A liberal global order also placed constraints on U.S. practices. Formal colonization was obviously not within the realm of possibility in 1950 because it would have called into question the identity of the United States: "Our aim must constantly be one of furnishing the necessary personnel for the particular needs of the individual country and at the same time avoiding the impression that the U.S. endeavors to 'colonize' or 'Americanize' those countries to which aid is being given" (FR51, vol. 6, part 1: 46).

But the promotion of U.S. goals and values required an unquestioned recognition of the legitimacy of those goals and values. Indeed, they must appear "natural." Situations in which competing interpretations came into play thus required that the United States define, manage, and control the outer limits of the sovereignty and independence of "third world" countries. The major objective of U.S. economic and military aid was "to secure strong, independent, cooperative countries, able to participate in a mature way in the world society. For that reason, the use of U.S. leadership should be clothed in every manner possible with the pretense, at least, of local action and responsibility" (Craig 1950: 4).

So while sovereignty, independence, and a commitment to pluralism would seem to imply noninterference, this second element pointed increasingly toward intervention in, and indeed the very definition of what constituted, the "internal affairs" of states such as the Philippines: "In the event that this proposed course is unsuccessful and proper remedial measures are not undertaken promptly it may be necessary for the United States to consider what further steps it should take to rescue the Philippines from its own mistakes" (memo from Secretary of State Acheson to President Truman, April 20, 1950, FR50, vol. 6: 1443).

Effective management of this tension, essential to the production of global purpose, was a never-ending task for the United States. "Third world" insurgencies such as the Huk rebellion entertained the possibility of an alternative social purpose and thereby politicized social purpose itself. They, thus had to be contained, not just in a physical sense but in a rhetorical sense as well. U.S. international identity and the social purpose to which it was fused were at stake. This identity was not based on an unproblematic and obvious self-presence, but rested on extremely precarious foundations that only existed by virtue of the fragile balance between the two ostensibly opposed elements of a balance that was always in danger of being undermined. The effective management of this tension required the production of self-disciplined subjects who were not obvious puppets of the United States nor obvious victims of U.S. domination, but whose goals, values, and ways of being were "naturally" consistent with those of the United States. Such self-disciplined subjects could be trusted to plan their "proper" and self-evident role in the free world:

> The American objective in the Philippines is to achieve and preserve a stable and self-supporting economy, and a reasonably honest and efficient government, in order that it may plan its proper role in the community of free nations, preserve and strengthen its basically anti-Communist attitude, and maintain the traditionally pro-American orientation of the Philippine people and government. (Draft paper prepared in the Department of State for consideration by the NSC, June 20, 1950, FR50, vol. 5: 1461)

Insurgency calls into question the self-evidence of the existing order. It undermines any naturalized way of being. Rules and the social purpose they presuppose are anything but self-evident. Further, insurgency reveals the play of power that is at the very heart of the production of social purpose. It suggests the possibility of alternatives — alternative political identities, alternative social arrangements and political orders at both the domestic and the international level. Insurgency can thus be understood as a crisis in effecting global purpose. We can conceive of this crisis as existing at and simultaneously blurring the distinction between the two levels, domestic and

international. The crisis at the "domestic" level of the country experiencing the insurgency is perhaps the most obvious, but a crisis
also exists at the international level. Indeed, the whole concept of
counterinsurgency, both in the cold war context and otherwise, implies a situation that exceeds and blurs the differentiation between
domestic and international. Counterinsurgency has always involved
the intervention of a colonial or neocolonial power to put down the
struggles of disaffected "domestic" groups and indeed to define
what the "domestic" order would be. This was especially true of the
insurgency in the Philippines, which was defined as a strategic issue
for the United States (Shafer 1988: 119), thus making it more than
a "domestic" Philippine issue:

> The U.S. is committed to the external defense of the Islands and can-
> not permit them to be taken by aggression or internal subversion.
> The strategic importance of the Philippines to the U.S. is such as to
> justify the commitment of the United States forces for its protection
> should circumstances require such action. Soviet domination of these
> Islands would seriously jeopardize the entire structure of anti-com-
> munist defenses in Southeast Asia and the offshore island chain, in-
> cluding Japan. Therefore, the situation in the Philippines cannot be
> viewed as a local problem since communist domination would en-
> danger the U.S. military position in the Western Pacific and the Far
> East. (NSC report, November 6, 1950: 3–4)

Equally if not more significant was the inextricable link between
U.S. international identity and what happened in the Philippines:
"Failure of the Philippines to maintain independence would discredit
the United States in the eyes of the world and seriously decrease U.S.
influence, particularly in Asia" (NSC84/2, FR50, vol. 6: 1515).

Insurgency in the Philippines was thus not only an "internal"
crisis, if indeed one could unproblematically say what "internal" signified. The situation in the Philippines was represented as an "internal" one with the ever present possibility of being re-presented as
an international one. The irony is, of course, that the situation was
already international in the sense that, for the Philippines there was
no pure, undisputed, and representable "internal" space that was
free from the international gaze, particularly that of the United States.
What was "internal" was defined externally by the United States.

Insurgency brought the problematization of this boundary to the
fore. In doing so, it constituted an "organic crisis" in which the sig-

nifiers *sovereignty* and *independence* assumed the character of floating signifiers whose meanings were unanchored. The discourses surrounding counterinsurgency worked to articulate these signifiers with others and thereby fix their meanings and reinscribe this boundary. At the same time, however, U.S. intervention, in its many aspects, itself problematized the internal/external boundary. An important element of U.S. policy thus became the simultaneous reinscription of this boundary and justification for violating it. Representational practices whereby the meaning of floating signifiers could be fixed and anchored within a dominant discourse were thus an important element of U.S. policy. It is the concern of the remainder of this chapter to show how meanings and identities were fixed and how counterinsurgency thereby became the only reasonable course of action to deal with the "internal" situation in sovereign and independent "third world" countries.

NATURALIZING INTERNATIONAL IDENTITIES: WORLD CITIZENS, PRECOCIOUS CHILDREN, AND INTERNATIONAL DELINQUENTS

Such continued participation in the affairs of an independent country has its undesirable aspects but in the context of the present world situation there is no acceptable alternative.

NSC STAFF STUDY ON U.S. OBJECTIVES, POLICIES,
AND COURSES OF ACTION IN ASIA

I believe we have no alternative at this time but to provide military assistance to the Philippines.

J. T. FORBES, REPORT TO CHAIRMAN OF JOINT MDAP
SURVEY MISSION ON THE PHILIPPINES

Those who have lined up with us in Asia have none of the sense of being the advance guard of a great and noble cause of which we are the base and Fatherland."

CHARLES OGBURN, POLICY INFORMATION OFFICER,
BUREAU OF FAR EASTERN AFFAIRS

These efforts of the Philippine Government to make itself stable and cope with the communist problem can, however, succeed only with American assistance. The alternative to this assistance is the loss of the Philippines.

CONFIDENTIAL MEMO FROM U.S. SECRETARY OF STATE
DEAN ACHESON, JANUARY 26, 1951

Underlying these statements of necessity were several metaphysical presuppositions regarding different subject identities. These presup-

positions were based on binary oppositions that derived their meaning from mutual opposition rather than from any inherent relation
to "reality." For example, Filipinos were emotional by virtue of being
Filipino and *not* American. These binaries were the operative principles that underlay the representational practices whereby meanings
were fixed and subject identities were constructed. The resulting conceptual system upon which U.S. foreign policy was based was organized around two guiding or core oppositions that served as a frame
of thinking, an economical way in which to divide self from other(s).
Several other oppositions can be subsumed under the core oppositions.

Reason/Passion

One presupposition was that there were different kinds of mentali-
ties. "Asian thinking" differed fundamentally from non-Asian thinking and was characterized by passion and emotion, in contrast to
reason and rationality: "Filipinos are more emotional than Americans and think more frequently in personal terms" (Office of Intelligence report, April 1952: 4). This rather primitive kind of mentality made it imperative that U.S. influence be brought to bear in the
Philippines. The "theory" of two types of mentality was not, of
course, unique to this particular case. It was prevalent among an-
thropologists in the 1920s and 1930s and was applied to the "West"
and its others: "Negroes," "American Indians," "Melanesians,"
"Australian Blackfellows" (Mudimbe 1988: 136). French historian
Robert Aron suggested in 1962 that Muslims lack the "taste for order and clarity we have inherited [from Descartes].... They do not
know how to reason and argue like us.... The true nature of Muslim
thought reappears—more emotional and sentimental than dialecti-
cal and logical" (quoted in Shafer 1988: 146). This is also a concrete
and more contemporaneous manifestation of the phenomenon Said
(1978) describes. This opposition has historically facilitated various
practices of interference ranging from formal colonization to more
subtle forms of domination. We find the same opposition at work
in the British discourse on the "Mau Mau" rebellion, which I examine in chapter 5.

Several of the orienting oppositions that were prevalent throughout the texts can be grouped under this core opposition. The most
recurring one rested on a parental metaphor. The theme of "political maturity" was widely disseminated. Filipinos were regarded as

precocious children who had assimilated the superficial aspects of U.S. culture but had failed to grasp its more fundamental implications (memo for U.S. Embassy in the Philippines, FR51, vol. 6, part 2: 1561). The United States had to be patient and sympathetic, yet firm, in using its constructive and guiding influence on its former ward. The ostensibly nurturing relationship invoked by the parent/child opposition obscured and justified practices of domination. Past practices of domination—colonialism itself, for example—were justified by pointing to the "progress" that had been made. Continued interference was also justified in order to facilitate the "development of Philippine initiative, leadership, and ability to function independently of outside assistance" (FR51, part 1: 57).

The parent/child opposition was not unidimensional, but rather contained several layers or levels. The first level served to differentiate countries such as the United States and countries such as the Philippines. The second level served to differentiate the "good child" from the "problem child." The good child was the self-disciplined, anticommunist, procapitalist, pro-U.S. subject. The goals, values, and social purpose promoted by the United States was unquestioned. This kind of subject stood firmly behind its parental model:

> For us now to equivocate, to declare that we are merely non-Communist, instead of standing foursquare that we are anti-Communist, to pursue a neutral course to join the third force counter-balancers on the fence or to coast along even as America is engaged in a bitter 'cold war' struggle to contain Soviet Communist expansion is, in my humble light, a breach of our sacred commitments, a betrayal of a trust, a travesty on our friendship and a blasphemy on gratitude. (Philippine Senator Tomas Cabili, *New York Times,* June 5, 1950)

The Philippine secretary of national defense, Ramón Magsaysay, was constructed as this kind of subject. While showing the qualities of a "self-made American executive" (*Congressional Record* 1946), Magsaysay was still in need of U.S. parental guidance and restraint. "Ramon Magsaysay was America's boy," *Time* magazine declared (November 23, 1953). Referring to U.S. Colonel Edward Lansdale's anti-Huk work with Magsaysay, Ambassador Myron C. Cowen said, "It is inconceivable to me that the Philippine situation would be as favorable as it is without Colonol Lansdale's superb performance. He has guided and advised [Magsaysay]. He has provided a driving power and when necessary a restraining one" (memo to

U.S. Secretary of State September 19, 1951, FR51, vol. 6, part 2: 1567).

With the guidance of the United States, the good Philippine child could be brought to understand and deal with the dangers that faced the Philippines: "Through the persuasive efforts of our representatives in Manila, the Philippine Government and people now give every evidence of being fully aware of the dangers of their position and are seemingly determined to take the necessary measures" (FR51, vol. 5, part 1: 24–25).

While the good child was the near ideal disciplinary subject, parental guidance and restraint were still necessary. The problem child, on the other hand, illustrated the failure of discipline. However, as Foucault suggests regarding the "delinquent," the problem child can be both part of the system and also its instrument, an object of surveillance and an instrument of surveillance (1979: 280–82). The problem-child category was characterized by a third level of differentiation. On the one hand the problem child was the proverbial "bad seed," in this case embodying the evils of communism. On the other hand, the problem child could be put to use. Political leaders labeled corrupt, dishonest, and inefficient could nonetheless be useful in promoting U.S. goals. In that the problem child was not a smoothly self-disciplined subject, constant surveillance was required in order to produce a delinquency that was controllable and could be put to political use in fighting communism and supporting capitalist economic and social relations.

Philippine president Elpidio Quirino exemplified the problem child. He was represented as politically inept and incompetent, someone who did not fully understand the difficulties facing the Philippines. The inferiority of leadership was attributed to noncommunist Asian countries more generally. It remained a task of the United States to consider "means to encourage the development of competent leadership and to stimulate its rise in the countries of Asia" (FR51, part 1: 45). The United States recognized that the Philippine people had the potential to develop competent leadership and become world citizens, but this development would take place under U.S. guidance through "firm patience and sympathetic understanding" (memo from U.S. Embassy in the Philippines, FR51, vol. 6, part 2: 1561).[7]

Another set of oppositions encompassed by the reason/passion core opposition was that of order/chaos. The Philippines were constructed as a place threatened by disorder, whose very definition as well as the strategies by which it should be managed were established by the United States. For example, "management" of disorder could not move away from policies consistent with U.S. strategic and economic interests. Such management would itself be defined as a source of instability. U.S. policies themselves could not be regarded as sources of disorder, that is, disorder could not be seen as the direct result of American colonialism/neocolonialism and Philippine integration into the American economy.

Good/Evil

Good versus evil was the second core opposition that structured this discourse, working in tandem with the reason/passion and parent/child oppositions. This guiding opposition formed an important element in the cold war discourse to which this particular case was inextricably linked. This battle for hearts and minds involved "the most basic conceptions of good and evil" (Secretary of State Acheson, March 16, 1950). The Manichaean opposition, which served to orient U.S. foreign policy discourses regarding the Philippines around 1950, worked at two levels. At one level it served to construct the United States and the Soviet Union as two distinct kinds of subjects: free world/communist world, moral/totalitarian, the latter terms falling under the classification of evil. Filipinos could then be divided according to where they fell along this opposition. The Huk leaders were evil, a problem that had to be eliminated. When it came to Filipino subjects, evil mixed with irrationality. This particularly dangerous combination, which was exemplified in the Huk leadership, could not just be "contained" but had to be eliminated: "But Andrea, like Taruc, was a mad dog of the jungle. That kind would have to be tracked down and killed or kept behind bars. The virus of Communism had infected them and made them immune from reason and compromise" (William O. Douglas, future U.S. Supreme Court Justice, 1953: 116).

At a second level, this opposition worked to objectify the Philippines as *objects* at stake in the worldwide struggle between good and evil. They were an essential "part" of the Asian offshore island chain of bases, a possible "key" to Soviet control of the Far East, a "show window" of democracy, a "testing ground" for American leadership. The Philippines were an object of desire for the United States and the Soviet Union, an object that might be needed for "operational use," an object that could "be denied to communist control," could be "retained" by the United States. The Philippines were an object to be acted upon rather than an initiator of action. They gained their significance by virtue of their utility and importance to the two opposed global powers.

CLASSIFICATION AND SUBJECT POSITIONING

The construction of subjects along the oppositional dimensions I have discussed simultaneously positioned these subjects in a hierarchical arrangement. The result was a classificatory scheme of international identities. The focus of the representational practices evident in this counterinsurgency discourse shifted from the colonial discourse that focused on kinds of people to kinds of states— "third world" states. This was not, however, a total break with the earlier discourse. We can note an overlap between this discourse and the colonial one regarding the representation and positioning of subjects. Various attributes were clustered together and then linked to terms such as "the *United States,* the *Philippines,* the *Soviet Union.* This, in turn, constructed a cultural code within which foreign policy was discussed, organized, and implemented.[8]

The hierarchical positioning of international subjects is evident in the kind and degree of agency assigned to the subjects of these texts. The United States, as a speaking, writing, and knowledgeable subject, implied an extensive and complex kind of subjectivity that encompassed a whole array of interconnected ideas, values, and goals that amounted to a "worldview." The United States was an initiator of action, a formulator of policy, an assessor of situations, and a definer of problems; it was endowed with a significant degree of agency. The United States and the USSR were complicated kinds of subjects who had worldviews and accompanying rational and coherent ideologies. Along the dimension of "good versus evil" the United States occupied a higher position than the USSR. Juxtaposed with the Philippines, however, the United States and the USSR became similar kinds of subjects.

In contrast, the subject position(s) available for Filipinos was much less complex. Filipino subjectivity did not include a rational, coherent worldview. Support for, as well as nonsupport of, communism was based on passion and emotion rather than a rational assessment and understanding of its tenets:

> World ideologies play little part in Asian thinking and are little understood. What the people strive for is the opportunity for a little more food in their stomachs, a little better clothing on their backs, a little firmer roof over their heads, and the realization of a normal nationalist urge for political freedom. (MacArthur 1951: 1114).

> Very few Filipinos, even very few Filipino Communists, have a rational understanding of Communist ideology. Communism finds most of its adherents in the Philippines among those who are predisposed, for racial or other reasons, to hate the United States or to hate the social, economic, or psychological restrictions upon their lives. Communism offers a rallying point for such individuals. Like the attitudes of Filipino anti-Communists, attitudes of Filipino Communists and Communist sympathizers also are largely irrational. (OIR report 1952: 10)

American policy discourse constantly highlighted the failures of Philippine leadership and marginalized its successes (Welch 1984: 287). Any improvement in the economic or political realm was regarded as the result of American influence: "The progress that the Filipinos have made under our guidance in the years in which we have been there has been notable" (*Review of the World Situation* 1949–1950: 253). In the economic realm (the bastion of rationalism), the Filipinos were regarded as particularly inept. In discussions regarding the composition of a proposed American economic mission (known as the Bell Mission) to the Philippines, U.S. officials repeatedly stressed that the mission should be composed exclusively of Americans, with no Filipino members. The State Department doubted that "any man of necessary caliber would be prepared to accept assignment on a Joint Mission since any joint report would require compromise on views and recommendations of both participants" (Secretary of State Acheson to U.S. Embassy in the Philippines, FR50, vol 6: 1426). In executive session hearings before the Committee on Foreign Relations it was asserted that the modern machinery of finance was devastating when the Filipinos "fool around with it" (*Review of the World Situation* 1949–1950). John Melby of the U.S. State Department suggested that, politically speaking, "the Filipinos are only one generation out of the tree tops" (quoted in Brands 1992: 236). Any positive attributes of the Filipinos were credited to the United States: "The widespread and intense Filipino desire for education is one of the more striking heritages of American occupation" (OIR report 1952: 7).

If we accept the premise that the attributes linked to human beings can become attached to geographical space, what can we say about the construction of the Philippines? I would suggest that U.S. foreign policy discourse constructed the Philippines as the kind of state found more generally constructed in policy circles and in North American social science literature: the "third world state." This kind of state is characterized by disorder, chaos, corruption, and general ineptitude.[9] At the same time, for economic and geopolitical reasons, this state was needed by the United States and the West more generally. The "good guys," the precocious children, who could be guided and cultivated to become mature "world citizens," existed in a precarious combination with the problem children, the bad seeds and the delinquents who were both subject to and instruments of international surveillance, together constituting the "third world state."

The representational practices examined in this chapter illustrate the discursive construction of this particular kind of nation-state. The *intertextual* nature of these texts becomes important here. To borrow a phrase from Barthes (1987: 135), these texts were "plugged in" to each other as well as to other foreign policy texts, social science texts, and nonacademic texts. Even a cursory examination of social science literature dealing with the "third world" reveals that it contains many of the oppositions shown here. This is most evident in the area of development studies, and particularly in the body of literature known as modernization theory. At the same time, we see the reproduction of a particular U.S. identity: moral, rational, efficient, honest.

DEFERRING SOVEREIGNTY

When the United States relinquished sovereignty over the Philippines in 1946 it was the culmination of a half century of effort to cultivate an independent democratic state in the Orient and it is

absurd to think the United States today would destroy the very inde-
pendence it had labored to create.

U.S. AMBASSADOR MYRON COWEN

Central to the tension I have discussed was the sign of *sovereignty.*
The promotion of independent and sovereign states in the "third
world" was part of the U.S. mission of creating a pluralistic, liberal,
and democratic world order, albeit one in which the outer bounds
of pluralism were defined by the United States itself. In one respect
it is reasonable to regard U.S. intervention in the Philippines around
1950 as a violation of sovereignty. Indeed, this was articulated as a
major concern of policy makers: "But such aid is extended only upon
request of the Government of the Philippines and only as assistance
extended by one friendly sovereign state to another" (Ambassador
Cowen, *New York Times,* June 11, 1950).

This view, however, presumes that we know what sovereignty
"is" — that sovereignty can be pointed to, defined, violated. While
the signifier *sovereignty* was firmly attached to the Philippines, what
this signifier pointed to could not be pinned down once and for all.
We could imagine some of sovereignty's possible signifieds — economic independence, political and military independence — but the
empirical evidence suggests that, at least in the case of the Philippines,
these were not what sovereignty signified. For example, economic
independence was vitiated by the Philippine Trade Act of 1946, which
set the terms of the economic relationship between the United States
and the Philippines.[10]

Military independence was also weakened by outside supervision
of Philippine arms purchases. This was illustrated in correspondence
between the British Embassy and the U.S. Department of State. In
November 1951 the British urged the United States to take action
to prevent Indonesia and the Philippines from purchasing more arms
from the United States than they needed for the purpose of maintaining internal security. To this end, it was suggested that the British
and Americans should consult jointly on any substantial orders these
countries might wish to place. This applied to all other Southeast
Asian countries as well (FR51, vol. 6, part 1: 118–25). All NATO
members and Commonwealth governments as well as Switzerland
and Sweden were advised of the dangers of excessive arms purchases
by Indonesia and the Philippines and asked to take appropriate steps

to ensure that these two countries did not accumulate more arms than they required.

One may correctly question just what "sovereignty" signified in a situation in which the United States had "to take appropriate measures to assure the institution of necessary political, financial, economic, and agricultureal reforms and in general to participate in the defence and administration of the country" (ibid.: 57). All of the empirical referents that one might generally associate with the term *sovereignty* seemed to be missing. Do we then say that the Philippines were not sovereign? This would not seem to be an appropriate interpretation, given the overwhelming U.S. rhetorical concern with violating sovereignty. At one level it would make sense to follow Jackson and Rosberg and make the distinction between "positive" and "negative" sovereignty, suggesting that the Philippines possessed "negative" sovereignty only.[11] Making this distinction may be analytically useful for some purposes, but I would suggest that it elides the inextricable link between positively sovereign states such as the United States and negatively sovereign states such as the Philippines. It marginalizes the importance of practices whereby positively sovereign states are actively engaged in producing the very conditions that cause negatively sovereign states to experience internal disorder and the inability to legitimize themselves to their own populations.

This distinction, while complicating and in some respects enriching the concept of sovereignty, implies that it is possible to fix the meaning of sovereignty. While sovereignty may have multiple meanings, the presumption is that sovereignty is decidable, that it is possible to say what sovereignty is in any particular situation. Positive sovereignty is implicitly what sovereignty "really" is. Negative sovereignty, which is juridically based, applies to states that are less than real, "not yet substantial realities in the conduct of public officials and citizens" (Jackson and Rosberg 1987: 528). These criticisms notwithstanding, the positive/negative distinction is, however, significant and can be further scrutinized. What I want to suggest is that, at least in the case examined in this chapter, sovereignty was a floating signifier whose meaning was always deferred. This is most obvious in instances of "third world" sovereignty such as the Philippines, where any stable and decidable signfieds for sovereignty are conspicuously absent and the signifier *sovereignty* floats, unanchored.

It is perhaps less obvious in instances involving what Jackson and Rosberg would refer to as "empirical" — that is, "real" — states. Yet the positive/negative opposition opens up space within which to pursue the links between the two and to pose the question of what the practice of making this distinction *does*.

Ashley and Walker suggest that the "word sovereignty is only spoken amid and in reply to a crisis of representation where paradoxes of space, time, and identity displace all certain referents and put origins of truth and meaning in doubt" (1990: 383). The participants in this counterinsurgency discourse, while not articulating in explicit theoretical terms the positive sovereignty/negative sovereignty opposition, nonetheless through their practices did in fact make the same distinction Jackson and Rosberg later laid out in an explicit theoretical manner. This distinction permitted the preservation of a domain of sovereign being exemplified by the United States. The United States was the living norm of sovereignty, the center of the structure in need of no explicit formulation of what sovereignty signified. The United States was the nodal point around which the meaning of sovereignty was fixed. The deferral of sovereignty stopped with the United States. The United States (and the West more generally) simply *was* sovereign.

In contrast, in the Philippines (and elsewhere in the "third world") modes of being were open to different interpretations. Social purpose and social relations were not unproblematic. Rather, social practices, social being in both the "domestic" and the international realm were politicized. There was no norm of sovereign being. What sovereignty and independence could possibly mean were political issues.[12] What sovereignty signified could, however, be infinitely deferred through representational practices that naturalized a particular way of being exemplified by the United States and that constructed the Philippines as its opposite, its "other." The problem of how to represent sovereignty in the Philippines was deferred by shifting the focus to the representation of the Philippine nation itself. The themes of political maturity, chaos and internal disorder, and corruption and inefficiency in leadership all became important elements in the construction of an international identity whose "positive" sovereignty was continually suspended. The Philippines were represented as having a "natural sensitivity to their recently acquired sovereignty" (NSC84/2, FR50, vol. 6: 1518). This was attributed to a "morbid psychology", that could lead them to misperceive certain U.S. practices that might appear to be an infringement of their sovereignty. This sensitivity was also attributed to Asia in general (NSC84/2, FR50, vol. 6: 1518).

As Ashley and Walker (1990) suggest, the word *sovereignty* was spoken amid and in reply to a crisis of representation. This crisis consisted of the dual problems of (1) representing the sovereignty of the Philippines (and other "third world" countries) in a liberal, democratic, and pluralistic international order and (2) simultaneously enabling U.S. practices that defined the outer limits of pluralism, democracy, and liberalism. It was within this context that sovereignty was spoken and deferred.

CONCLUSION

This chapter has attempted to show how U.S. counterinsurgency discourse created spaces for certain kinds of international subjects to exist in particular relations with one another and thereby to naturalize certain global arrangements. Representational practices that relied upon a series of oppositions and other relations created a hierarchy of identities that in turn made certain practices possible and precluded others. These representations produced a world in which all states could be sovereign but sovereignty itself was a floating signifier anchored only by the United States' exemplary mode of being and its will to authority.

This chapter should also serve to broaden our conception of what counterinsurgency and foreign policy more generally are.[13] Counterinsurgency is a knowledgeable practice par excellence, an international disciplinary technology that often substitutes for overt force and violence the "gentle efficiency of total surveillance" (Foucault 1979: 249). Remembering the continuities between the identities represented in this discourse and those of the colonial discourse examined in chapters 2 and 3 suggests that the "third world" and "first world" policies toward it are not solely or even primarily products of the cold war. The "third world" has always been already there, waiting to be written and rewritten by the West. It has always been represented as a realm of disorder and passion, to be managed, controlled, and molded by the West. At the same time, it has been a site wherein the identity of the West has been instantiated, disrupted, and continually reconstructed.

Resistance in Colonial Kenya

Mau Mau is a movement which in its origins and in its development is wholly evil. It is the worst enemy of African progress in Kenya. It has about it all the horror of the powers of darkness; of spiritual wickedness in high places. There can be no compromise, no common ground between Mau Mau and the rest of the civilized world. It must be utterly destroyed if the peoples of Kenya are to live together and build up their country.   FATHER TREVOR HUDDLESTON

There has been an attempt to disguise Mau Mau as a liberation movement. It is an evil, malignant growth, a dark, tribal, septic focus, and it has to be destroyed.

IONE LEIGH, *In the Shadow of Mau Mau*

We cannot hide Mau Mau-ism. We cannot hide the causes of Mau Mau-ism. In cold water flats in Harlem and in the hot, tropical parts of the British possessions, coloured people, coloured races, colonial peoples are discussing what is going on in Kenya today.

SIR LESLIE PLUMMER, HOUSE OF COMMONS
NOVEMBER 7, 1952

What has been termed the Mau Mau rebellion also has been described as the "first great African liberation movement," which "precipitated what was probably the gravest crisis in the history of Britain's African colonies," and the first struggle between black Africans and white minority rule in modern Africa (Edgerton 1989: vii, x). Few mass movements have elicited as much controversy as this one did (Rosberg and Nottingham 1966: xvi).[1] This rebellion occurred against the background of massive "third world" upheavals after the Second World War, when European empires were being dismantled by Nehru in India, Nasser in Egypt, and Sukarno in Indonesia. Despite the proclamation of a senior British colonial official in 1939 that "in Africa we can be sure that we have unlimited time in which to work," this revolutionary wave exploded in Africa as well (Stavrianos 1981: 665). Ghana (formerly the Gold Coast), Sierra Leone, and Gambia in British West Africa and Senegal, the Ivory Coast, and Niger in French Africa were just a few of the places where struggles were going on during this period. The British response to the struggle in Kenya constituted one of the casebook examples of classic counterinsurgency.[2] Like U.S. operations in the Philippines, British policy in Kenya in the 1950s was deemed to be largely successful in putting down rebellion.

The enduring significance of the rebellion in Kenya, however, perhaps lies less in the counterinsurgency policies per se than in the power of the representations that enabled them and that were subsequently reproduced. These representations were to be found in the commentaries, debates, and discussions that took the form of official reports and investigations, parliamentary debates, journal articles, books written by those who had "knowledge" of and experience in Kenya, and media coverage, as well novels such as Robert Ruark's *Something of Value,* which became a major motion picture starring Rock Hudson and Sidney Poitier. Representations surrounding this event encompassed the nature of the African in general and the Kikuyu in particular, the British colonial administration, and the white settlers, as well as notions of what constituted the legitimate means, ends, and reasons for protest and struggle. This resistance struggle and Britain's attempts to deal with it were part of an ongoing imperial encounter in which identities and hierarchical relationships were constructed and reconstructed. It thus constitutes an important piece of the mosaic of North-South relations.

BACKGROUND

Four elements constituted the resistance movement that became known as Mau Mau: (1) urban African political organizations, (2) squatters, (3) trade unions, and (4) ex-soldiers who fought in World War II. In this section I briefly discuss each of these elements and the events that led up to the declaration of a state of emergency in 1952.

The first important urban African political organization established in colonial Kenya was the East African Association, founded in 1919; its rural counterpart, the Kikuyu Association, was established in either 1918 or 1919 (Maughan-Brown 1980; Rosberg and Nottingham 1966). The East African Association was closed down in 1922, and its place was taken by the Kikuyu Central Association (KCA). This organization had three main concerns: constitutional reform that would permit African participation in the political system and a say in policy making, the return of land alienated for white settlement, and the assertion of the worthiness of Kikuyu tribal custom. The KCA pressed for reforms throughout the 1930s; it was banned in 1940 for alleged communication with the king of England's enemies in Ethiopia (Maughan-Brown 1980). When World War II broke out, the KCA, along with two other African associations, the Taita Hills Association and the Ukamba Members Association, had sent a joint memorandum of loyalty to the governor, though their opposition to government policies and their demands for land reforms did not slacken. Despite the proclamation of loyalty, the administration considered their activities to be subversive, and on May 27 and 28, 1940, twenty-three of their leaders were arrested under the Defence Regulations of 1939, the same law that was used for detaining Italian and German aliens in Kenya. Despite their denials of any association with foreign powers, they were all sent to prison, thus leaving the KCA leaderless, powerless, and effectively banned (Rosberg and Nottingham 1966: 185–87). Still, the KCA did not die. Members helped the British war efforts during the day and talked of freedom and getting back their stolen lands at night.

In 1944 the Kenya African Union (KAU) was founded and gained the support of many members of the banned KCA, especially when Jomo Kenyatta assumed its presidency in 1947. It continued to press the demands that the KCA had made. The KAU was a legal political organization whose objective was expressing to the government the grievances of the people. Its strength lay chiefly among the Kikuyu, but it sought to extend its influence throughout much of the country (Odinga 1967: 107). As Odinga (ibid.: 107–12) points out, there were other political movements operating at this time. A network of land committees for the protection and return of clan lands had started up at the village level. These committees owed their inspiration to the Kikuyu Land Board founded in the 1930s for people whose land had been alienated. The land committees took on a variety of forms and had many different names. Despite the fact that the KCA had been outlawed by the government, it still functioned. It deputed clan elders to organize the land committees in villages. KCA membership and allegiance had been bound by oaths. These oaths were used in the land committees, whose leadership and members were secret. The work of the committees brought new members to the KAU and the KCA; there was much overlap in both leadership and rank and file members among the land committees and the KAU and KCA.

The years after the end of World War II also witnessed an active trade union movement in Kenya. As more Africans became part of the urban economy, urban working and living conditions and a spiraling cost of living stimulated the growth of the trade union movement. There were spontaneous workers' strikes. In January 1947 a general strike involving nearly the entire African labor force in Mombasa was led by Chege Kibachi. During this strike the African Workers' Federation was founded with Kibachi as its president. The successful strike resulted in a general minimum wage (Rosberg and Nottingham 1966: 209; Odinga 1967: 108). Kibachi sought to develop the federation into a Kenya-wide trade union movement; he traveled to Nairobi, Nakura, Nanyuki, Naaivasha, and other places urging people to organize and not to be intimidated by the government. There was a rash of local strikes. As might be expected, the government viewed Kibachi and the new union with suspicion. He was arrested in August 1947 and deported in September "on account of activities subversive of law and order" (Rosberg and Nottingham 1966: 210). Other officers were arrested and the African Workers' Federation began to dissolve. Its successor organization, the East African Trades Union Congress (EATUC), was led by Makhan Singh and Fred Kubia. Singh sought to develop the trade union movement in Africa and linked up with Fred Kubia, then general secretary of the Transport and Allied Workers Union, and Bildad Kaggia, then president of the Clerks and Commercial Workers Union. Six other unions were affiliated with the EATUC, which rapidly gained strength in Nairobi, openly eschewing the possibility of separating politics from labor issues in a colonial situation. The government refused to grant legal recognition to the EATUC on the grounds that it did not represent any single trade (ibid. 1966: 241). It continued to operate, however, and became much more militant than the KAU, whose leadership it overlapped with.

Fred Kubia, president of the EATUC, was also chairman of the KAU Nairobi branch. His arrest in 1950 on charges of being an officer in an unregistered union organization brought on a general strike in protest and an influx of trade union membership into the KAU as well as an increased militancy. By 1951, as a result of this influx of trade union strength into the KAU and the accompanying pressure for recognition, the government was forced to recognize the trade union movement, though it refused to recognize the EATUC because its leadership was considered too militant. Instead it encouraged a rival trade union organization, the Kenya Federation of Registered Trade Unions. The leader of the KFRTU was Aggrey Minya, soon to be replaced by Tom Mboya.

After the war, Africans who had served with the British army in India, Burma, Ceylon, the Middle East, and Europe joined the struggle. This new generation of ex-soldiers had fought not only to protect their own country but also for the preservation of liberty and democracy, ideas that would not be quickly forgotten after the war ended. Some of the more prominent of these ex-soldiers included Waruhiu Itote (General China), Bildad Kaggia, J. D. Kali, Dedan Kimathi, and P. J. Ngei. These people came to play an important part in the KAU. A new inner core of leadership prepared for a new type of struggle: they wanted immediate independence. In 1951 KAU elections threw out some of the moderates, and the constitution was changed to include a demand for independence.

Another important element of the movement was the squatters who provided support for the KCA. One of the main dynamics behind Mau Mau was the agrarian revolution that was taking place, and the people most affected by this revolution were the squatters (Furedi 1989: 60–67). The active intervention of the KCA in the squatter movement was stimulated by events that were taking place in Olenguruone, which came to be a symbol of Kenyan anticolonial resistance and an occasion in which unquestioned unity had been achieved and resistance to the power of the government had reached an unprecedented level.[3] It also provided a unifying link between the squatter movement and the subsequent revolt in the Kikuyu reserves. Olenguruone became a symbol of national resistance and sacrifice. It had a critical impact on the KCA, forcing it to open its doors and extend its core of activities. The fusion of the squatter movement with that of the Olenguruone settlers provided a powerful stimulus to the spread of resistance, which was now a grassroots movement.

The willingness to support political activity that directly challenged the laws and institutions of the colonial government increased. Attacks on European-owned property were frequent in 1950. Resistance members set up roadblocks on isolated roads at night, cut telephone wires, and sabotaged the machines and equipment of European farmers (Furedi 1989: 110). The European settlers and the colonial administration, increasingly uneasy, sought declaration of a state of emergency and the neutralization of African political activity (Rosberg and Nottingham 1966: 235). On October 20, 1952, a state of emergency was declared in Kenya. This was followed by operation Jock Scott, which resulted in large-scale arrests of prominent Kikuyu throughout Kenya and of 183 KAU leaders. Kenyatta, Paul Ngei, Achieng Oneko, Bildad Kaggia, Fred Kubia, and Kung'u Karumba were charged in the notorious Kapenguria trial with managing or assisting the society of Mau Mau (Odinga 1967: 112). These first arrests were followed by waves of others, which sparked off armed resistance. After the initial arrests, the government began a counterinsurgency program designed to destroy Mau Mau and win over the "people."

REASON IN THE SERVICE OF EMPIRE

In making the distinction between liberation and nationalist independence, Said (1993: 264) uses the phrase "dynamics of dependence" to describe the process that produced independent states in once-colonial countries across the globe. Nationalist independence was the culmination of collaboration between colonial powers and indigenous elites who worked within a Western cultural framework (ibid.: 263). This dynamic exemplified the process of modern statecraft within a colonial setting. The political life of the nation was absorbed into the body of the state (Chatterjee 1986: 168). Liberation, on the other hand, involves a resistance that does not necessarily fit within the bounds of the Western nation-state, a resistance that questions nationalists' often friendly agreement(s) with colonial powers. A tension can thus develop within resistance movements that is exacerbated and used by colonial authorities. Liberationist politics are silenced and often made illegal. The encounter between colonial power and resistance movements can be seen as an instance of a strategy (without a strategist) in the reproduction of a particular kind of social order, here the reproduction of the Western nation-state and global capitalist systems.[4]

Seen in this light, resistance and the responses it elicits become part of a long series of imperial encounters. Decolonization involved not just winning sovereignty and independence, but also suppressing alternative possibilities.[5] The Mau Mau rebellion becomes interesting from this perspective because the colonial responses to it were based upon discursive and disciplinary mechanisms designed to master and control rebellion, to isolate the kind of rebellion that was not acceptable, and to make this kind of rebellion deviant, abnormal, and incomprehensible to the rational mind. This was perhaps discipline's ultimate dream: to delimit and master that which would resist discipline in the first place. The representational practices entailed in these responses spanned both time and space in their linkage to earlier and later texts as well as their replicability across diverse locales. The significance of the representational practices present in the narratives surrounding Mau Mau rebellion lay in their complicity in the reproduction of particular international identities and their hierarchical positioning vis-à-vis one another. In a more immediate sense, their importance lay in the practices they made possible.

Kenyan soldiers who had fought for the preservation of liberty and democracy during World War II played an important part in the formation of a new inner core of KAU leadership that demanded liberty, democracy, and immediate independence — signifiers that lay at the heart of the Western liberal values colonial Britain saw itself as epitomizing. The appropriation of these signifiers by the Mau Mau movement unmoored them from their fixed meanings within Britain's colonial discourse and created a space for alternative understandings. Mau Mau rejected Britain's colonial mission and all that it entailed: the superiority of Europe and its mission to spread its civilization based upon that superiority. Yet Mau Mau did not reject democracy, liberty, and independence. These signifiers could be linked to signifieds — the return of lands stolen by the British and the Europeans, the retention of indigenous cultural practices, and the rejection of European superiority—not possible within the colonial discourse.

Britain was faced with the dilemma of rearticulating these signifiers into its own discourse. Britain's counterinsurgency policy involved representational practices that sought to reappropriate within their dominant discourse the meanings of these signifiers. Dealing with this dilemma was of no small concern and indeed animated much of the discourse surrounding the Mau Mau rebellion: "Both the Colonial Office and the Colonial Governments have been caught in the ever-present struggle of our nation to resolve the dilemma of being autocratic abroad and democratic at home" (Corfield 1960: 28). The solutions involved representations and other disciplinary practices that delegitimated Mau Mau and at the same time defined an acceptable form of resistance. Laclau (1990: 28) suggests that hegemonizing a content amounts to fixing its meaning around a nodal point. Different political projects strive to articulate a greater number of social signifiers around themselves. Periods of organic crisis occur when hegemonic articulations weaken and an increasing number of social elements assume the character of floating signifiers. The Mau Mau rebellion signaled just such a crisis. The solution involved fixing the meaning of this rebellion around evil, darkness, irrationality, criminality, and abnormality—all opposed to Western reason.

MADNESS, IMMATURITY, AND MODERNIZATION: REPRESENTING MAU MAU

The parent/child relationship and the accompanying theme of political immaturity discussed in chapter 4 are also found in this case. African people, like children, were characterized by "smiling faces and carefree laughter" (Wyatt 1953: 207). The parent/child analogy also helped to explain the emergence of the Mau Mau movement:

> A child with inconsistent indecisive parents spends his unhappy life ever trying to get more; ever trying unsuccessfully to discover the length of the chain that binds him. The African must do the same with his employer, and it seems likely that this principle has played no little part throughout the development of Mau Mau, but especially in its early stages. (Carothers 1955: 13)

In the case of Mau Mau, the theme of political immaturity was grafted onto the theme of the African in transition. This resulted in a focus on the mental makeup of the African, and especially how it was affected by and reacted to change. Transition, it was suggested, brought to the fore the basic forces of savagery, superstition, and evil that lurked just below the surface of the African mind. Understanding the African in transition meant understanding "the mental or psychic make-up of the African" (Wyatt 1953). This theme was widely disseminated throughout official government narratives, scholarly works, and the media. Mau Mau was characterized as a virtual collapse of the African mind:

> When this strange collapse of the structure of the African mind takes place, usually on a tribal basis, we should do everything possible to help and encourage the moderate and responsible members and representatives of the African tribe to defeat that slide-back into barbarism. (Alport, November 11, 1952, British House of Commons, 483)

Nowhere was the emphasis on the African mind more prominent than in the report written by Dr. J. C. Carothers. Carothers, Kenya's most respected psychiatrist, had practiced medicine in Kenya for twenty years before becoming the psychiatrist in charge of Mathari Mental Hospital outside of Nairobi. During the emergency a committee—Harry Thuku, one of Kenya's early political leaders, Louis Leakey, a prominent missionary, and Carothers—was formed to deal with Mau Mau (Edgerton 1989: 174). The "findings" of this committee were widely accepted by the government and settlers. Several important policies such as the "cleansing process" and "villagization" followed from their "findings." These policies are discussed later in this chapter. Here, I examine Carothers's report in detail because the representations it contains are illustrative of those that were at work more generally.

Dr. Carothers's report consisted of four parts: (1) a "study of indigenous African psychology with special reference to certain Kenya tribes," (2) "a study of African psychology in transition between the old ways and the new," (3) "a study of the Mau Mau movement," and (4) recommendations. The indigenous African psyche was characterized by a lack of conscious personal integration, Carothers wrote: "Social rules are not meaningfully synthesized within the individual.... A man is not weighed down by preoccupation with past sins or by preoccupation with a need to order his future life on certain lines" (1955: 19). Stability, however, was achieved to some degree within the group. In the group the African "was courteous, socially self-confident, and in effect, a social being" (ibid.: 3). Outside of the group, the African became anxious and insecure. This led to the "highest degree of unconstraint and violence — a common experience in psychiatric practice in Africa" (ibid.). While the Kikuyu psychology followed the general African pattern, their relatively isolated patterns of living created a "forest psychology" that made them so individualistic that they were isolated from group pressure and therefore lacked "general moral principles." They tended to secretiveness, suspicions, and scheming (ibid.: 4–5). While the Kikuyu had lost their close attachment to the forests, the "forest psychology" persisted. Carothers's analysis of the African individual and the African community presupposes that the morality of an African, unlike that of the Western subject who is guided by enlightened thought upon which the principles of morality are grounded, is grounded on an external source — the group. The African, then, is posited as fundamentally different from the Westerner.

European contact and the changes that accompanied it had disrupted and led to the collapse of African traditions and culture. The breakdown of traditions had removed constraints on behavior: "His respect for his parents, relations, and his clan, which was previously upheld and reinforced by strict rules of behavior and by supernatural sanctions, is now much undermined and may well, in many instances be replaced by positive contempt" (ibid.: 8). The African's lack of personal integration exacerbated this and led to even greater insecurity. In addition to lacking personal integration, the African lacked the ability to "look critically at himself and the world and see that neither the goodness nor the badness is absolute, and accept himself and the world as the mixture of potential good and potential bad" (ibid.: 3). This lack of critical reflection led the African to identify the malevolent world with the Europeans and lay all his troubles at their door. How did Africans deal with this anxiety and insecurity?

> By virtue of the type of mental structure that develops in Africans, misfortunes are seldom seen as one's own fault. They are seen as the work of evil "wills" and, since the power of these wills is now largely

replaced by the power of the European, the latter is apt to be re-garded nowadays as the sole author of all evil. (ibid.: 12)

From these understandings of the psychology of the African, an explanation for the rise of Mau Mau followed:

> It arose from the development of an anxious conflictual situation in people who, from contact with the alien culture, had lost the sup-portive and constraining influences of their own culture, yet had not lost their magic modes of thinking. It arose from the exploitation of this situation by relatively sophisticated egotists. (ibid.: 15)

Jomo Kenyatta was considered one of those egotists who exploited the situation:

> If one substitutes pagan culture and Christianity for the Catholic faith, and Jomo Kenyatta for the Devil, the two are often virtually identical. Jomo Kenyatta is very certain to have made some study of European witchcraft; he had the opportunity and it is easy to imag-ine more than one incentive. (ibid.: 16)[6]

Carothers's report was an intertext of widely shared meanings regarding the identity of the African, the meaning of Mau Mau, the definition of "true" nationalism and legitimate liberation struggles, and appropriate policies. Another important piece of this intertext was a study of Mau Mau commissioned by the colonial government in Kenya and undertaken by F. D. Corfield, a veteran of the colonial civil service in the Sudan and Kenya. The resulting study, *Historical Survey of the Origins and Growth of Mau Mau,* presented to Par-liament by the secretary of state for the colonies in May 1960 as Command Paper 1060, was regarded as the official government his-tory of the revolt. The report echoes Carothers's psychologism. The primacy of the individual in the Western world was contrasted with the primacy of the group in Africa: "Original modes of thought and action are the very life blood of western society," while the group or tribal system "has kept the African secure, but at the very heavy price of social and mental stagnation" (Corfield 1960: 8). The Afri-can in Kenya, having come into contact with an outside culture, was going through a transition stage that had placed a great strain on him, producing

> a schizophrenic tendency in the African mind—the extraordinary facility to live two separate lives with one foot in this century and

the other in witchcraft and savagery. A Kikuyu leading an apparently normal life would, in one moment, become a being that was barely human. (ibid.: 9)

Mau Mau was the prime example of the lengths to which this tendency could go.

Significantly, chapter 2 of Corfield's report, entitled "The Psychological and Sociological Background," is devoted entirely to Kikuyu claims regarding land in Kenya. This discussion depends upon the opposition characterizing Europeans as reasonable and Africans as passionate:

> It is not easy to convey to those who have had little contact with, or understanding of, primitive societies, the intense emotional attachment those societies have to land.... As anyone who has had to deal with land disputes well knows, passions are inflamed and reason and truth go by the wind. (ibid.: 11)

African claims to land taken by Europeans were attributed more to the passion and irrationality of the African and less to legitimate claims that land was stolen from them:

> However conclusively it can be shown that the settlement of Europeans in the empty spaces of the White Highlands was fully justified in the prevailing circumstances, and was fully in accord with the declared policy of Her Majesty's Government, no Kikuyu would be convinced either by truth or by logic.... The African's attachment to land is so emotional that it is almost impossible for him to take a detached view whenever land is mentioned. (ibid.: 20)

It follows from this representation that no meaningful or rational discussion of the land issue would be possible. The reason/passion opposition was widely disseminated throughout the texts dealing with Mau Mau. Even those occasions in which resistance voices were permitted to be heard could be used to reinforce the oppositions upon which colonial authority depended. An example of this was Margery Perham's foreword to Tom Mboya's *The Kenya Question: An African Answer* published in 1956 by the Fabian Colonial Bureau. Though she does not agree fully with Mboya, Perham seems compelled to comment on Mboya's "clear head," his "restrained manner," and his public speaking style, which "avoids emotion and maintains a very rational manner" (Perham 1956a: 2). These same ostensibly complimentary but ultimately condescending comments would be unnecessary—indeed, would seem out of place—were they to precede, for example, a text written by Winston Churchill, whose rationality would be assumed as given. This ostensible compliment to Mboya works to reproduce a reason/passion, rational/irrational opposition that can be used to discredit liberation struggles that do not conform to a Western definition of the norm and indeed reject the superiority of the West: "Their sense of increasing oppression was more psychological than reasoned" (Perham 1963: xvii).

Oppressive, nondemocratic practices could be defended as "necessary" to protect the naive and easily influenced from the corrupt and evil leaders of Mau Mau. Nowhere was this more evident than in dealing with freedom of the press and freedom of assembly and speech. After World War II indigenous presses began to proliferate.[7] They published "pernicious propaganda and seditious" and thus constituted "a grave menace to the future of the Colony," as they generally had a serious effect on the "uneducated and politically immature Africans" (Corfield 1960: 191). The situation became graver as the Mau Mau emergency progressed.

The Penal Code was amended in 1950 to give the courts the power to confiscate presses used in the printing of seditious literature. On October 3, 1952, the Printing Press (Temporary Provisions) Ordinance was enacted, giving the registrar of printing presses, after consultation with the member for law and order, the power to cancel license if "it appears to him that the licensee has kept or used, or is likely to keep or use, a printing press for unlawful purposes, or for the printing of any document prejudicial to, or incompatible with, peace or good order in the Colony" (ibid.: 193).

While the right to speak, to have a voice, and to express dissent is at one level a function of the law, it is simultaneously and inextricably linked with dominant modes of representation. The representation of the African as politically immature and vulnerable to propaganda permitted practices of restriction and censorship in their most severe form: "The African is only beginning to read newspapers and is apt to take the written word as truth. These papers, therefore, have a much greater influence on readers than they would in a more civilized country" (ibid.: 192).

In the name of reason, order, and the promotion of civilized values, voices had to be silenced.

One of the many books written during the state of emergency was by Sir Philip Mitchell, governor of Kenya from December 1945 until his retirement in June 1952. These seven years were crucial ones, coinciding with events that led up to the declaration of the state of emergency by his successor, Sir Evelyn Baring, three months after his retirement (Carter 1971: 29). Mitchell promoted the idea of multiracialism.[8] In his contributions "towards some understanding of what had been happening," Mitchell suggested that "forest and mountain-dwelling primitive people were particularly given to black and foul mysteries, to ritual murder, and to cults of terror" (Mitchell 1954: 252). The Kikuyu were forest-dwelling people and were thus so prone. Mau Mau was but one of many of the cults that had developed from time to time. It resulted from the fear and confusion of "simple and primitive people being thrown into the twentieth century" (ibid.: 260). By far the greater cause, however, was "the black and blood-stained forces of sorcery and magic, stirring in the vicious hearts and minds of wicked men" (ibid.). These "wicked men" were the leaders of Mau Mau. Mitchell reasserted the mission of the British in Kenya:

> For the truth is that the only way in which the multitude of East African tribes can hope to enjoy the benefits of civilized government, both central and local, now and for generations to come, before they have become themselves civilized, and thereby to have the opportunity to become civilized, is under the forms of colonial government—the flexible and continuously developing forms of colonial government—administered by a strong and enlightened colonial power and directed, as British colonial policy has been for centuries, to the achievement not of any particular political system but of a state of society in which the men and women of which it is composed—or at least a large part of them—have reached a stage of spiritual, moral, social, cultural, and economic development capable of supporting and operating such democratic forms of government as may then appear desirable to them. (ibid.: 276)

Another important text written about Mau Mau was by Louis B. Leakey, world-renowned anthropologist and son of a Church Missionary Society missionary. Born and raised in Kenya, Leakey was fluent in the Kikuyu language and considered himself more Kikuyu than English.[9] Leakey played a significant role during the rebellion, explaining Mau Mau to the West, the colonial state, and the British

Army. He was a Kikuyu translator at the famous Kapenguria trial of Mau Mau suspects at which Kenyatta was convicted, and he was part of the Committee on Rehabilitation along with psychiatrist J. C. Carothers. While Leakey was ostensibly sympathetic to the Kenyan people and recognized that they had legitimate grievances, he shared the belief that the explanation for Mau Mau lay in the mental state of the African. In his book *Defeating Mau Mau,* Leakey suggested that there were legitimate grievances; the result was that "the vast majority of the Kikuyu people had very certainly drifted into a state of mental instability and irresponsibility, and were thus an easy prey to Mau Mau religion and hysteria" (127).

The Mau Mau emergency called into question the success of Britain's civilizing mission. Like the Huk rebellion, it signified a failure of the normalization of a particular social purpose—the legitimation of white rule and empire—both "internally" within Kenya and internationally. The portrayal of this rebellion as the result of political immaturity, the African mentality in transition, and a dark, evil, and irrational force performed a delegitimating function. These representations served to reproduce a particular hierarchy of identities that justified the colonial enterprise. They were also complicitous in making possible the more immediate and local practices that constituted Britain's counterinsurgency policies. The portrayal of Mau Mau as an aberration of normality enabled the justification of policies aimed at restoring normality.

Mental breakdown, irrationality, primitiveness, political immaturity, and criminality were linked together to constitute the Mau Mau rebellion as a form of collective mental breakdown or social disease. Even those who admitted to the existence of legitimate grievances on the part of the Africans shared an affinity with those who attributed the rebellion to psychological causes in terms of their shared presuppositions and the practices these presuppositions made possible. Mau Mau was not a legitimate struggle. It was an "outbreak of ferocity" and "corrupted savagery," prompted not by reason but by "unreasoning anger" (Perham 1956b: 6). Thus, despite differences between blatantly racist narratives and more sympathetic liberal ones, their similarities enabled the same kind of practices.

The practices so enabled were blatantly at odds with freedom and democracy according to almost any understanding of these concepts. Principles of freedom and democracy were simultaneously promoted and violated by colonial authorities. Indeed, they were violated in order to promote them. Representational practices present in the various mechanisms of domination enabled the deferral of freedom and democracy for the good of those to whom they were denied.

DISCIPLINARY TECHNOLOGIES AND THE DEFERRAL OF DEMOCRACY

In analyzing the emergence of new forms of power, Foucault (1979: 209) discusses two images of discipline. One takes as its model the plague-ridden town. Here there exists an exceptional situation in which power is mobilized against an extraordinary evil. Power makes itself visible; it separates, immobilizes, and partitions. Power performs the negative functions of arresting evil, breaking communications, suspending time (ibid.: 205–9). The other image of discipline takes as its model the panopticon. This disciplinary model seeks to improve the exercise of power by making it lighter, more rapid, a design of subtle coercion for a society to come. Its aim is to strengthen social forces — to increase production, develop the economy, spread education, raise the level of public morality (ibid.).

We can detect elements of both of these models in the British response to the Mau Mau emergency. Policies implemented under the state of emergency drew upon the image of a plague-ridden town. Colonial military power was mobilized against the evil that was Mau Mau in order to arrest and immobilize it like a disease, to separate those infected from those merely susceptible to infection:

> One thing is certain. Those Kikuyu who are incurably afflicted by Mau Mau must be as rigorously isolated as lepers. They must be kept in the forests and there exterminated one by one so that they can never again contaminate the healthy. And those of the stricken who have been proclaimed cured, must be carefully watched for any signs of another epidemic." (a white settler, quoted in Maughan-Brown 1985: 51)

It was also recognized, though, that the exceptional discipline required to restore law and order as quickly as possible by isolating those infected with the Mau Mau disease was not a permanent solution. There was no "short cut or a substitute for the necessarily arduous and slow task of winning the people over," Sir Frederick Crawford of the colonial office wrote to General George Erskine, commander in chief of East Africa, in August 1953 (Mockaitis 1990: 129). "Winning the people over" would require a whole array of policies and practices more consistent with the image of the panopticon and the multiple and varied uses to which this mechanism of power can be put: "It serves to reform prisoners, but also [to] treat patients, to instruct school children, to confine the insane, to supervise workers, to put beggars and idlers to work. Whenever one is dealing with a multiplicity of individuals on whom a task or a particular form of behaviour must be imposed, the panoptic schema may be used" (Foucault 1979: 205). Thus we find in Britain's counterinsurgency policies modes of discipline that have the dual purpose of "arresting the plague" and creating a disciplined society of individuals whose collective social purpose would coincide with that of the West.

Separation and Enclosure

General Erskine produced a military plan designed to restore law and order to the areas contaminated by Mau Mau. Operation Anvil involved a massive sweep of the entire city of Nairobi in order to clear it of Mau Mau supporters. Twenty-five thousand military men surrounded the city and swept through every conceivable section. All Kikuyu, Embu, and Meru tribesmen were screened on the spot and sent either to detention camps or to reserves. Operation Anvil lasted for one month, at the end of which twenty-four thousand Africans, almost all Kikuyu, had been sent to detention camps (Edgerton 1989: 91).

Operation Anvil destroyed Mau Mau's urban base, but it was obvious that the campaign to separate Mau Mau from the "people" would have to be won in the countryside (Mockaitis 1990: 129). Nearly 2 million Kikuyu, Meru, and Embu in the reserves around the Mau Mau–occupied forests were still supplying them with food, weapons, clothing, and ammunition. Erskine's next military plan was to restore control to these areas. Towns and Kikuyu locations were swept as Nairobi had been in Operation Anvil. Those who supplied food, clothing, and ammunition to the Mau Mau were separated from the rest of the population and sent to detention camps. The rest of the people were put in guarded villages (Rosberg and Nottingham 1966: 293; Edgerton 1989: 92). These villages were surrounded by fifty-mile-long ditches that cut off the sympathetic populace from the forest-based freedom fighters. In most places the ditch was ten feet deep and sixteen feet wide and was filled with impenetrable mazes of booby-trapped barbed-wired and sharpened bamboo stakes. Every half mile there was a police post that was patrolled day and night. This barrier was constructed with the forced labor of thousands of Kikuyu. Kikuyu laborers were also forced to build access roads for military patrols. Every loyalist chief was empowered by the government to call up labor for such tasks. Anyone who resisted was beaten (Edgerton 1989: 92).

This mobilization of power for the purpose of destroying Mau Mau was extended throughout entire Kikuyu communities. With the support of Governor Baring, Louis Leakey, and Dr. Carothers, Kikuyu were forcibly moved from their traditional pattern of widely scattered homesteads into villages, which Carothers thought would reduce the individualism of the Kikuyu. Many thousands of Kikuyu were forced to build dwellings, access roads, barbed-wire fences, watchtowers, schools, and all the other necessary features of their new life. Curfew regulations required everyone to be inside their villages from nightfall to dawn. By the end of 1954, one million Kikuyu had been resettled into 800 newly constructed and completely controllable villages (ibid.: 93). The major Kenyan newspaper, the *East African Standard,* reported that the villagization program

> represents nothing less than a major revolution in the traditional conditions of life among the African people — the Kikuyu in particular — and its benefits as well as its problems, should be understood from the outset. It is not a punitive measure. It is a direction of change which time would have brought, but it is being hastened in the life of one tribe by the circumstance which they have themselves created for very different ends. (February 19, 1954)

In 1955, two years after the villagization program had been started, the chief native commissioner for Central Province reported:

> Of one thing there is no doubt. The original horror at the idea of living in villages has disappeared. The vastly improved standard and layout of the villages, as well as the security afforded, has resulted in a complete volte-face by the bulk of the population, who are more than content with their new mode of living. (Central Province 1955: 35)[10]

Rehabilitation: Confession and the Correct Means of Training

The confession is a ritual of discourse in which the speaking subject is also the subject of the statement; it is also a ritual that unfolds within a power relationship, for one does not confess without the presence (or virtual presence) of a partner who is not simply the interlocutor but the authority who requires the confession, prescribes and appreciates it, and intervenes in order to judge, punish, forgive, console. MICHEL FOUCAULT, "TRUTH AND POWER"

By the end of 1954 the implementation of the military plan to restore order to Kenya resulted in such a large number of assorted detainees that this situation itself threatened a new kind of disorder. Partly as a result of Operation Anvil, there were more than 50,000 detainees in prison. Some who had already been convicted of Mau Mau crimes were deemed so infected with the disease that permanent isolation in exile settlements was required. Many awaited execution in Nairobi's notorious Kamiti prison (Edgerton 1989: 176). A significant number of the detainees, however, were regarded as "passive supporters who had been hypnotized by agitators and now might well be amenable to cure" (Rosberg and Nottingham 1966: 335).

Tom Askwith, once municipal Africa affairs officer in Nairobi, was sent to Malaya to study the work of rehabilitation of the communists there. His report formed the basis for the policies devised by a special committee set up by the colonial government. The committee made up of Carothers, Thuku, and Leakey was convinced that people who took the Mau Mau oath became so deranged that they were literally diseased or infected. It was decided that the way to rehabilitate them was to force them to confess and then to put them through a "cleansing process." As Governor Baring put it, rehabilitation required full public renunciation and denunciation (Edgerton 1989: 174). While it was recognized that the most effective confessions would be those made freely and voluntarily, confession by whatever means had to be made. After 1956 the colonial government increasingly accepted the legitimacy of the use of force to extract confessions from detainees. This was the foundation of the government's rehabilitation program (Rosberg and Nottingham 1966: 337, 341).

The "cleansing process" was seen as the first step toward returning Mau Mau supporters to "normal" Kikuyu life. It began with an interrogation intended to screen out the innocent and send the guilty to detention camps. Those who refused to confess would be sent down a pipeline through repatriation camps of increasing severity until they saw the error of their ways, then sent back up the pipeline toward full rehabilitation and eventual freedom (Edgerton 1989: 177). Screening took place in a variety of police- and civilian-run centers until 1954 when all detainees were screened at Langatra, a former military base on the outskirts of Nairobi. Each detainee was classified as white (innocent of Mau Mau involvement), gray (some Mau Mau activity), or black (hard core Mau Mau). Eighty thousand Kikuyu passed from detention to stages of rehabilitation between 1953 and 1959 (White 1988: 19). The chief native commissioner reported in 1954:

> The camps served a dual purpose: to provide a channel through which Kikuyu from elsewhere could be reabsorbed into the life of the tribe; and, at the same time, to screen them and prevent undesirables from filtering back. It has always been a cardinal principle that these camps are not prisons, but centres for reabsorbing and rehabilitating the expatriate members of the tribe. (Central Province 1954: 37)

Foucault (1980b: 59–62) suggests that the confession has become one of the West's most highly valued techniques for producing "truth" as well as for producing intrinsic modification in the person who articulates it. He who confesses purifies and redeems himself. However, truth does not reside within the subject who confesses. Rather, truth is constituted in the one who listens, says nothing, deciphers and records the confession. It is this latter subject who is the master of truth, the agency of domination, and the former subject upon whom truth works its effects (ibid.: 62–67). The whole notion of confession rests upon what Foucault calls the "repressive hypothesis," which presumes that truth is inherently opposed to power, that truth is liberating, that truth will expose and eliminate power. This of course obscures the inextricable link between power and truth.[11]

We see this confessional technology at work in Britain's counterinsurgency policies. Confession was the first essential step in the rehabilitation process. The goal was not to silence the subject, as was the case with the closing down of indigenous presses, but rather to control the signifying practices by which the subject came to know himself and the truth. In one respect, the confessional aspect of Britain's counterinsurgency program might be regarded as a failure in that many refused to confess or confessed only under duress (Edgerton 1989: 175–80; Rosberg and Nottingham 1966: 340–41). On the other hand, more than seventy-seven thousand people "successfully" passed through the rehabilitation process (Rosberg and Nottingham 1966: 342). At another level, though, it is not a matter of success or failure that is the main point. Rather, it is to point to the fact that the technologies at work in complex structures of domination have been at work globally in the international realm as well as the domestic realms that are the concern in studies such as Foucault's. Secularized confession was based upon an opposition between the normal and the pathological (Foucault 1980b: 67). Colonial Britain's use of this technology worked to represent the Mau Mau resistance members as abnormal and in need of either rehabilitation or permanent exile.

The rehabilitation process, which followed the confession, emphasized hard work, reeducation, washing, discipline, and games. Askwith (1958) noted that "hard physical labour has a very cleansing influence." Much of the reeducation program was based on Askwith's *The Story of Kenya's Progress,* originally published in 1953. Askwith noted that Africans and particularly the Kikuyu had been mistakenly misled to believe "in the crazy notion that they could manage their own affairs without the European" (Rosberg and Nottingham 1966: 338). As part of the reeducation program, the detainee would learn how the "unoccupied land which lay between African tribes who were frequently at war with each other was reserved for farming by Europeans or Indians. In this way a barrier was placed between the tribes, and fighting was prevented" (a white settler, quoted in Askwith 1958: 4). The detainee could also learn that European farming had been necessary because there "was little possibility of the African inhabitants being able to produce crops for exports, as they could hardly grow enough for their own needs, owing to their primitive methods of agriculture" (ibid.).[12] Reeducation also included coming to understand that "God Save the King" or "God Save the Queen" was a "prayer for our Sovereign, whom they respect and honour." Perhaps most important of all, detainees were to learn that the Europeans and Indians "understand better what democratic government means" and that "freedom is a great privilege. It cannot be given but can only be earned. It is only safe in the hands of those who know how to use it" (ibid.: 120).

The rehabilitation program overlapped with the villagization policy. Many of the same programs were emphasized in both. Upon reading Askwith's report, Carothers had commented that villagization should become much more than a policy to meet the needs of the emergency. It should be a policy for the whole future of Kikuyu rural life (Carothers 1955: 22). Carothers noted that it was not just the persons in detention for involvement with Mau Mau who needed rehabilitation. Rehabilitation for the "general Kikuyu people who remain at large" was also required. "Villagization would be of the greatest benefit (immediate and long-term) for all Kikuyu people and that, whether they accept it willingly or not, they should have no option but to do so" (ibid.: 23). Villagization was seen as a policy that offered multiple advantages, from protecting the personal security of the Africans, especially the Kikuyu, to promoting development: "Their isolation, suspicion, and longstanding social insecurity needs a development of this sort" (ibid.: 22). The colonial office also stressed that relocation and villagization should be considered "a new and permanent feature of the country's development and not merely ... an emergency security measure" (Mockaitis, 1990: 139). Carothers envisaged the villages "developing their local industries, their shops, their churches and health centres, schools, and clubs (Carothers 1955: 22).

CONCLUSION

Throughout this discourse, "reason" was repeatedly invoked, sometimes explicitly and often implicitly, as a privileged signifier, the nodal point around which the meaning of other signifiers was fixed. Western reason functioned to define a particular kind of individualism as good and a particular relationship between the individual and the community as desirable. The kind of individualism attributed to the Kikuyu—the "forest psychology"—was a bad kind of individualism that resulted in suspicion, scheming, and a general lack of social conformity (Carothers 1955: 5). The kind of individualism attributed to the British/European was a good individualism, consistent with the Kantian notion of a community of rational individuals who in exercising ethical judgment dictated by the laws of their own intelligible nature establish a public sphere of agreed-upon rational laws and constraints such that each individual concurs in the desirability of these laws and constraints for the good of the community.[13]

The African had not attained the good kind of individuality nor the proper relationship between the individual and the community. Social rules and constraints prevailed only within the group. They were not synthesized within the individual (ibid.: 19). Rational and ethical judgment, for the African, was dictated by an external source rather than within the nature of the individual. This was the problem of the African in transition. The external source had been disrupted or removed. While the Kikuyu were individualistic, it was not an individualism based upon the enlightened thought of Western reason.

The reason/unreason opposition enabled the array of practices that constituted Britain's counterinsurgency operations. The cleansing and rehabilitation processes as well as the villagization program and all that it entailed aimed to construct the rational individual subject on the model of the Western individual. Democracy and independence could be deferred until the African became this kind of subject.

The whole notion of a rational subject exercising ethical judgment in its own interest but also freely abiding by the rules and norms of the community's interest required that the definition of that community be severely circumscribed so as to exclude the majority of the people who might "reasonably" be considered to make up that community — the Africans themselves. What could not be questioned, what was understood to exist outside of history and outside of any relations of power, was Western reason itself. This privileged status of reason and the Africans' inherent lack of it, enabled and arguably necessitated the counterinsurgency practices colonial Britain engaged in to crush the Mau Mau resistance.

III

Contemporary Encounters

Introduction to Part III

Contemporary encounters between the North and the South have been extremely varied and have occurred in several different arenas and within the context of a rapidly and permanently changing world. In Part III I focus on (1) three prominent and interrelated issues (foreign aid, democracy, and human rights) that have been more recent focal points in North-South relations and (2) academic and scholarly representations of North-South relations. While foreign aid, democracy, and human rights are very much contemporary issues, it is possible to locate within them traces of concerns I expressed in earlier chapters about other encounters.

Being democratic, freedom-loving, and humanitarian have been important constitutive elements in the construction of the Western "self." When these qualities were called into question—when they became floating signifiers, unanchored to a specific discourse—rhetoric was intensified and hegemonic practices accelerated. As I have demonstrated, practices of domination that were seemingly at odds with humanist values were enabled by the fixing of meaning around dominant signifiers, or what I have referred to as nodal points. These nodals point functioned as the center of the structure that both enabled and limited meaning; the dominant signifer was the reference point for the oppositions by which identities were constructed. Practices that would seem to be at odds with the values embodied in the concepts of civilization, trusteeship, sovereignty, and democracy were enabled through the deferral of the meaning of these concepts and the shifting of the object of representation from these signifiers themselves to subjects whose identities were constructed through sets of oppositions. Thus, for example, the practice of colonization was enabled by the positing of "white man" as the reference point by which civilized could be distinguished from uncivilized. The United States was the reference point for sovereign identity. The actual meaning of sovereignty, or the encounter with the thing itself, was deferred by shifting to the representation of the Philippines vis-à-vis the United States, the exemplar of sovereign being. Western reason was the nodal point that enabled the Mau Mau rebellion to be constructed as the anathema of reason.

In moving to more contemporary encounters, then, it behooves us to ask what is being deferred, what practices are being enabled, and how. It might be tempting to take on an air of superiority and suggest that the kind of representational practices we have examined are a thing of the past. Whether this is true is what I examine next. In moving to more contemporary encounters, I shift the focus somewhat from that of the previous empirical chapters. Chapters 6 and 7 share no unifying theme other than being more contemporary than the other encounters. They also depart from the previous chapters in that they are more general, not anchored in a specific geographic locale. Though academic discourses have been included in several of the earlier chapters, chapter 7 is devoted exclusively to this genre of writing about North-South relations. Scholars can be considered what Foucault calls the "community of experts." North-South relations is perhaps one of the most doubtful "sciences" one can imagine, the realm in which the relationship between power and knowledge can be most readily discerned.

6

Foreign Aid, Democracy, and Human Rights

In a sense, only a single drama is ever staged in this "non-place," the endlessly repeated play of dominations. This relationship of domination is no more a "relationship" than the place where it occurs is a place; and precisely for this reason, it is fixed, throughout its history, in rituals, in meticulous procedures that impose rights and obligations.

MICHEL FOUCAULT, "NIETZSCHE, GENEALOGY, HISTORY"[1]

Since the end of World War II, foreign aid has been one of the major issues in North-South relations.[2] Aid has not just been about giving assistance to needy countries. Rather, foreign aid has and continues to be linked to other important issues such as democracy and human rights. These other issues have animated much of the discourse surrounding foreign assistance. In this chapter I view these three interrelated issues as contemporary sites (or "non-places") of North-South encounter wherein meanings and international identities have been constructed and reconstructed.

My concern is not with foreign aid, democracy, or human rights per se. I am not offering theoretical explanations for foreign aid practices or philosophical arguments for or against the promotion of human rights. There is already a vast amount of literature that does this. Rather, I am using these issues and the debates, discussions, and narratives surrounding them as instances in which we can gain insight into the representational practices that inform contemporary encounters between the North and the South. I am particularly concerned in this chapter and the next to explore the continuities and discontinuities with earlier encounters in terms of the constitutive elements of global identity construction and the politics of representation at work in the construction of North-South relations. In contrast to explanations for foreign aid practices that would focus on the self-interest of donor nations or the development of international norms of humanitarian concern with "third world" poverty, I suggest that it is important to grasp the *productive* aspect of the practices that have gone into the giving of aid and the promotion of democracy and human rights. My analysis is not a hermeneutic endeavor whereby I try to get at shared norms and understandings that can explain the development of foreign aid. It is not the anticipatory power of meaning that is at issue here but the hazardous play of dominations (Foucault 1977: 148). Foreign aid, as a set of productive representational practices, made possible new techniques within an overall economy of power in North-South relations. It put in place permanent mechanisms by which the "third world" could be monitored, classified, and placed under continual surveillance.

A key underlying theme of this chapter is that one can no more unproblematically point to what democracy and human rights signify than one could, at the turn of the century, unproblematically point to what "civilized" signified. Rather, these signifiers have always pointed to other signifiers, continually deferring encounter with the things themselves, that is, with the presence of democracy and human rights. The signifying chains, the deferrals, and the nodal points that attempt to fix meaning and the practices they make possible are the substance of this chapter.

FOREIGN AID AND DEMOCRACY: CONSTRUCTING THE "OTHER"

> Assisting the poor is a means of government, a potent way of containing the most difficult section of the population and improving all other sections.
>
> GIOVANNA PROCACCI
> "SOCIAL ECONOMY AND THE GOVERNMENT OF POVERTY"

Foreign assistance has been conceptualized by scholars and policy makers alike according to two conventional viewpoints. One stresses aid as an instrumental tool for the promotion of national security and economic interests. The other views aid as the result of humanitarian concerns related to alleviating poverty, fostering economic development, and promoting democracy.[3] The problem with these understandings is not inaccuracy per se. As Lumsdaine (1993: 32) points out in his study of foreign aid, human action is a mixture of principled and humane acts and self-interested calculation. No doubt both understandings are partially correct as far as they go. The problem is that they do not go far enough in terms of elaborating the continuing drama of domination. They give power numerous places to hide.

By placing foreign aid in the wider context of power relations, I suggest that it should be regarded as a specific technique in the more general field of exercising power. The importance of conceptualizing foreign aid in this manner is that it focuses not on the conscious, intentional aims of the aid givers, be they narrowly self-interested or humanitarian, but rather on what foreign aid, as a practice, *does*. Foreign aid enables the administration of poverty, the surveillance and management of the poor. Foreign assistance does at the global level what welfare institutions do at the domestic level.[4] That foreign aid has not eliminated poverty or produced economic development or led to democracy is not necessarily an indication of its failure. Foreign aid is but one of the numerous domains for the deployment of disciplinary techniques. So understood, the practice of foreign aid no longer appears as such a recent and anomolous departure from past practices.[5] Rather, it is part of the continuing drama in which meticulous rituals of power are played and replayed with various twists, turns, and modifications.

Lumsdaine (ibid.: 182) traces the origins of foreign aid to the growth of humanitarian internationalism, social democracy, and a concern for poverty. While it is no doubt true that in the absence of the ideas associated with these concerns the articulation of foreign aid programs would not have been possible, it is also true that intertwined with perhaps genuine concerns for the welfare of poor countries were fears and a sense of social danger incited by poverty and the poor. Poverty was linked with danger both at the domestic level and internationally: failure to achieve practical improvements in the lives of people throughout the world would provoke unrest and bring political extremists to power (Staley 1961: 20). Fear was generated by widespread poverty in Europe after World War II, but the danger of poverty associated with the "third world" was of an essentially different nature. In the case of Europe, poverty itself was the object of concern, the thing to be eliminated. In the case of the "third world," the subjects who personified poverty were the objects of concern. Eliminating poverty was secondary to "knowing" the mentality, the behaviors, the tendencies of those who were impoverished.

In the mid-1960s, as a hegemonic global power, the United States was especially aware of such international social dangers: "The United States is confronted with crises and problems all over the world. There is not any part of the world which we can ignore, where we can say that it does not matter what happens there" (Congressman Morgan of Pennsylvania, House of Representatives, *Congressional Record,* July 12, 1966: 15328).

One of the crises that Morgan referred to involved the "undeveloped" countries:

> It is very difficult to get these countries to take a long-range view of their problems, not just economic problems but social and political problems as well. It is in their interest and in the interests of world peace and prosperity to have them think ahead and not, in trying to deal with their current problems, get themselves into situations which they cannot cope with. (ibid.)

Hence, one of the objectives of U.S. foreign aid was to "encourage the people of the less developed countries in their efforts to better themselves." Foreign aid would provide this encouragement. While one may surmise a sense of humanitarian responsibility here, the notion of danger is also implicit. Foreign aid was not just for the purpose of alleviating poverty, but also for dealing with an international social danger. This was not a danger solely in the sense of the possibility that communism would provide an attractive alternative to capitalism for the poverty-stricken countries, but something more profound that required the transformation of populations into particular kinds of subjects.

Colin Gordon notes in his discussion of the social economists of the first half of the nineteenth century that "the personality and mentality of economic man cannot be implanted among the populations of the poor except as part of a broader strategy, a political technology designed to form, out of the recalcitrant material of the dangerous classes, something more than economic man, a social citizen"

(1991: 38). The countries that received foreign aid were not merely those in need of economic assistance (as was the case in rebuilding Europe after World War II), they were those that, as Pasquino suggests of criminals, "can be identified comprising those individuals and groups who, outpaced and left behind by the proper rate of evolution, endanger by their existence the orderly functioning of the whole" (1991: 38). Seen in this light, foreign aid can be usefully understood as a strategy for combating the dangers that confronted the project of an international liberal, capitalist social order. The discourses surrounding foreign aid in the 1960s suggest that the danger was not in poverty itself, but in the identities of those who were impoverished, those who could not take a long-range view of their situations.

The Foreign Assistance Act of 1966 was the largest single authorization bill in the history of foreign aid (*Congressional Record,* July 12, 1966: 15333).[6] Democracy was also put on the foreign policy agenda with Title IX of this act, "Utilization of Democratic Institutions in Development," which called for the assurance of

> maximum participation in the task of economic development on the part of the people of the developing countries, through the encouragement of democratic private and local institutions.... In particular, emphasis should be given to research designed to increase understanding of the ways in which development assistance can suport democratic social and political trends in recipient countries. (MIT report: xiii)

The agency charged with carrying out the provisions of Title IX was the Agency for International Development (AID). After passage of Title IX and various amendments to it, there was some uncertainty within AID and elsewhere about how the provision should be interpreted and implemented. In the fall of 1967 AID requested that the Center for International Studies at the Massachusetts Institute of Technology engage in an intensive examination of this subject. A study group was formed and met in continuous session from June 24 to August 2, 1968. Members of the study group consisted of academics from MIT and Cornell, Duke, and Columbia Universities and policy makers from the Department of State and AID. The group's report and congressional discussions and debates on foreign assistance constructed a particular understanding of what democracy and par ticipation were, how they were to be promoted, and, importantly, when they were not to be promoted. Most significantly, they were intertexts linked with earlier representations of international identities, demonstrating important continuities with earlier North-South encounters.

The purpose of U.S. aid was to provide opportunities for self-help and self-achievement for the "emerging peoples" (*Congressional Record,* July 13, 1966: 15405). What is presumed in such a designation? One is tempted to suggest that this term, put in the proper historical context, refers to the emergence of a people from darkness, from an uncivilized condition. A kinder interpretation might suggest the emergence of peoples (and nations) from colonial domination and dependence. In either case, the presupposition is that these "emerging peoples" did not exist in any meaningful or significant sense before the West recognized them as a "new" or "emerging" entity entitled to be labeled a "people" or a nation. This replicates the representational practices of the turn of the century when U.S. colonizers denied existence as a "people" to the "heterogeneous mass of humanity" inhabiting the Philippine Islands. The history that matters is the history of the West, and human beings emerge as "a people" when they are recognized in the eyes of the West.

An equally important and related goal of U.S. foreign assistance was to "reconcile the unreconciled among men and nations to the continued validity and viability of the present world system" (Zablocki, House of Representatives, *Congressional Record,* July 13, 1966: 15405). "Unreconciled" implies unsettled, potentially unstable, and unpredictable. It implies a dangerous population in need of transformation. Like "pauperism" in the nineteenth century, "unreconciled" invoked images of indefiniteness, a dangerous fluidity, at once massive and vague. Restraint and guidance thus became important bases of policies for reconciling the unreconciled, for transforming "emerging peoples" into social citizens.[7]

Unreconciled populations were a threat to stability, which was an important goal of U.S. foreign assistance. Political stability thus required their transformation, and to this end Title IX was important. Democratic institutions and popular participation were recognized as necessary elements in the achievement of political stability (ibid.: 15405). Activities that were part of Title IX were considered important in helping the "new nations" ultimately to "stand on their own."

For Congressman Donald Fraser of Minnesota, sponsor of Title IX, political development meant "the fostering, stimulation, and guidance of fundamental social structures and behaviors that make effective self-government possible" (ibid.: 15454). The problem with existing U.S. policy and interaction with the "new nations" was that "we usually treat those nations as though they already have the capacity to run their own affairs, if we only give them substantial additions to their material resources" (ibid.). To explain the problems with this policy, Fraser used the following analogy:

> A child matures to adulthood, at least physically, pretty much without human intervention, given a reasonable diet and protection against the harshest threats to his life. We don't really teach a child to stand or walk—we merely encourage him to follow our example when he is physiologically ready. Without our intervention doubtless he would stand and walk and run as soon and as well on his own as with our coaching.
>
> Our present international policies have largely relied on economic and military aid—analogous to the food and security needed by a child. I suspect that we have assumed these measures would allow the recipient young nations to mature politically by some automatic inner-directed process toward stable, responsible nationhood.
>
> But we know far too little about political development of societies to rest our hopes on such an assumption of automatic political maturation. I for one am convinced that we must take a far more deliberate and more comprehensive role toward developing nations. We should systematically try to trigger, to stimulate, and to guide the growth of fundamental social structures and behaviors among large numbers of people in other countries if we are to insure political development commensurate with the technological and defensive military prowess we are already striving for.
>
> To return to the human analogy I warned against earlier, sophisticated parents know that the emotional and social maturation of their children requires far more conscious effort on their part than their physical development does. Surely we can alert ourselves to the need for encouraging political growth if we hope them to become well rounded nations. (ibid.: 15454–55)

Fraser's rhetoric is reminiscent of earlier encounters in its representation of the South as lacking the capacity to run its own affairs. An important difference is revealed between dealing with poverty in post–World War II Europe and in the "third world." In the former case, Secretary of State George Marshall urged the countries of Europe to draw up a joint program for economic recovery and submit it to Washington; the American-financed European Recovery Program began in 1948. No such initiation was invited when it came to foreign assistance to the South. The earlier mission to uplift and civilize was replaced with the intent "to trigger, to stimulate, and to guide the growth of fundamental social structures and behaviors." Once again the West must breathe life into a base and lifeless (though always potentially volatile) element of humanity, giving it an identity and beginning its history. The motive force remains outside of the "third world" society and its indigenous culture, social structures, and inhabitants.

The parent-child (problem child) analogy found in earlier encounters is again prominent in these texts. The "emerging peoples" are the childlike subjects of previous encounters. The parents in this relationship cannot simply turn them loose in a dangerous world of competing forces of good and evil. Rather, they need to be nurtured, guided, and aided until they are capable of handling their own affairs and making their own decisions. As children — and children are always potentially problem children — they presented their parents with many potential problems. Not yet fully developed, unreconciled, they are always subject to the dangers stemming from their own immaturity. They are prone to getting themselves into situations they cannot handle. Parents should encourage and teach them to think ahead, to take a long-range view so they will not find themselves in situations they are not prepared to deal with.

The crises the United States faced in 1966 were attributable to its past mistake of treating the children, the "new nations," as if they had the capacity to run their own affairs. Having assumed that they only needed economic or technical help, the United States had failed to encourage and guide them into full political and social maturity. The Fraser text exemplified this parent-child analogy. The inability of the "new nations" to run their own affairs, coupled with their poverty and the potential attractiveness of communism, led to an inherently unstable and dangerous situation in which U.S. interests were at risk. It was not poverty per se that was the source of this danger, but the people who personified poverty, dependence, and at least potential delinquency and deviance.

The report of the MIT study group is illuminating because, while democracy and participation were the goals of Title IX, in studying how these goals could be realized, the group explicitly set forth conditions under which they should *not* be encouraged. For example, in Indonesia, "just recovering from a disastrous demagogic regime and suffering acute economic and national disintegration symptoms, it may be inappropriate to press for greater participation at present; its oligarchic regime must first have time to improve its ability to govern and promote economic growth" (MIT report: 47). The report also notes that "we must recognize that increased political participation may subject regimes to domestic political pressures which lead them to adopt policies counter to long-run U.S. interests" (ibid.: 49). In regard to military, communications, and other facilities:

> The interest of reliable access will usually be served by the persistence in power of the regime which originally granted these rights in the first place.... If the political process brings to the threshhold of power groups which are ideologically or for other reasons opposed to our continued presence, normally the United States should not encourage change. (ibid.: 55)

The presupposition that ran throughout the MIT study was that when, how, and if democracy should be promoted would be determined by members of the study group and U.S. policy makers. The presumption was that some subjects were the definers, delimiters, and boundary setters of important practices and ideas such as participation and democracy and that others not capable themselves of making such definitions, would have these things bestowed upon them and would be permitted to enjoy them only under the circumstances deemed suitable by the United States.

The contrast between postwar Europe and the South is significant. None of the participants in the MIT study group were from any of the countries that were the object of discussion and policy. It was beyond the realm of imagination that those whose participation was to be encouraged would actually participate in articulating the parameters of that participation. The MIT text constructed one kind of subject identity who could engage in studies that determine how to promote democracy in the development process of the other kind of subject. While the latter were the subjects to be encouraged to participate in the development process, they were the objects to be studied in order to determine how and under what conditions democracy should be encouraged.

Closely associated with this parent-child opposition was the reason-passion opposition. The MIT document implicitly drew on it in constructing two distinct kinds of subject identities. This was evident in the study group's suggestion that greater participation would convince "third world" leadership that it was necessary "to meet internal questions with greater pragmatism and less ideology and this may translate to the international stage" (51). Later in the report, the group asserted that "third world" leaders "rarely make the sharp distinction between politics and economics" (60); the implication is that politics is the realm of passion and ideology and economics the realm of reason and rationality. "Third world" leaders have difficulty making this distinction. The thrust of these statements is that with U.S. encouragement for increased participation, these "other" countries could reach a point where pragmatism and rationality replaced ideology and passion as guiding forces.

The parent/child, reason/passion oppositions complemented one another. Those guided by passion and ideology were dangerous, potential disrupters of the international social order. Rational parents imposed both self-restraint and external restraint upon irrational children. This discourse was directed not toward the disappearance of poverty and inequality but toward the elimination of difference — the transformation of childlike subjects, guided by emotion and ideology, into adults guided by the rationality compatible with a liberal international order. As was the case with the earlier encounters, however, the representational practices present in the foreign aid discourse constructed the very differences that transformation ostensibly would eliminate.

Focusing on the subjects of aid enabled the deferral of democracy itself. What democracy signified in the foreign aid discourse was never the *presence* of a clear and unambiguous signified, but rather the *absence* of certain characteristics in "third world" subjects, characteristics that were deemed essential prerequisites for full-fledged, mature membership in the international community. This obscured the undemocratic character of policies ostensibly aimed at promoting democracy and of the international order itself—institutions such as the International Monetary Fund and the World Bank. Democracy and participation were constructed as relevant internally—inside the bounds of domestic societies—but not at the level of the international community.

FOREIGN AID AND HUMAN RIGHTS: CONSTRUCTING THE "SELF"

In 1974, after a period of realpolitik during the Nixon-Kissinger years in which the utility of force replaced concern with democracy and participation, Congress strengthened section 502B of the 1974 Foreign Assistance Act.[8] The amendments to toughen 502B were introduced by Senator Alan Cranston, Congressman Don Fraser, and Senator Stephen Solarz. They called for two types of reports: one to accompany security assistance recommendations about to be presented, the other to be at the request of either the House International Relations Committee or the Senate Foreign Relations Committee for any country receiving security assistance. In addition, Congress adopted Section 116 of the Foreign Assistance Act (on international development) in 1975. Authored by Congressman Tom Harkin of Iowa, it addressed economic assistance, making the observance of certain basic human rights within recipient countries a condition for U.S. bilateral economic aid (Harkin 1978: 17). Thus, by the end of 1976 a substantial amount of legislation on U.S. policy on human rights practices in other countries, all of it initiated by Congress, was in place.

The effect of this legislation (intentions notwithstanding) had less to do with the promotion of human rights than with the promotion of U.S. security and the representation of the United States as a world power capable of exercising moral leadership.[9] These two effects, not surprisingly, often contradicted one another. It was, after all, within the context of U.S. linkages with repressive military regimes—in Greece, Brazil, and East Timor, to mention a few—the coup in Chile, and the moral issues surrounding Vietnam that the human rights issue arose. In the international realm the United States was a latecomer to the human rights issue and had actually failed to ratify many human rights treaties (Ajami 1982: 378).[10] In effect, these actions had called into question the morality of the United States as a hegemonic leader. Promoting human rights became a practice whereby the United States re-presented itself as a global hegemonic subject:

> Strict adherence to the principles of internationally recognized human rights will be necessary if the United States is to regain the moral leadership it possessed at the end of World War II. A United States firmly and visibly in defense of human rights will be in a better position to give leadership in the search for solutions to the urgent problems of this planet. (Bruce Cameron, Legislative Representative, House International Relations Committee, April 18, 1977)

Attention to the human rights issue during this period was not limited to the U.S. government. In September 1976 a conference titled "Renewed Concern for Democracy and Human Rights: Special Bicentennial Program" was attended by members of the U.S. Congress and European Parliamentarians. The general theme of the conference was, in the words of Republican congressman Philip Crane, "how ... the United States and the European Community, through political and economic relations with other countries, [can] try to promote democratic development and respect for human rights."

Paul Tsongas, a Democrat from Massachusetts, presented a paper entitled "Economic Assistance in Human Rights" that opened with a statement of credentials establishing him as an expert on non-Western societies. His experiences in the Peace Corps in 1962 and 1964 in Ethiopia and the West Indies respectively enabled him to "gain some insight into the dynamics of the non-Western societies" (51). Tsongas pointed to the need to be careful in trying to influence human rights practices in some of the "less developed countries":

> I am convinced that in the dealings between North and South, between the developed and less developed worlds, there exists a mind set of skepticism at best and the outright hostility at worst on the part of the recipient countries".... The fact is that most Third World countries do not have a democratic tradition, and there are very few John Lockes or Rousseaus or Magna Cartas in the Third World Legacy. Indeed the historic tradition in most Third World countries is based on social institutions that are mostly authoritarian, such as tribes, religious institutions, and the extended family. (51–52)

The lack of democractic traditions in most Third World countries led Tsongas to suggest that U.S. policy should not tie aid to the development of democratic institutions but should make aid contingent upon human rights practices: "Human rights should be substituted as a primary criteria for assistance in economic development" (54).

Philip Crane, a Republican from Illinois, asserting that U.S. foreign policy had historically been based on morality rather than power politics, suggested establishment of "an association of freedom-loving nations" that would be an alternative to the United Nations. Ironically, membership in this association would be more restrictive than in the United Nations. Such an association would "provide a vehicle for the United States and its European friends to promote self-government and human rights" (29). There would be two categories of membership: "full membership for nations with a proven record of guaranteeing individual rights; and associate membership for those nations who do not meet the requirements for full membership but which are nonaggressive and anti-Communist" (22). A commission consisting of elected representatives from member states would be assigned the responsibility of investigating allegations and filing charges, which would then be referred to a special court, which, in turn, would have the responsibility for adjudication and recommendation of penalty (30).

Fraser of Minnesota suggested how the United States and the European Community could promote democratic development and respect for human rights: "the European Parliament and members of the U.S. Congress might consider conducting joint study missions to countries where widespread human rights abuses have been reported" (35). The two groups should hold meetings to discuss topics such as implementation of the Helsinki Accords, encouragement of democratic development in Spain, white minority rule in South Africa, and "major problems of repression in individual nations" (35).

These texts set up the United States (and Europe) as subjects who inherently knew what human rights and democracy were. As they were inherently civilized in earlier encounters, they were now inherently humane and democratic. Being themselves living exemplars, heirs to the traditions of Locke and Rousseau, they were uniquely qualified to promote these values and demonstrate them to others. The human rights discourse also functioned as a site wherein the issue of U.S. security became linked up with the parent-child opposition. This was evident in the cases of South Korea and the Philippines, where the "hard questions" regarding human rights practices and foreign assistance presented themselves.

On June 24, 1975, Philip Habib, assistant secretary in the Bureau of East Asian and Pacific Affairs, U.S. Department of State, testified before the Committee on International Relations regarding human rights in South Korea and the Philippines and the implications they had for U.S. policy. He recognized the consequences of martial law, the suspension of certain democratic processes and of human rights, wide-ranging arrests, and the curtailment of freedom of the press. He said, however, that there was no evidence that torture and mistreatment of prisoners was the policy of the government of the Philippines or a general practice (312). He also expressed support for the "Philippine Government's avowed intention to promote improvement in the social, economic, and administrative areas" and said that there has been measurable progress in some of them (312). He added:

> The Philippines has had a long association with the United States; first as a colony; then as the Philippines Commonwealth; and since 1946, as a close and valued ally. Regarding the question of human rights and fundamental freedoms, we can only express our concerns, as we have and hope that governments will realize that free people inevitably come down on the side of that which is good for the country as a whole. (312)

Habib's invocation of the long association between the United States and the Philippines was an implicit plea that the United States not abandon the Philippines even if they were violating international norms regarding human rights principles. The same theme can be found in the testimony of Richard Holbrooke, assistant secretary designate of state, East Asian and Pacific Affairs, in hearings before the Committee on International Relations regarding foreign assistance legislation for 1978. East Asia in general was portrayed as "undergoing its own transformation from an unfortunate past to an uncertain future." Like delinquent children, the countries of east Asia "still [had] far to go in their development efforts (Holbrooke 1977: 5). The parent/child analogy enabled the continuance of security assistance despite doubtful commitments to democracy and human rights: "Selective military assistance supports the security of our friends and allies, thus providing them with greater opportunities for social and economic development" (ibid.: 7).

Parents cannot abandon their children, even if the children are misbehaving. Even a "symbolic slap in the face" risks alienating them and forcing them to turn elsewhere—to communist countries—for guidance and assistance. A parent must offer unconditional love, support, nurture, and even defense of children's actions:

> We did receive some independent estimates that most Filipinos prefer the martial law regime to the chaotic democracy of the past years. Nonetheless we wish to emphasize again the continued congressional interest in human rights and a desire for movement in the Philippines toward democratic constitutionalism. (14)

The portrayal of martial law as relatively benign was also found in 1976 hearings entitled "Shifting Balance of Power in Asia: Implications for Future U.S. Policy." These hearings were held before a subcommittee of the House Committee on International Relations. On May 18, Lewis Purnell, former deputy chief of mission at the U.S. Embassy Manila, made the following statement:

> While martial law applied in the Philippines is far different from the picture that term normally raises in our minds, it has involved the setting aside of numerous political liberties and human rights. The effect has been felt less by the great majority of the population than by the small articulate class which has dominated the political processes and the public media. (190)

Robert Oakley, deputy assistant secretary for East Asian Affairs, in appropriations hearings on foreign assistance for 1978, recommended that security assistance for the Philippines be continued:

> [Elimination of security assistance] could lessen the ability of the U.S. to influence the Philippine government on a range of U.S. interests in the Philippines, including the promotion of human rights, adversely affect our security position in the East Asian region and elsewhere, and decrease confidence in U.S. security commitments to many important nations who have for decades been closely aligned with the U.S. (1977 hearings: 614)

Putting human rights on the foreign policy agenda made surveillance of other societies possible without the United States itself being monitored. Despite the different positions on the human rights issue, there was an unspoken consensus regarding the need for surveillance of the countries in question. For those opposed to tying foreign aid to adherence to human rights principles, surveillance was required in order to stop the spread of communism. For security purposes it was necessary to be informed on all relevant events in these countries. Surveillance was also necessary in order for policy makers to be answerable to Congress and to defend countries against cuts in foreign assistance. The 1974 amendments to section 502B required human rights reports to be prepared *on any country* receiving security assistance at the request of the House International Relations Committee or the Senate Foreign Relations Committee. For those who favored tying assistance to human rights, continuing surveillance was necessary in order to assure that countries receiving U.S. assistance did not engage in human rights abuses. Thus, to receive assistance was to be put under surveillance.

This is the reversal of visibility that is characteristic of disciplinary power (Foucault 1979: 191): those who are monitored have the greatest visibility, while the sovereign is relatively invisible. The United States was comparatively invisible in this exercise of power. The United States and other Western democracies were constructed as exemplars of human rights practices, without themselves being subjected to the normalizing gaze of the international community.[11]

This was an effective and efficient mechanism, not because the stated goals — the adherence to human rights principles — were realized, but because it was a productive power that constructed and simultaneously hierarchized particular kinds of subjects. What was normalized was not the norm of acceptable human rights practices but rather the hierarchical relationship between the United States and the rest of the world. Section 502B created a system of individualizing and permanent documentation, a system of "moral accounting" (Foucault 1979: 250). Some international subjects were subject to this accounting; others were not.

Activities of the United States were not subject to global scrutiny. Inherently moral subjects did not need to account for their practices. It was unthinkable that their practices could be anything but moral. What was a human right and when violation warranted punishment was to be determined by the United States. U.S. security interests served as the nodal point around which the meaning of human rights was constructed and that enabled the United States to ignore violations (and even participate at least indirectly in violations) and still be capable of exercising international moral leadership. Like democracy, human rights were constructed as relevant within national boundaries — between a government and its own citizens — but not in international practices. This enabled international practices such as the training of dictators and members of death squads (the School of the Americas), intervention that overthrew elected leaders (Guatemala, Chile), and later military action that caused extreme suffering and death among civilians (Panama and the Gulf War). The United States could be implicated in such practices and still not be considered a violater of human rights.

Foucault (1979: 279–80) speaks of a "useful delinquency," a controlled illegality, as an agent for the illegality of the dominant groups. This is a useful concept in discussing the U.S. position on international human rights. The implicit hierarchy of countries and the system of surveillance made it possible for the United States to profit by the violation of human rights (in the sense of keeping order and preventing leftists from coming to power in "third world" countries) and still condemn those practices. In this sense, human rights violators were privileged instruments, useful delinquents, of the very system that created and supported them.

CONCLUSION

Concern with democracy and human rights has been manifested in various forms that are not always linked with official foreign aid. During the Reagan administration, aid and democracy were privatized, so to speak. Despite drastic cuts in foreign aid and severance of its ties with human rights practices, democracy remained an important concern. For example, in a well-known speech before the British Parliament, President Reagan, reiterating the goal of promoting democracy throughout the world, said, "If the rest of this century is to witness the gradual growth of freedom and democratic ideals, we must take actions to assist the campaign for democracy." He also reiterated the inherent British identity, reminiscent of earlier discourses: "Here among you is the cradle of self-government, the mother of parliaments. Here is the enduring greatness of the British contribution to mankind, the great civilized ideas: individual liberty, representative government and the rule of law under God."[12]

Britain and the United States, despite widespread practices that had denied self-government to millions of people, retained an identity associated with self-government and the promotion of liberty. This, of course, is not a startling revelation, but perhaps it behooves us to express incredulity at this fact and to recognize it as evidence that material practices have no inherent meaning. What a practice *is* is inextricably linked with the constructed identity of the subjects/agents engaging in it. This bears directly on the issue of promoting democracy and human rights internationally. It is not to suggest that these things should not be promoted; it is rather to call attention to the meanings and identities that are constructed in the process of promoting democracy and human rights *and* the meanings that these signifiers themselves are given.

The promotion of democracy during the Reagan administration, for example, resulted in the privatization of aid and democracy. It also enabled a particular construction of the meaning of democracy. In 1983, for the first time, the U.S. government created an agency expressly for the purpose of promoting democracy abroad, the National Endowment for Democracy (NED). Consistent with Reagan's fear of the "threat posed to human freedom by the enormous power of the modern state," it was ostensibly a private organization, but it was (and is) funded almost entirely by Congress through an annual grant from the United States Information Agency (Promoting Democracy 1986: 1).[13] Working through a web of civic organizations, research institutes, trade unions, business associations, and media outlets and enjoying bipartisan support, the NED has created nodal points by which the meaning of democracy is linked with private enterprise and conservative political and labor organizations.

Democracy and human rights continue to be important concerns in North-South relations. Indeed, the "building of democracy and respect for human rights" is currently one of the top objects of U.S. security assistance programs.[14] I am not suggesting that it should not be. I am suggesting that what needs to be examined are the representational practices that occur in the process of promotion. What meanings and identities are being (and will be) constructed? One can question what signifieds are being linked with democracy and human rights by the portrayal of Islam as inherently undemocratic, thereby justifying the military coup that denied electoral victory to the Islamic Salvation Front in Algeria.[15] One can pose the same question regarding the representation of Haiti and Aristide.[16] Similarly, one may ask what meaning of democracy is signified by the continued U.S. military exercises in Guatemala, one of the most outrageous violators of human rights imaginable. The pursuit of democracy requires careful and critical analyses rather than claims to a self-evident exemplary mode of democratic being on the part of the United States.

Repetition and Variation: Academic
Discourses on North-South Relations

*In societies like ours, the 'political economy' of truth is characterized
by five important traits. 'Truth' is centered on the form of scientific
discourse and the institutions which produce it; it is subject to constant economic and political incitement (the demand for truth, as
much for economic production as for political power); it is the object,
under diverse forms, of immense diffusion and consumption (circulat-
ing through apparatuses of education and information whose extent
is relatively broad in the social body, not withstanding certain strict
limitations); it is produced and transmitted under the control, dominant if not exclusive, of a few great political and economic apparatuses (university, army, writing, media); lastly, it is the issue of a whole
political debate and social confrontation ('ideological' struggles).*

MICHEL FOUCAULT, "TRUTH AND POWER"

In the previous chapters I have examined how power has worked
through various discursive practices that have produced different
"truths" and the practices those "truths" made possible. The missions to civilize, to fight communism, to promote democracy and
human rights have often masked the workings of power, not because the individuals involved (the speakers of the discourses) were
consciously and intentionally engaged in a game of deceit with an
underlying ulterior motive. Rather, power was masked because power
was (and is) generally understood to be separate from "truth" and
knowledge. Coming to "know" is not conceived as an exercise of

power. But coming to "know" is a productive practice of constructing identities and relationships, and power inheres in this. This is perhaps most obvious in situations where the production of truth and knowledge coincides with the military and economic power that facilitates control and domination. It is often a good deal less obvious in discourses that are ostensibly not connected to the aims and interests of military and economic power—academic discourses, for example. Foucault suggests that the relationship between power and knowledge can readily be discerned in the social sciences—the "doubtful sciences"—which have not crossed the "threshold of epistemologization," have not become "normal" science in the Kuhnian sense. Such an understanding of power and knowledge prompts the substitution of the apparent internal intelligibility of social science discourses on North-South relations with a different intelligibility: their place within a larger discursive formation.

In this chapter I examine how the "third world" has been incorporated into one area of social science discourse, the discipline of international relations. There are, of course, numerous ways that this has been done. The literature on "third world development," especially from the perspective of modernization theory, is the obvious place to begin, but so much has already been said about this literature that to focus exclusively on it would be redundant.[1] Yet to exclude it would miss an important set of representational practices that have significant linkages with past practices and have been important in producing certain widespread "truths" as well as legitimating certain practices. Rather than examining political development theory per se, I include within my examination of international relations discourses the ways in which important aspects of development theory have worked their way into these discourses and have been accepted as truth.

For my examination of international relations discourses I have chosen two sets of texts that deal with issues of central importance to the field. I chose them for their recognized contribution to international relations scholarship, particularly in the area of North-South relations. The first involves the topic of sovereignty and statehood in the "third world," the second the goals and demands articulated by the "third world" that run counter to the global liberal doctrines institutionalized in international regimes. These two sets of texts share an underlying and often implicit—some would argue marginal—

theme: a fear or sense of danger regarding the entry of the "third world" into the international society of states and an accompanying apprehension about the diminishing value of power as a constitutive element of international politics. Both were produced in times of crises of representation wherein naturalized understandings of foundational concepts and normative ideals such as sovereign statehood and the ability of a liberal global order to "deliver the goods" were problematized. In responding to such crises, both put into play replicable and widely circulated practices of representation by which international identities have been produced and reproduced.

In analyzing these texts I am not imputing any specific intentions or bad faith to the authors. I am not deciphering the texts to get at the true intentions of the authors. Rather, I am suggesting that these texts, like those I examined in previous chapters, are intertexts linked with a wide array of discourses and representational practices. Academic theorizing, like any practice of generating "knowledge," is never a neutral or autonomous endeavor. The text(s) of such theorizing belong to language, not to the generating author (Spivak 1976: xxv). In this sense, the meaning and significance of the texts cannot be limited to the purposes and intentions of the authors.

THE SOVEREIGNTY OF SOVEREIGNTY: "REAL" STATES,
"QUASI" STATES, AND THE "THIRD WORLD" IN
INTERNATIONAL RELATIONS THEORY

> *Many Third World states are scarcely self-standing realities but nevertheless are completely sovereign jurisdictions recognized by international legitimacy and law. Rugged individualism in international relations hardly applies to these entities which for the most part are creatures of a novel international protectionism.*
>
> ROBERT H. JACKSON, *Quasi-States: Sovereignty, International Relations and the Third World*

One of the ways that the South has been incorporated into the international relations literature has been through the attempt to make sense of "third world" sovereignty and statehood. As I noted in chapter 4, the words *sovereign statehood* often look quite different attached to "third world" states than to "first world" states. Scholars of international relations have not ignored this. One of the most impressive and widely recognized efforts to come to grips with sovereign statehood in the "third world" can be found in the works of Robert Jackson (1987, 1990, 1993) and Robert Jackson and Carl Rosberg (1982, 1986). Prompted initially by the inadequacy of realist-oriented theories that could not explain the persistence of weak states (i.e., "third world" states), Jackson and Rosberg (1982) attempted to provide an explanation for their endurance despite their lack of important empirical conditions for statehood. Their arguments subsequently have been generalized to include much of the "third world." Here I examine these texts as tissues of meanings drawn from a variety of other texts and as productive political practices of generating truth and knowledge. My aim is to foreground the representational practices that make them complicitous with other texts and other imperial encounters.

The posing of questions about sovereign statehood by Jackson and Rosberg occurred within the context of a crisis of representation of sovereignty itself. What foundational meaning could one attribute to sovereignty if it could also signify its opposite—anarchy—as it seemed to do in much of Africa and other "third world" countries? At one level, in recognizing the paradox of "third world" sovereign statehood, these texts work to undermine conventional international relations theory. Black Africa, as represented by Jackson and Rosberg, makes problematic the core hierarchical sovereignty/anarchy opposition that undergirds conventional international relations theory. Ashley refers to this opposition as the "deep structure" of international relations theory that functions to demarcate the internal realm of order and civility from the external realm of violence, disunity, and disorder: "Sovereignty signifies a homogeneous and well-bounded rational order of politics finding its focus in a hierarchical center of decision to which all questions of interpretation can be referred; and anarchy is then defined residually, as an opposed domain of practice which, for lack of a center, involves the undecidable interaction of plural interpretations and practices" (1988: 238). Statehood in Africa turns this opposition on its head. Jackson and Rosberg suggest that in contemporary black Africa, "an image of international accord and civility and internal disorder and violence would be more accurate" (1982: 24). What sovereignty demarcates is reversed when it comes to black Africa and much of the "third world." The crisis in Africa is thus also a crisis of representation, of how to represent the fundamental meaning of sovereignty.

So far, so good. However, there is within these texts an attempt to save sovereignty itself, so to speak. While suggesting that political realism, with its dependence on the sovereignty/anarchy opposition, cannot explain statehood in the "third world," these texts nonetheless work to preserve a domain of "genuine" sovereign statehood wherein power is the key element. There is an important, if implicit, lament over what might be called the diminishing value of power as the primary constitutive element in the "sovereignty game" and an accompanying fear of what the alternative grounds for sovereign statehood might portend. While suggesting that the alternative grounds for sovereign statehood could mean a radical new development in international relations that would legitimate an international theory of morality based on assumptions of social justice (Jackson and Rosberg 1982: 22), the texts acquire their productive force via a desire to reaffirm the "real" and "true" foundations of sovereign statehood.[2] This reaffirmation entails the garnering of conceptual resources whereby the idea of a normal and authentic sovereign state is reproduced and juxtaposed to a different and inferior kind of state, a "category mistake," lacking "real substance and value" (Jackson and Rosberg 1987: 543). The conceptual resources are the focus of this section, for it is here that we find important intertextual linkages with earlier texts in the representational practices that construct international identities.

In trying to make sense of "third world" sovereignty, Jackson and Rosberg draw upon a whole array of hierarchical oppositions, the most notable being positive sovereignty/negative sovereignty. In an important respect the distinctions entailed in this opposition complicate and enrich our understanding of sovereignty. Sovereignty is not a unitary category with the same basis at all times and in all situations. Rather, the norms by which states are constituted as sovereign are subject to change. Still, one should question what is entailed in making the distinction between positive and negative sovereignty. This is important because it is not just two different but equally valid bases of sovereign statehood at issue here. Rather, it is a question of the kinds of sovereign subjects that constitute international society, and there is a strong implicit suggestion of differential moral value attached to different kinds of subjects. The two different bases of sovereignty apply to different kinds of international identities and indeed are implicated in the very construction of those identities. When they are placed in historical context, the positive sovereignty/negative sovereignty opposition and the other oppositions that support it bear remarkable resemblances to earlier differentiations that prepared the way for various imperial practices.

The positive sovereignty/negative sovereignty opposition depends upon the real state/quasi state opposition (Jackson 1987). Real states are exactly what the term would seem to imply. They are simply there in unquestioned presence. "Sovereign statehood ... originated both logically and historically as a de facto independence between states. States had it 'primordially': 'the nature of the sovereign state as constitutionally insular is analogous to that of the individual as a developed personality, dependent indeed upon society, yet at the same time inner-directed and self-contained' " (ibid.: 532, quoted by Wight). The analogy here between the sovereign state and the inner-directed and self-contained individual is significant. Following the logic of this analogy, if the positively sovereign, real, empirical state is analogous to a particular kind of individual, then the negatively sovereign quasi state is analogous to an individual who is not inner-directed, not yet fully developed as an individual.[3]

Real statehood and positive sovereignty are consequences of successful state building characterized by development, military power, socioeconomic capabilities and resources, internal unity and legitimacy, science and technology, education, and welfare (ibid.: 536). States to whom these attributes apply are found in the developed West and the Soviet bloc. Political realism's focus on power and competition fits well with real states. The East/West conflict was only the latest version of a historical and endlessly developing system in which the power and prestige of states depend upon achievements in government, science, and technology (ibid.).

Realist theory falters, however, when it comes to quasi states. The foundation for quasi statehood and negative sovereignty, in contrast, is to be located in "the contemporary moral-legal framework of the accommodative juridical regime" (ibid.). The moral and legal basis of the states system has changed in the direction of equality (ibid.: 537). This change, however, is not necessarily for the good because it has resulted in the delinking of international legitimacy and national capability. Quasi states, which have international legitimacy but lack national capability, are characterized by a public community segmented ethnically into several publics, by widespread corruption, and by incompetence. Quasi states are maintained by international courtesy (ibid.), by a benevolent international society, a global democracy (Jackson and Rosberg 1982: 16). In the absence of this, they could not survive.

At one level this characterization seems unobjectionable. The concept of negative sovereignty and those associated with it—juridical or quasi statehood—ostensibly add a layer of complexity to the construct of sovereignty and to our understanding of sovereign statehood. Still, these texts contain a productive force that warrants examination. Jackson and Rosberg's initial concern implicitly recognized a certain paradox: that sovereignty could itself signify anarchy in the case of the "third world." This recognition could have served to problematize the opposition between sovereignty and anarchy, to expose its arbitrariness and thereby acknowledge that sovereignty depends upon widely circulated practices that produce and reproduce it as somehow natural and beyond question, be it in the "developed West" or the "underdeveloped third world." To recognize the inherently fragile nature of the sovereignty/anarchy opposition suggests, as Walker has noted, that "states are constantly maintained, defended, attacked, reproduced, undermined, and relegitimized on a daily basis" (1993: 168). It would recognize, as Ashley and Walker have suggested, that "the problem of sovereignty is profoundly paradoxical.... It is preoccupied with the problem of foundation: a fundamental principle, a supporting structure, a base on which society rests, a fund of authority capable of endowing possibilities, accrediting action, and fixing limitations" (1990: 382).

These texts, however, stop short of doing this and instead function to preserve a domain of true, genuine, and unquestioned sovereign statehood. They work to reconstruct the problematic foundation upon which the problem of sovereignty rests. This is accomplished by splitting sovereignty into positive and negative, and positing to each an essence that invokes images of identity that have been present in many of the past imperial encounters between the North and the South. Consider the following list of attributes.

- positive sovereignty
- real states
- possess sovereignty by merits or deserts

- negative sovereignty
- quasi states
- possess sovereignty by international courtesy

- integrated political community resting on common culture etc.
- effective government organization

- rugged individualism (Jackson 1990: 81)

- absence/lack of political community
- "soft" state, characterized by corruption and disorder, devoid of moral value
- backwardness (Jackson 1990: 131)
- collective ideologies (Jackson 1990: 114)

We can observe in this list a certain symmetry. The attributes on the left seem to fit together "naturally," as do the ones on the right. We can also note that the terms on the left are the superior terms; the ones on the right are characterized by a lack, an absence of some desired quality. This "structure" of representations bears significant resemblances to those discussed in earlier chapters. Indeed, we could expand this list to include some of the earlier representations without violating its symmetry. Many of the earlier colonial stereotypes are present in the real state/quasi state opposition: inability to handle power and authority responsibly and humanely, incapacity for self-government, general incompetence.

Like the earlier representations, the concepts of juridical statehood, quasi statehood, and negative sovereignty move insistently toward a questioning of the capacity of states so labeled and those who inhabit them. Jackson and Rosberg note that the African crisis goes back to independence, when "the question of the readiness and capacity of the colonies for self-government was bypassed" (1986: 19). They note that General Principle XIV of the 1964 Conference on Trade and Development "assumed that the indigenous capacity for exercising control already existed or could be rapidly developed" (ibid.: 19–20). The effect of these statements, whether it is intended or not, is to raise doubts regarding the indigenous capacity for self-government in Africa and elsewhere in the "third world." This skepticism is made explicit by Jackson:

> Most non-European peoples were deemed to be not yet conversant with (Western) ideas and institutions of modern self-government. It was feared that if they were granted independence prematurely, some members of their populations would simply impose an authoritarian regime on the remainder, thus obstructing the movement toward authentic political freedom. (*The fact that this scenario was frequently*

played out after decolonization is perhaps an indication of the valid-
ity of the argument). (1993: 121; emphasis added)

This same doubt has characterized most of the imperial encounters we have examined. As in the U.S. colonization of the Philippines and British justification for African labor, the readiness and
capacity of particular kinds of subjects is a primary issue. This doubt
reduces the integrity of African and other "third world" societies and
indeed provides advance justification for future interference. It provides a ready set of explanations for "third world" failure and silences
the historical as well as contemporary global relationships that contribute to this "failure." For example: "We must conclude that international society is at least partly responsible for perpetuating the underdevelopment of the empirical state in Africa by providing resources
to incompetent or corrupt governments without being permitted to
ensure that these resources are effectively and properly used" (Jackson
and Rosberg 1982: 22–23). While blame is attributed to international
society, the fundamental cause of failure is assigned to "third world"
incompetence and corruption, which international society permits
and often, albeit unintentionally, facilitates. The implicit assumption is that international society could, if permitted, ensure the effective and proper use of resources: "Alternative arrangements
which could supply greater expertise, responsibility, and probity in
government decision-making" are unthinkable because they would
invite "accusations of paternalism, neocolonialism, and even racism
and so international society for the most part remains silent" (Jackson 1990: 191). While Jackson's text explicitly suggests that these
alternatives are unthinkable, its rhetorical force does just the opposite—makes them thinkable and even desirable. The benevolent,
democractic "international society" in these texts replaces the "superior West," the "white man" of earlier imperial encounters. "International society" itself is characterized by a certain ambiguity. While
the term ostensibly includes all the world's nation-states, the distinction between "real" states and quasi states implies that it consists
of only those "real" states found in the "developed" world.

REINSCRIPTIONS: BENEVOLENT IMPERIALISM

Key to the negative sovereignty game is self-determination of former colonies and the development of a norm of entitlements for impoverished countries (Jackson 1990: 40). In so defining the nega-

tive sovereignty game, it becomes not just a formal legal principle regarding mutual recognition and norms of noninterference among states, a principle that has always supplemented positive sovereignty. Rather, it becomes inextricably linked with decolonization and the recognition of the right of self-determination on the part of former colonies. It is this self-determination that is regarded as troubling because it is attached to states that need and assert the right to economic assistance in various forms. This, according to Jackson, creates a normative dilemma involving the contradictory nature of demanding both sovereign independence and development support: "In the real world of international relations one cannot have one's cake and eat it" (ibid.: 138).

In explicating this normative dilemma, something of a cleansing operation is performed for colonialism, which is portrayed as "the moral, legal, and material aid structure that maintained Africa" and that subsequently has been replaced by the international community centered on the United Nations (Jackson and Rosberg 1986: 10). Colonialism, which was a product of the international norm of positive sovereignty, is represented as a basically bloodless episode in the unfolding and development of the state system (ibid.: 7). Following the logic of the hierarchical oppositions that structure these texts, quasi statehood takes on the character of inferiority: "By enforcing juridical statehood, international society is in some cases also sustaining and perpetuating incompetent and corrupt governments" (Jackson and Rosberg 1982: 22). Sovereignty undergirded by power is implicitly the more desirable condition, the term marked by moral and cultural superiority. Incompetence, corruption, and injustice are seen as arising from the new norms that characterize the principle of international recognition. That incompetence, corruption, and injustice have been linked with positive sovereignty and empirical statehood is not an issue, though such examples are certainly not lacking.[4] Power is inextricably linked with competence, efficiency, and progress. As Goldberg (1993: 166) points out, the term *progress* has, since its inception in the fifteenth century, assumed moral and cultural judgments of civilized superiority. The existence of quasi statehood is seen as antithetical to progress and thus as a potential danger the international community should be wary of.

In these texts on "third world" sovereignty we bear witness to the creation of several new signifiers—negative sovereignty, quasi states, juridical states — that function as a condensation of the attributes that differentiate African and other "third world" countries from the West. These new signifiers are only the latest in a long series of hierarchical binary oppositions that have served to construct various international identities. One cannot consider the positive sovereignty/negative sovereignty or real state/quasi state oppositions without implicitly resurrecting traces of prior historical oppositions. Jackson notes that dualisms have characterized the states system since Grotius's original conception of an outer circle that embraced all humankind and an inner circle bound by the law of Christ (1987: 533–35). These dualisms are portrayed as historical progressions from one set to the next that result from normative changes in international society regarding the criteria for statehood and sovereign recognition. What is missing in Jackson's admittedly brief review of the changing images of dualism in international relations is an elaboration on the connection between the dualisms and the oppositions contained in them. From the perspective offered in this study, these dualisms can be viewed as structures of exclusion consisting of (1) a privileged inner core (characterized alternatively as Christian-European nations, civilized sovereign states, and, currently, empirical states possessing positive sovereignty) and (2) inferior peripheries (characterized as uncivilized dependencies and, later, as quasi states possessing negative sovereignty). In an important sense, the earlier oppositions are embedded in the present ones, having paved the way for them. As Foucault (1988: 3–38) suggests in his study of madness, one structure of exclusion creates niches for others. Just as the poor vagabond, the criminal, and the deranged person took up the niche previously occupied by the leper, the quasi state characterized by incompetence and corruption takes up the niche previously occupied by the uncivilized and unfit for self-government.

While the terms "traditional man" and "modern man" are not used in these texts, they are nonetheless implicitly present. Development theory's focus on modern man constitutes a background set of assumptions. "Vattel's famous remark that a dwarf is a man" is not the correct analogy to make for the "third world" quasi state, Jackson writes; rather, the quasi state is one that "someday might be developed into a real state" (1987: 542). Implicit here is the discourse of development. Modern man embodied in a benevolent international society has bestowed on traditional societies a modern institution, the state, that has not lived up to the Western ideal model. This failure is implicitly attributed to a lack of readiness or capacity. The necessity for external support to "third world" societies is constructed as evidence of incompetence and failure at self-government. "Third world" countries are constructed as freeloaders on the international system who demand and take handouts and contribute little or nothing in return. Quasi states require Western attention, which is precluded by the institution of negative sovereignty. Several things become unthinkable in these texts, particularly the possibility that the international system itself is partially responsible for generating the conditions that give rise to "quasi states." I am not referring here to the changes in norms that these texts emphasize, but rather to the possibility that the benefits of a liberal international system are distributed in an extremely asymmetrical fashion or that Northern practices, such as the stockpiling of raw materials in the 1950s, distort and dilute the benefits that "quasi states" might reap from participation in the international system. "External support" is defined solely in terms of the support received by the "third world." Cheap raw materials, access to oil and other resources, and cheap labor provided by the South and enjoyed by the North are not considered "external support." The possibility that the South could indeed require support and at the same time be competent enough to have a meaningful voice in defining the kinds and terms of that support becomes unthinkable.

THEORIZING THE INEQUALITY OF NATIONS

> This is the most important book on North-South relations which I have ever read.... This book will be read and cited by political scientists for years. It will also be required and controversial reading in the broader community debating American foreign policy and the future of the international system.
>
> PETER KATZENSTEIN, COMMENTING ON
> STEPHEN KRASNER'S *Structural Conflict*

> The frontiers of a book are never clear-cut: beyond the title, the first lines, and the last full stop, beyond its internal configuration and its autonomous form, it is caught up in a system of references to other books, other texts, other sentences: it is a node within a network.
> MICHEL FOUCAULT, *The Archaeology of Knowledge*

"The history of the international system is a history of inequality par excellence" (Tucker 1977: 3). Inequality has for the most part been more of an accepted state of affairs from which international relations begins than a problem to be investigated. What has, however, caught the attention of international relations scholars is a particular challenge to inequality posed by "third world" states. As Jackson notes, "Third World states have radicalized international society by introducing collectivist ideologies and goals that challenge classical positive sovereignty doctrine particularly in the area of international economics" (1990: 114). Negative sovereignty has provided an opening for the "third world" to articulate demands designed to redress global inequality. It is not the demands themselves, though, that I am concerned with here. Rather, it is the narratives, explanations, predictions, and prescriptions that these demands have elicited on the part of North American international relations scholars. They have taken the form of inquiries into "what the third world wants," why, and the consequences of meeting or ignoring its demands.[5]

In this section, I examine a text that is representative of what Murphy (1983) refers to as the "common wisdom" regarding the South's proposals for change in liberal international regimes. These demands for the most part centered around the call for a New International Economic Order. As this was arguably the most unified and comprehensive articulation on the part of the South of specific policies to redress global inequality, it gained a great deal of attention in the North and was the subject of much scholarly interest. It occurred within the context of growing recognition of increased interdependence, declining U.S. hegemony, and the North's perceived vulnerability to the "commodity power" of the South. Here I should stress that I am not providing yet another interpretation of or explanation for the "third world" demands. Rather, I am using these demands as a site that elicited from North American social scientists narratives that participated in the production and legitimation of world ordering possibilities, specifically possibilities for relations between the North and the South. These narratives reproduce, by virtue of presupposing as valid background knowledge and truth, some of the same representations we encountered in previous chapters.

As I have noted, the discourse of development constitutes a background of preunderstandings, of given assumptions regarding types of individuals and societies, change, progress, and the desirability of particular kinds of social arrangements. While the discourse of development has for the most part not been a major element in international relations as an academic discipline, it has in important respects formed the basic "knowledge base" about the "third world" and the take-off point, so to speak, regarding the place of the "third world" in international society. Said (1993: 290) suggests that the discourse of development deployed "a truly amazing conceptual arsenal" that commanded the attention of strategic planners and policy experts. This conceptual arsenal also caught the attention of international relations scholars and underlies attempts to theorize North-South relations. This is particularly significant because, as presumed background knowledge in theories of international relations, the discourse of development is not open to scrutiny and criticism as theory. On the contrary, it constitutes given preunderstandings.

Coming from a structural realist perspective, Stephen Krasner addresses the conflict between North and South that results from their inequality; this perspective suggests that "the behavior of states is determined by their relative power capabilities" (1985: 12). Such an "objectivist" approach would seem to suggest that the identities of international subjects are not an issue because they are all basically the same. The most important international subjects are states, and states are essentially alike—they seek to "maximize their power—their ability to control their own destinies" (ibid.). This appears to be at odds with any kind of focus on subject identities. Yet occupying an apparently marginal position in this text (only two pages out of more than three hundred) is the opposition between traditional and modern societies that invokes all kinds of other oppositions that serve to focus attention on international identities.

The traditional/modern opposition enters Krasner's work under the heading "Domestic Structures" as one of the elements that has "driven Third World states to attempt to alter regimes fundamentally" (ibid.: 38). Krasner writes:

> The ability to cope with environmental disturbances depends on the mobility, flexibility, and diversity of a country's resources. A country with highly mobile, flexible, and diverse factors can absorb shocks emanating from the international system. It can reallocate its factors of production when environmental conditions change. (ibid.: 39)

"Less developed countries," goes the argument, cannot absorb and adjust to external shocks because of their political weakness and social and economic rigidity. The latter factors are captured in the distinction between traditional and modern societies. This opposition, which is the foundation of the much criticized modernization theory, is brought into Krasner's analysis not as a controversial proposition, a problematic distinction that is part of an even more problematic body of "knowledge," but rather as foundational fact. Its presence is all the more significant for the scant elaboration of it. From this one might conclude that it is marginal to this text as a whole, but the small amount of explicit discussion given to the traditional/modern opposition is actually indicative of its "givenness." It "goes without saying" that this opposition accurately and objectively captures the distinctions in the societies that are the subject/object of this text. Its apparent marginality in terms of space should not be taken as marginality in terms of its productive force in reproducing the dichotomies that historically have functioned to construct the Western self and the non-Western other.

To examine the importance of the traditional/modern opposition in Krasner's work one must look to the syntagmatic relationship that the signs "traditional" and "modern" entertain with other signs that surround them, particularly the signs of "flexibility" and "ability to adapt."[6] The text relies on a strategic positioning of groups of statements regarding the characteristics of traditional societies and their inability to respond to external shocks. Drawing on Hirschman's earlier work, Krasner (ibid.: 40) suggests that the mobility of resources is crucial in explaining flexibility and the ability of a country to adapt to external shocks and pressures. This is ostensibly a purely neutral fact determined by a country's objective environment—the nature of its resources, for example. In the paragraph immediately preceding this one, however, Krasner juxtaposes the characteristics of a traditional society to the characteristics of a modern society. His invocation of the traditional/modern opposition immediately preceding his explanation of the ability or inability to adapt implicitly draws a connection between the mobility of resources (and thus the ability of a society to adapt to external changes) and traditional versus modern "man" and society.

Describing one of the characteristics of a traditional society, Krasner points out that "the world is seen composed of concrete and discrete elements—that is, indivisible units—economic, social, cultural, and political resources are seen as being finite and immobile rather than expanding and flexible" (ibid.). Without making an explicit connection between this statement and the next, he goes on to say that "modern societies are less vulnerable to external changes because their factors of production are more mobile." Two things can be noted about these statements: (1) either the mobility of resources is an "objective fact"—that is, they are either mobile or immobile as a result of their nature (agricultural and mineral vs. industrial/manufacturing, for example)—in which case the traditional/ modern opposition becomes unnecessary or, alternatively, (2) mobility and flexibility can be seen as products of an ontology. The ontology of traditional "man" is such that resources are regarded as finite and immobile. They are not objectively so. A particular ontology that makes them so. The ontology of "modern man" thus becomes an important element in accounting for resource mobility. Immobility and rigidity are not objective facts but consequences of a particular worldview. "Traditional man" thus becomes important in accounting for the South's inability to adjust to changes in the external environment.

Krasner's text implies the latter, in which case the fundamental reason the "third world" seeks to alter international regimes is to be found in its own incompetence and lack of modern attitudes and ways of thinking. Coming from a perspective much different from the one taken here, Murphy comes to a similar conclusion: "The common wisdom has it that Third World governments choose their economic analyses and moral principles to project their own inability to solve crucial domestic economic problems upon the international system and thus deny responsibility for their incompetence in economic matters" (1983: 56). The syntagmatic organization of Krasner's text implicitly links this presumed incompetence to the traditional/modern opposition. After all, how could one expect sound economic analysis and policy from members of traditional societies where "general principles that can be applied in a wide range of situations are eschewed" (Krasner 1985: 40). Economics, if nothing else, requires the acceptance of general principles.

Despite the enormous amount of criticism directed at theories of modernization, it is a given for Krasner that societies in the "third world" do progress from traditional to modern. That societies can experience political decay (à la Samuel Huntington) is also recognized. Indeed, Krasner's broader argument regarding the place of the South in the international realm bears a striking similarity to Huntington's argument on political order in domestic societies. Krasner, like Huntington, places supreme political value on order. Access to international institutions has enabled the "third world" to voice demands for regime change and in some instances to effect change. The result generally has been a move toward instability: "Third World accomplishments only rarely contribute to a stable international environment" (ibid.: 30) and "the most prudent policy for the North is to limit the membership of regimes" (ibid.: 306). The South, for Krasner, is a potential disrupter of order. Its very existence poses a danger to the stable functioning of the international system. Calls for reforms and changes in international regimes are to be judged not on their merit, but in terms of whether they promote stability or instability. The conclusion Krasner reaches is that only if "third world" societies can develop the capacity to adjust to the perturbations of the global system will they reconcile themselves to liberal international regimes and by implication cease their efforts to move regimes away from market principles (ibid.). As long as domestic structural weakness — "a manifestation of traditional social norms and political underdevelopment" — persists, the South will seek change and North-South conflict will persist. In what seems to be a remarkably "traditional" attitude that views states, like individuals, as locked within a rigid structure, Krasner closes with the prognosis that "there are some problems for which there are no solutions" (ibid.: 314). The practical implication of this conclusion is to promote the status quo and preclude the imagining of alternative world ordering arrangements.

CONCLUSION

An important question that arises in regard to the texts examined in this chapter and the series of oppositions they have both implicitly and explicitly drawn upon is whether or not it would be possible to recognize difference — in the basis of sovereignty, in the distribution of benefits from liberal regimes, or any other kind of difference, for that matter — between the "first world" and the "third world," the North and the South, without invoking the hierarchical oppositions reminiscent of the superior/inferior classifications that have justified the practices characteristic of earlier imperial encounters. Would it be possible to recognize crisis in Africa without attributing it to an inherent lack of indigenous capacity for efficient self-government? Would it be possible to discuss the attractiveness of regimes based on authoritative principles without attributing it to the lack of modernization? Krasner's himself recognizes that some international regimes have in fact been based on the principle of authoritative allocation even prior to demands made by the South. Interestingly, he invokes "market failure" rather than the modern/traditional opposition to explain this.

The texts examined in this chapter attest to the power of earlier representations, the continuity amid discontinuity. They form a sort of cultural unconscious that always comes back to the presumption, generally unstated, especially in more recent texts, of different kinds of human beings with different capacities and perhaps different inherent worth and value. "We" of the West are not inefficient, corrupt, or dependent on a benevolent international society for our existence. "We" are the unquestioned upholders of human rights. "We" attained positions of privilege and authority as a result of our capacities. "We" of the West are different from "them." "Their" fate could not befall "us." "They" can succeed only if "they" become more like "us." These intertexts begin with the presupposition of a clear and unambiguous boundary between "us" and "them," between the North and the South, between "real states" and "quasi states." They thus disallow the possibility that rather than being independent and autonomous entities, these oppositions are mutually constitutive of each other. Their production as separate and unconnected realms requires constant work of differentiation and naturalization. The North is constituted vis-à-vis the South as modern, efficient, competent. The South is constituted as its lack, its other. Imperial encounters have always contained the element of "modern man" confronting his "traditional" other, characterized alternatively as uncivilized, incompetent, childlike, and incapable of handling power and authority. The incapacity to exercise agency in the same manner as the Western "self" is repeatedly inscribed in the identity of the non-Western "other." The civilization of the "other" requires intervention. The transformation of "quasi states" into "real" states requires the intervention of the West.

Conclusion

*The starting point of critical elaboration is the consciousness of what
one really is, and is "knowing thyself" as a product of the historical
process to date which has deposited in you an infinity of traces, without leaving an inventory.*

ANTONIO GRAMSCI
Selections from the Prison Notebooks

Said (1979: 25) points out that the only available English transla-
tion of Gramsci's *Prison Notebooks* inexplicably leaves out the last
line of the Italian text, which goes on to say that "therefore it is imperative at the outset to compile such an inventory." In an important
sense, this study can be considered an inventory, though admittedly
only a very partial one, of some of the representational practices
that have enabled the North to "know" both itself and the South.
Objections will undoubtedly be raised that the inventory I have provided in this study is focused too heavily on Northern practices and
thereby excludes important Southern representations that may have
provided alternative forms of "knowledge." In one sense I would
have to plead guilty to this. On the other hand, my occasional mention of local discourses is meant to convey recognition that they did
exist, but the dominant discourse for all intents and purposes could
and did dismiss them. Just as Filipino voices were systematically silenced by Western members of the Paris Peace Conference at the
turn of the century, so too are current "third world" voices ignored

by the mainstream international relations community. Perhaps even more significantly, mainstream international relations continues to ignore the issue of representation itself.[1] The exclusion of the issue of representation from "legitimate" international relations scholarship is simultaneously an exclusion of any such inventory that would illuminate the infinity of traces that have enabled the Northern self to know itself and its "other."

Against this mainstream politics of refusal, this study accepts that a politics of representation is pervasive and that to some degree we cannot escape the infinity of traces that have been deposited in "us" and have served to constitute "us" vis-à-vis "them." This has implications both for scholarly theorizing and for foreign policy. In an important sense it means that we are always caught in a kind of double bind, much like the bishops in colonial Kenya. When a country such as the United States engages in an operation to "restore hope" to Somalia, it carries with it a whole array of historical traces. An inventory of these traces calls attention to the double bind entailed in what is perhaps a genuine humanitarian concern. Prior traces also inevitably accompany attempts to theorize poverty, inequality, and democracy. In the absence of an inventory of those traces they remain invisible, and language is understood in a purely referential sense with identities presumed to be given rather than constructed.

This is evident in the resurgence of attention to the realm of culture in explaining development and democracy or their absence. One example is a June 1993 *Atlantic Monthly* article about Haiti entitled "Voodoo Politics." The article was written by Lawrence Harrison, 1977–79 director of the USAID mission to strengthen democratic institutions in Haiti and a member of the 1991 Organization of American States mission that attempted to negotiate President Jean-Bertrand Aristide's prompt return to power after the military coup that deposed him. The article suggests that the only hope for Haiti lies in a cultural transformation that will be made possible only by the return of diaspora Haitians from the United States, Canada, and France who have been "exposed to the progressive values and institutions that largely explain the success of those societies." The abuse of power that "has been an unrelenting fact of Haitian life since the country's emergence as a French slave colony 300 years ago," according to Harrison, can only be explained by culture: "The values and atittudes of the average Haitian are profoundly influenced by traditional African culture, particularly the voodoo religion.... The Haitian people see themselves, their neighbors, their country, and the world in ways that foster autocratic and corrupt politics, extreme social injustice, and economic stagnation." Such a representation obscures the historical reality of the abuse of power by just those societies — the United States and France, for example — from which Haitians are supposed to learn progressive values. It also ignores the number of Haitians who have died or have been jailed, tortured, or exiled for their opposition to corrupt politics and social injustice. The very title of the article, "Voodoo Politics," conveys the notion of irrationality, superstition, and incompetence; one really need read no further to "know" that without outside intervention and control Haiti is beyond hope.

Traces are also evident in Samuel Huntington's widely read and cited "clash of civilizations" thesis, which suggests that the answer to the question "What are you?" is a given that cannot be changed (Huntington 1993: 27). Balibar (1991) makes clear the function of cultural explanations in the emergence of "neoracism," a racism without race. Culture, like nature, functions as a way of locking individuals and groups a priori into an immutable determination. This is especially evident in the issue of immigration in Western Europe and the racist backlash that has resulted. Nor is the United States immune either to the anti-immigrant, racist backlash that has occurred in Europe.

Accepting the pervasiveness of the politics of representation also has significant implications for two important concepts that figure prominently in the discipline of international relations: power and agency. It is ironic that a concept as central to international relations as power remains so impoverished in terms of how it is defined and how it is understood to operate in global politics. Foucault has suggested that "there can be no possible exercise of power without a certain economy of discourses of truth which operates through and on the basis of this association" (1980b: 93). Foucault's alternative understanding of power shifts the focus of analyses in several ways that have been crucial to this study. In contrast to the prevailing conceptualizations of power, which continue to draw heavily on metaphors associated with Hobbes and the social contract, Foucault's work suggests that power is implicated in the very possibility of meaning. The naturalness of the world and the categories through which we know it and its subjects are manifestations of power. Neither subjects, nor subjectivity, nor structured social relations exist before the workings of power. Both agency models and structural understandings of power presuppose that agents and structures exist prior to power, rather than themselves being effects of power. This study, in contrast, has elucidated a variety of representational strategies or modes of making meaning by which agency was made possible and structures were produced.

Perhaps the most serious flaw in existing understandings of power in international relations is the absence of any acknowledged relationship between power, truth, and knowledge. As Foucault suggests, a discourse of truth is essential to the exercise of power. Subjects are constituted according to notions of truth and knowledge. Foucault's formulation of the relationship between power, truth, and knowledge conveys an ontological skepticism that is perhaps disturbing to an enterprise such as international relations that to a large degree depends on the presumption of foundational grounds for its very existence.[2] To remove those grounds is not only to question the basis upon which scholars make knowledge claims, it is also to politicize the very practice of generating knowledge. Scholars then become implicated in the production of "regimes of truth," the practice of disciplinary power, and the obliteration of the inventories of traces that have constructed our current "reality." Rather than being an "objective," detached intellectual endeavor, international relations scholarly discourse on North-South relations becomes imbued through and through with the imperial representations that have preceded it.

One of the deadly traces that has been deposited in our current "reality" and that figures prominently in this study is "race." The inventory of this trace has been systematically ignored by international relations scholarship. It seems fair to suggest that most international relations scholars as well as makers of foreign policy would suggest that "race" is not even a relevant issue in global politics. Some might concede that while "race" may have been a significant factor internationally during particular historical periods—as a justification for colonialism, for example—"we" are past that now. The racial hierarchy that once prevailed internationally simply no longer exists. To dwell upon "race" as an international issue is an unproductive, needless rehash of history. Adlai Stevenson rather crudely summed up this position when he complained that he was impatiently waiting for the time "when the last black-faced comedian has quit preaching about colonialism so the United Nations could move on to the more crucial issues like disarmament" (quoted in Noer 1985: 84).

This view is unfortunately, although subtly, reflected in the very definition of the field of international relations, whose central problems and categories have been framed in such a way as to preclude investigation into categories such as "race" that do not fit neatly within the bounds of prevailing conceptions of theory and explanation and the legitimate methods with which to pursue them. As Walker (1989) points out, current international relations research agendas are framed within an understanding that presumes certain ontological issues have been resolved. Having already resolved the questions of the "real" and relevant entities, international relations scholars generally proceed to analyze the world with an eye toward becoming a "real science." What has been defined as "real" and relevant has not included race. As this study suggests, however, racialized identities historically have been inextricably linked with power, agency, reason, morality, and understandings of "self" and "other."[3] When we invoke these terms in certain contexts, we also silently invoke traces of previous racial distinctions. For example, Goldberg (1993: 164) suggests that the conceptual division of the world whereby the "third world" is the world of tradition, irrationality, overpopulation, disorder, and chaos assumes a racial character that perpetuates, both conceptually and actually, relations of domination, subjugation, and exclusion. Excluding the issue of representation enables the continuation of this and obscures the important relationship between representation, power, and agency.

The issue of agency in international affairs appears in the literature in various ways, ranging from classical realism's subjectivist privileging of human agents to neorealism's behavioralist privileging of the state as agent to the more recent focus on the "agent-structure problem" by proponents of structuration theory (e.g., Wendt [1987], Dessler [1989]). What these accounts have in common is their exclusion of the issue of representation. The presumption is made that agency ultimately refers back to some prediscursive subject, even if that subject is socially constructed within the context of political, social, and economic structures. In contrast, the cases examined in this study suggest that the question of agency is one of how practices of representation create meaning and identities and thereby create the very possibility for agency. As Judith Butler (1990: 142–49) makes clear and as the empirical cases examined here suggest, identity and agency are both effects, not preexisting conditions of being. Such an antiessentialist understanding does not depend upon foundational categories—an inner psychological self, for example. Rather, identity is reconceptualized as simultaneously a practice and an effect that is always in the process of being constructed through signifying practices that expel the surplus meanings that would expose the failure of identity as such. For example, through a process of repetition, U.S. and British discourses constructed as natural and given the oppositional dichotomy between the uncivilized, barbaric "other" and the civilized, democratic "self" even while they both engaged in the oppression and brutalization of "others." The spector of the "other" was always within the "self." The proliferation of discourse in times of crisis illustrates an attempt to expel the "other," to make natural and unproblematic the boundaries between the inside and the outside. This in turn suggests that identity and therefore the agency that is connected with identity are inextricably linked to representational practices.

It follows that any meaningful discussion of agency must perforce be a discussion of representation. The representational practices that construct particular identities have serious ramifications for agency. While this study suggests that "race" historically has been a central marker of identity, it also suggests that identity construction takes place along several dimensions. Racial categories often have worked together with gendered categories as well as with analogies to parent/child oppositions and animal metaphors. Each of these dimensions has varying significance at different times and enables a wide variety of practices. In examining the construction of racialized identities, it is not enough to suggest that social identities are constructed on the basis of shared understandings within a community: shared understandings regarding institutional rules, social norms, and self-expectations of individuals in that community. It is not enough to examine the shared social criteria by which one identity is distinguished from another. Two additional elements must be considered: power and truth.

"Race" has not just been about certain rules and resources facilitating the agency of some social groups and denying or placing severe limitations on the agency of other social groups. Though it has been about these things, this is only one aspect of what "race" has historically been about. "Race" has most fundamentally been about being human. Racist discourses historically have constructed different kinds and degrees of humanness through representational practices that have claimed to be and have been accepted as "true" and accurate representations of "reality." Racist discourses highlight, perhaps more than any other, the inextricable link between power and truth or power and knowledge. A theory of agency in international relations, if it is to incorporate issues such as "race," must address the relationship between power and truth. This realization in turn implies a reconceptualization of power and how it works that transcends those present in existing theories of international relations.

The cases examined in this study attest to the importance of representational practices and the power that inheres in them. The infinity of traces that leave no inventory continue to play a significant part in contemporary constructions of "reality." This is not to suggest that representations have been static. Static implies the possibility of fixedness, when what I mean to suggest is an inherent fragility and instability to the meanings and identities that have been constructed in the various discourses I examined. For example, to characterize the South as "uncivilized" or "unfit for self-government" is no longer an acceptable representation. This is not, however, because the meanings of these terms were at one time fixed and stable. As I illustrated, what these signifiers signified was always deferred. Partial fixation was the result of their being anchored by some exemplary mode of being that was itself constructed at the power/knowledge nexus: the white male at the turn of the century, the United States after World War II. Bhabha stresses "the wide range of the stereotype, from the loyal servant to Satan, from the loved to the hated; a shifting of subject positions in the circulation of colonial power" (1983: 31). The shifting subject positions—from uncivilized native to quasi state to traditional "man" and society, for example—are all partial fixations that have enabled the exercise of various and multiple forms of power. Nor do previous oppositions entirely disappear. What remains is an infinity of traces from prior representations that themselves have been founded not on pure presences but on differance. "The present becomes the sign of the sign, the trace of the trace," Derrida writes (1982: 24). Differance makes possible the chain of differing and deferring (the continuity) as well as the endless substitution (the discontinuity) of names that are inscribed and reinscribed as pure presence, the center of the structure that itself escapes structurality.

North-South relations have been constituted as a structure of deferral. The center of the structure (alternatively white man, modern man, the United States, the West, real states) has never been absolutely present outside a system of differences. It has itself been constituted as trace—the simulacrum of a presence that dislocates itself, displaces itself, refers itself (ibid.). Because the center is not a fixed locus but a function in which an infinite number of sign substitutions come into play, the domain and play of signification is extended indefinitely (Derrida 1978: 280). This both opens up and limits possibilities, generates alternative sites of meanings and political resistances that give rise to practices of reinscription that seek to reaffirm identities and relationships. The inherently incomplete and open nature of discourse makes this reaffirmation an ongoing and never finally completed project. In this study I have sought, through an engagement with various discourses in which claims to truth have been staked, to challenge the validity of the structures of meaning and to make visible their complicity with practices of power and domination. By examining the ways in which structures of meaning have been associated with imperial practices, I have suggested that the construction of meaning and the construction of social, political, and economic power are inextricably linked. This suggests an ethical dimension to making meaning and an ethical imperative that is incumbent upon those who toil in the construction of structures of meaning. This is especially urgent in North-South relations today: one does not have to search very far to find a continuing complicity with colonial representations that ranges from a politics of silence and neglect to constructions of terrorism, Islamic fundamentalism, international drug trafficking, and Southern immigration to the North as new threats to global stability and peace.

The political stakes raised by this analysis revolve around the question of being able to "get beyond" the representations or speak outside of the discourses that historically have constructed the North and the South. I do not believe that there are any pure alternatives by which we can escape the infinity of traces to which Gramsci refers. Nor do I wish to suggest that we are always hopelessly imprisoned in a dominant and all-pervasive discourse. Before this question can be answered—indeed, before we can even proceed to attempt an answer—attention must be given to the politics of representation. The price that international relations scholarship pays for its inattention to the issue of representation is perpetuation of the dominant modes of making meaning and deferral of its responsibility and complicity in dominant representations.

Notes

1. INTRODUCTION

1. The "new missions" of the post–cold war world have been described as "counternarcotics, counterterrorism, and peace-keeping, all intended to deal with North-South, Third World problems" (Snow 1993: 115). Continued concern with North-South relations is illustrated by the following remark: "More than ever before, the United States is vulnerable to threats emanating from Third World Regimes or from people living in Third World Countries" (Cingranelli 1993: xi). Concern with the South is at least implicit in Samuel Huntington's (1993) anxiety over "the West versus the Rest."

2. The literature on North-South relations from various theoretical perspectives is simply too voluminous to be cited here. Some of the major works of international relations scholars include Tucker 1977, Bull and Watson 1984, Krasner 1985, and Jackson 1990. Useful historical studies include Wolf 1982, Stavrianos 1981, and various works of Immanuel Wallerstein. Much of the literature on North-South relations focuses on the issue of "third world" "development" (e.g., Rostow 1960, Packenham 1973, and Wallerstein 1979).

3. My understanding of representation is informed by numerous works that do not honor the arbitrary disciplinary boundaries that generally distinguish international relations from other fields. I have drawn particularly on the works of Michel Foucault and Jacques Derrida as well as on numerous secondary literatures (e.g., Dreyfus and Rabinow 1983, Culler 1982, and Norris 1987. I have also found the work of Laclau and Mouffe (1985), Bhabha (1983, 1990), and Shapiro (1988) exceedingly helpful in my think-

ing through this project. The issue of representation figures prominently in works that are generally considered "international relations" but that at least implicitly question a whole range of dichotomies that serve to define this field. These works include Campbell 1992, Weber 1990 and 1992, Klein 1990, Der Derian 1987, and various works of Richard Ashley and R. B. J. Walker. For especially useful discussions, see Ashley and Walker 1990, George and Campbell 1990, and George 1989.

4. The conceptualization of power suggested here is that offered by Michel Foucault (1977, 1979, 1980b, 1980c). Useful secondary sources are Dreyfus and Rabinow 1983 and Clegg 1989, chapter 7.

5. For exceptions see Campbell 1992, Weber 1990 and 1992, Klein 1990, Der Derian 1987, and various works of Richard Ashley and R. B. J. Walker.

6. Obviously, I owe a debt here to numerous scholars who have called attention to the performative nature of language—John Austin (1975) and John Searle (1969) as well as Campbell 1992, Weber 1990 and 1992, Klein 1990, Der Derian 1987, and various works of Richard Ashley and R. B. J. Walker. One should also note Wittgenstein's (1953) notion of language games that encompass the totality of language and the actions interconnected with it. See also Laclau and Mouffe 1985: 108.

7. Foucault (1987: 49) suggests that discourses are formed through both the operation of desire, which wants discourse to be unrestricted and infinitely open, and the operation of institutions and power, which pin down meaning. Derrida also calls attention to the fact that totalizations never fully succeed. Perfectly closed structures of inclusions and exclusions are never effected with any finality. Drawing upon psychoanalytic theory, Bhabha (1983) makes a similar suggestion regarding the colonial subject.

8. Pietz (1988) offers a good example of this in his reading of Hannah Arendt's argument that totalitarianism was the historical product of colonialism, thus locating its "true" origin outside of Europe, in "tribal" Africa. Totalitarianism then becomes not a part of the integral totality that is Europe, but rather a corruption of or deviation from what is truly European. Africa, then, is Europe's different and deferred other. This, however, should not be taken to imply that the "third world other" be thought of solely in terms of the West's desire for presence and its subsequent appropriation of its universal other as constitutive of that presence. As Bhabha (1983) stresses, otherness is implicated in specific historical and discursive conditions, requiring constructions in different practices. These constructions (and the instabilities inherent in them) give rise to varying and often contradictory possibilities. It is specific historical constructions (and their instabilities) that are the focus of this study.

9. Understandings of hegemony in world politics have ranged from the narrow conception of hegemony as a preponderance of material resources (as in hegemonic stability theory) to broader conceptions that draw upon a particular reading of Gramsci's work. This latter understanding suggests that hegemony prevails to the extent that the consensual aspect of power is in the forefront and coercion is applied only in marginal, deviant cases (Cox 1983: 164). Several theorists of international relations have drawn upon this understanding of hegemony: "Where a great power exercises hegemony over the lesser powers in a particular area or constellation, there is resort to force and the threat of force, but this is not habitual and un-inhibited but occasional and reluctant" (Bull 1977: 215). Onuf and Klink take up a similar position in their view of hegemony as "that instance of hierarchy in which the position of the ranking state is so overwhelming that it can dispense with the chain of command and cast directive-rules in a benign form as mere suggestions, and still have its rule effectuated" (1989: 165). Others, still drawing upon hegemony as consensual, have suggested that hegemonic power works at the level of the substantive beliefs of leaders (Ikenberry and Kupchan 1990: 283). Also see Augelli and Murphy 1988 and Gill and Law 1988 for Gramscian approaches to global politics.

10. On a priori givenness, see Laclau and Mouffe 1985 for a sympathetic critique and a Foucauldian reading of Gramsci's work.

11. Laclau and Mouffe (1985: 138) suggest that the hegemonic dimension of politics expands as the open, nonsutured character of the social increases. The term *social* here refers to the infinite play of differences implied by the concept of differance. Hegemonic practices are those that attempt to limit that play, to institute a finite order or structure. Laclau (1990) uses the term *society* to refer to such an impossible finite order or fully closed structure. A discourse or discursive formation would be analogous to "society" understood in this sense.

12. What Laclau and Mouffe call an organic crisis can be likened to what Derrida (1978) refers to as a rupture, that is, a disruption of thought in the human sciences in which the "structurality of structure" begins to be thought. As I will discuss later, crises or ruptures call into question identities and the existing order. Naturalization becomes more difficult to maintain.

13. Rather than use scare quotes around the term *Mau Mau* throughout this study, I take this opportunity to call attention to its problematic nature. As one author has suggested, any unqualified use of the term is implicitly an endorsement of a particular view—that of the Kenyan European community—of the movement (Maughan-Brown 1980). *Mau Mau* was the white man's name for the movement. There is no accepted Gikuyu or Swahili lit-

eral meaning for this word. Members of the movement never applied this name to themselves. In the words of one member of the movement, "I must make it clear that it did not have any special name. The world knows it by a title of abuse and ridicule with which it was described by one of its bitterest opponents" (Kariuki 1963: 24).

2. TO BE OR NOT TO BE A COLONIAL POWER

1. Kipling wrote "The White Man's Burden" in 1899, urging the United States to seize the Philippines. The poem was published in *McClure's Magazine* shortly before final action on the Paris Peace Treaty. It was also published in the *Times* of London with the subtitle "The United States and the Philippine Islands." It has been suggested that this was a call for the United States to assume the kind of responsibilities embodied in British colonial rule and thereby replace the old colonial mercantile world of Spain and Portugal with "an Anglo-Saxon Imperial mission that would be wide-thinking and modern" (Spurr 1993: 113). Senator Benjamin Tillman recited this poem in full during the Senate debates on Philippine annexation. See the *Congressional Record,* 55th Congress, 2d session, 1531–32.

2. Quoted in "Mark Twain on American Imperialism," *The Atlantic* 269, no. 4 (April 1992).

3. See Brands 1992.

4. See Kalaw 1916.

5. The Philippine Commission was a civilian commission established by President McKinley on January 20, 1899. Its purpose was to facilitate the "most humane, pacific, and effective extension of authority throughout these islands and to secure, with the least possible delay, the benefits of a wise and generous protection of life and property to the inhabitants" (Report of the Philippines Commission to the President, vol. 1, 1900: 185). The commission was to report on the conditions of the inhabitants of the Philippines and on "what improvements in public order may be practicable." To these ends they were to study "attentively the existing social and political state of the various populations." The first report was issued on January 31, 1900, as Senate Document 138. The volume of this commission's work indicates the importance attached to gaining "knowledge" of the Philippines and its inhabitants.

6. Drinnon (1980: 285) notes the continuation of this preoccupation with virility and manhood in Richard Nixon's rejection of a premature withdrawal from Vietnam. Campbell (1992: 73–74, 176–77) also notes the prevalence of gendered hierarchies in both international relations theory and foreign policy practices. For related suggestions see Jeffords 1989 on how the war in Vietnam and its representations were vehicles for a renewed sense of American masculinity. Also see Milliken and Sylvan 1991.

7. These are the words of Senator Turner, January 19, 1898 (785), and Senator Allen from Nebraska.

8. On a related topic, see Klein 1990 for an analysis of NATO and cold war representations in constructing Western identity.

9. See Drinnon 1980: 293.

10. Contradicting these representations of a fragmented and nonhomogeneous people, a 1903 Philippine census revealed a lower level of ethnic diversity than in the United States. See Drinnon 1980: 291.

11. The Katipunan, or Kataastaasan Kagalanggalang Katipunan ng mg Anak ng Bayan (The Highest and Most Honorable Society of the Sons of the Country), was a nationalist movement founded in 1892 by Andres Bonifacio. See Brands 1992: 41–44.

12. This, of course, was not the first time reason and the intellect had been deployed as a basis for differentiating identities. Jara and Spadaccini (1989: 21) note that Sepulveda, in trying to advance the political agenda of the Crown of Castile, contrasted the "mental ability, prudence, and common sense" of Cortes and his followers with the "feeble-mindedness and docility" of the conquered. This served as "proof" that the conquered were slaves by nature.

13. The animal metaphor is still alive and well. Note George Bush's reference to former Nicaraguan president Daniel Ortega as "an unwanted animal at a garden party" and a television reporter's comparison of Ortega to a "skunk at a picnic" (New York Times, October 29, 1989). Metaphors (including the animal metaphor) are intricately linked with practices and have serious consequences. Note General William Westmoreland's use of metaphor regarding U.S. strategies in Vietnam: "If you crowd in too many termite killers, each using a screwdriver to kill the termites, you risk collapsing the floors or the foundation. In this war we're using screwdrivers to kill termites because it's a guerrilla war and we cannot use bigger weapons. We have to get the right balance of termite killers to get rid of the termites without wrecking the house" (quoted in Drinnon 1980: 448–49). See Lakoff and Johnson 1980 on the significance of the use of metaphor.

14. For discussions of the water torture and U.S. massacre of Filipinos, see Brands 1992 and Drinnon 1980.

15. Professor Alden, University of Pennsylvania, quoted by Carnegie (1899: 365).

16. Young (1990: 175) uses the term "colonial intertext." This was also a specific historical and geographic manifestation of Said's Orientalism (1978).

17. It is interesting and significant that, while "manhood" and "masculinity" are generally thought to be constructed vis-à-vis their "feminine" other, the intertext examined here suggests that this construction is also

linked with other "others," e.g., a racial "other." There are an extraordinary number of references to "race" and very little explicit reference to
gender, other than that implied by the references to "American manhood."
This, of course, does not imply that gender was absent. Rather, it suggests
that the "other" to man is not confined to a gendered identity, but extends
to many "other" identities. Gender may, in specific situations, as Jeffords
(1989) suggests, work to overcome or erase racial difference and construct
a masculine bond. It is also likely that this is not always the case and that
"race" and "gender" work in a variety of complex and historically specific
ways. It has been suggested that categories such as "sexuality" and "race"
as well as "illness" have at various points in history overlapped and supplemented one another (Gilman 1985: 23). Nancy Leys Stephan suggests
that " 'lower races' represented the female type of the human species and
females the 'lower races' of gender" (1990: 123). Torgovnick (1990: 57)
suggests that when the West confronts the "primitive," power and sex, geo-
politics, and gender politics come into play. I would add that "race" also
comes into play, though how these different elements play off one another
is complex, contingent, and variable. It is interesting to note that in the discourse examined here, man and manhood are always linked to American
or Western but never to Filipino or "native." I speculate that this is because
Filipinos are alternatively regarded as children or as animal-like, both opposites to "man."

18. The following incident illustrates the denial of agency and margin-
alization of Filipinos and shows that the Philippines were most definitely
not recognized as international actors. After the establishment of the Philippine Revolutionary Government under Aguinaldo on January 23, 1899, a
commission was appointed to work abroad to encourage other nations to
recognize the Philippine Republic. The president of this commission was
Felipe Agoncillo, who proceeded at once to Paris to represent the interests
of the Filipinos before the treaty conference. The members of the Hispanic-
American Commission refused to see him. After the signing of the treaty,
Agoncillo entered a formal protest. This too was ignored. He then proceeded to Washington. On January 5, 1899, his secretary, Sixto Lopez, addressed a letter to the secretary of state, John Hay, requesting an audience
with him. No acknowledgment was received. On January 11 Agoncillo himself sent a letter to Hay. Again, it was ignored. Another letter was sent and
ignored on January 24. On January 30, a memorial was sent to Hay with
the request that it be presented to the Senate of the United States (Kalaw
1916: 63). This long statement set forth the history of relations between
the Americans and Filipinos and the grounds upon which the Philippine
Republic based its claim for recognition. Agoncillo was allowed to deliver

the memorial to Hay's office and was then dismissed. Again, no reply was forthcoming.

In the memorial Agoncillo argued that the United States had no jurisdiction to adjudicate in any matter on the rights of the Philippines and their people. The Philippines had achieved independence and were free from any danger of losing it at the hands of the Spaniards prior to the signing of the Paris treaty. Before the appointment of the commission members, American officials had fully recognized that Spain was no longer able to regain possession of the Philippines. Spain thus had no power to deliver possession of the Philippine Islands to the United States. Spain's sovereignty had been destroyed by the Filipinos.

On April 5, 1899, Apolinario Mabini, Aguinaldo's chief adviser—who was often referred to as the brains of the revolution—published a manifesto on behalf of the Philippine government in response to the U.S. Philippine Commission's invitation for interviews with Filipino residents in Manila. Mabini's manifesto presented the Filipino version of U.S. intentions. Like Agoncillo, Mabini argued that the U.S. claim to sovereignty over the Philippines was not valid because it was based on the Treaty of Paris, which had ceded the islands to the United States when Spanish domination had already ceased, thanks to the triumph of the Filipinos. Thus, at the time of the signing of the treaty, the Philippines did not belong to Spain. Moreover, there had been no representation of the Philippine people, who had sovereignty by natural right and international law.

In both of these texts, "reality" was quite different then it was in the Western texts. The Philippines were not objects that could be traded between sovereign powers. The Filipinos and Philippines were subjects inscribed with the attribute of sovereignty. Independence was not something that could be granted by the United States or Spain. It was not theirs to grant. This position was effectively silenced by the dominant discourse of both those opposed to and those who favored annexation.

19. The fact that Britain is sometimes characterized as being like the United States and sometimes unlike it merely serves to indicate the instability of social constructions.

20. The purpose of this critical analysis is not prediction, but rather to suggest how certain practices became thinkable, possible, and regarded as unremarkable. This analysis can usefully be contrasted to those of Strang (1991) and Wendt (1992), who suggest that the absence of recognition by others—the absence of sovereignty—explains Western practices of conquest, domination, and even genocide. I would certainly agree with this. Strang and Wendt's analyses do not go far enough, however, in that they leave unaddressed how some peoples and states come to be recognized as sovereign and others as not sovereign.

21. I am drawing here on Derrida 1978.

22. This parallels the distinction Ashley (1988) makes between a monological reading and a dialogical reading.

3. GETTING THE "NATIVES" TO WORK

1. The very designation of this situation as the "native labor problem" is significant, carrying with it the implication that "natives" were somehow naturally linked to labor, and if there was a shortage of labor, it was a shortage of "native" bodies. This is not, of course, the only designation imaginable today, though at the time it was. The indigenous inhabitants of Kenya just as surely had a "white settler problem." Such a designation was not thinkable within the discursive parameters of British colonial rule in Kenya, circa 1920.

2. The similarity between British colonial policy and U.S. policy toward the indigenous inhabitants of North America hardly needs pointing out. Reducing American Indians' landholdings as rapidly as possible—not to mention making their land available for white settlement—was the quickest way to force them to assume white culture (Horseman 1981: 103).

3. McGregor Ross points out that annexation of Kenya as a colony in 1920 (as opposed to its prior status of protectorate) had the effect of extinguishing any land rights of the indigenous peoples of Kenya before the courts. Citing a case of ownership dispute, he quotes Chief Justice Jacob Barth, who dismissed a claim by a member of the Kikuyu, saying that under the Crown Lands Ordinance of 1915 and the Kenya Annexation Order of 1920, "all native rights in such reserved land, whatever they be under the Gethaka (Kikuyu) system, disappeared, and the natives in occupation of such Crown Lands become tenants at will of the Crown on the land actually occupied" (McGregor Ross 1927: 87). Such inequities were not ignored by the Africans themselves. Various indigenous organizations such as the Young Kavirondo Association were organized to protest hut and poll taxes, land alienation, and labor issues. Largely as a result of the lack of indigenous political organization and institutions through which their presence could be felt, the British were able to ignore their demands (Rosberg and Nottingham 1963: 63). It is worth noting the contradiction between the official position that land ownership was "foreign to the mind of any African" and the reality that Africans did make claims to their land and sought legal action to uphold these claims.

4. There were several reasons for this. After the war, settlers who had served in the armed forces returned to their farms and undertook to rejuvenate them. In addition, new settlers arrived in Kenya as a result of a soldier settlement scheme that had been introduced by the Land Settlement Commission in 1917. This had derived from an East African War Council reso-

lution in late 1915 favoring a land settlement scheme for former servicemen. The heart of the scheme consisted of the sale at market price of more than a thousand farms, each approximately a thousand acres, to ex-servicemen who met a minimum capital requirement. This scheme proved the single most significant source of white immigrants in the interwar years (Kennedy 1987: 54–58). The participants in this scheme were predominantly officers from "gentlemanly origins" (ibid.: 57). The requirement of one thousand pounds savings, later increased to five thousand pounds, effectively excluded other immigrants. Both the returning and new settlers were anxious to develop their estates and thus were in need of African labor.

For various reasons, the number of Africans leaving their reserves to go to work on European farms was not sufficient to meet the demands of the settlers. One was that Africans had been subjected to more than three years of forced recruitment for the military and the Carrier Corps. In addition, there had been famine and epidemic disease in 1918 and 1919 (Maxon 1980: 350). Dr. John S. Arthur of the Church of Scotland Mission Station at Kikuyu estimated the combined Kikuyu death toll from the war and the Spanish influenza epidemic of 1918 at 120,000 in a population of less than one million (Rosberg and Nottingham 1963: 31).

5. The colonial office did not receive a copy of the circular until June 1920, nearly nine months after it was issued.

6. See chapter 3 for a discussion of "native" reserves.

7. The Masters and Servants Ordinance of 1910 regulated relations between employers and servants. On October 20, 1919, it was amended, giving the governor the power to appoint labor inspectors to inspect labor camps, check contracts, and report on working conditions, including sanitary arrangements, medical inspections, and food and housing conditions. This amendment was very much the result of the influence of John Ainsworth, chief native commissioner, who believed that Africans would benefit from working on European farms and that the colonial government should instill habits of discipne and hard work in them. His primary concern was helping the white settlers secure needed labor and in the process advancing the welfare of the "native." Ainsworth advised all labor inspectors "to work as amicably as possible with employers.... Every possible effort must be made to avoid appearing as holding a special brief for the native only. In visiting a camp or an estate an Inspector must not as a rule put to the natives any leading questions" (quoted in Van Zwanenburg 1975: 114).

8. Said (1993: 164) notes the work of Sir Henry Main, in which Foucault's history in *Discipline and Punish* is prefigured. Empire became a sort of laboratory for proving Main's theory of the shift from sovereign to administrative surveillance.

9. See Kennedy (1987) on Kenya and Rhodesia. Foucault's image of the leper was also present in these societies. Kennedy notes the "sanitation syndrome" and "the imagery of infectious disease" as a metaphor for social dangers produced by colonial urbanization (149–52). In Rhodesia and Kenya the dangers of disease transmission justified the removal of Africans from urban areas. Fear of the bubonic plague justified such practices in the Cape Colony even though the disease neither originated among nor inordinately afflicted the African population.

10. This system of identification was deemed necessary because the contract laid down in the Masters and Servants Ordinance lacked any means of identifying deserters (Van Zwanenburg 1975: 185).

11. See Alatas 1977 for additional discussion on idleness and the "native." This attribution, which dates back to the sixteenth century, played an important role in colonial capitalism.

12. This is clearly illustrated in the Masters and Servants Ordinance. In 1912 further specification was added to the definition of the term *servant*: "The principle Ordinance shall be and is hereby amended as follows: (1) By the addition to the interpretation of the word 'Servant' in Section 2 of the Principal Ordinance of the words following: 'and any Arab or Native to be exhibited in any capacity in any circus, show or exhibition' " (23).

4. PRECOCIOUS CHILDREN, ADOLESCENT NATIONS

1. From the message of President Truman to the people of the Philippines, July 4, 1946. The text appears in the U.S. *Department of State Bulletin,* July 4, 1946.

2. These are the words of the officer in charge of economic affairs of the Philippines and South East Asian affairs (Shohan) to the director of the office (Lacy), January 12, 1951, FR51, vol. 6, part 2, 1494).

3. From a memo prepared by the U.S. Embassy in the Philippines in August 1951 (FR51, vol. 6, part 2, 1561).

4. Twelve years after passage of the Tydings-McDuffie Act, the United States relinquished its formal hold and granted nominal independence to the Philippines. The Tydings-McDuffie Act, passed by the U.S. Congress in March 1934, mandated a ten-year transition to Philippine independence.

5. The recovery of much of Western Europe depended on a resolution of the struggles for decolonization — Indonesia's struggle with the Dutch, Indochina's fight for independence from the French — under way in this area. Additionally, raw materials from this area were vital to both Europe and the United States. U.S. anticolonial rhetoric notwithstanding, policies often supported the continuation of colonial ties. The United States continued full Marshall Plan aid when Dutch troops returned in force to Indone-

sia in late 1948 and formally initiated aid to the French in Indochina in 1950 (Kolko 1988: 30–33).

The reconstruction and reintegration of Japan into the regional economy also meant that Southeast Asia would become an important source of raw materials and markets if Japan was to be free of dependence on U.S. aid. It was deemed essential to U.S. security that Japan become an alternative anchor for U.S. power in Asia as China ceased to play that role. The Korean War had also served to alter the U.S. geopolitical vision in the region.

Part of the concern evident in all of these situations was either directly or indirectly related to the "communist threat." Despite U.S. support for the Dutch in Indonesia, in 1949, when opposition leader Sukarno's forces were challenged increasingly from the left, Washington threatened a total aid cutoff for the Dutch if they failed to compromise. After the Indonesians won their independence, U.S. policy was to aid the police and military with equipment to maintain order against the Communist Party. In December 1954 the National Security Council asserted that it would use "all feasible covert means," including "armed force if necessary," to prevent the richest parts of Indonesia from falling into communist hands (Kolka 1988: 174 and FR1952–54, vol. 12: 1066).

6. My understanding of global social purpose can be contrasted with that of Ruggie (1982), who criticizes the prevailing interpretations of international authority, which focus only on power and ignore social purpose. For Ruggie, the internationalization of political authority refers to the fusion of power with legitimate social purpose. While Ruggie complicates the idea of international political authority by adding the element of social purpose, he leaves unquestioned the production of social purpose itself. Relatedly, and perhaps even more significantly, he implicitly draws on an understanding of power that is distinct and separate from social purpose. Thus, one can suggest that power and social purpose become fused, but one cannot explore the possibility that power is inherent in social purpose, indeed that power *produces* social purpose. In contrast, Ashley (1989: 254) asks how it comes to be that recognition is elicited for pervasive structures of global life whereby a definite direction is effected despite the diversity and specificity of local experiences. This, Ashley suggests, is the problematic of "imposing global purpose." Ashley's "how" question regarding global purpose highlights an important kind of power that Ruggie's analysis neglects. It recognizes the possibility that the very existence of social purpose is an effect of power in its productive aspect.

7. Other "delinquent statesmen" who were both objects of U.S. surveillance and useful to the United States included Somoza in Nicaragua, Mobutu in Zaire, and later Marcos in the Philippines, to mention just a few.

8. The term *cultural code* is from Barthes (1974), who uses it to designate a conceptual system that is organized around key oppositions and other relations.

9. The theme of corruption, inefficiency, and ineptitude in "third world" governments is prevalent in North American social science literature. There are numerous illustrations of this. Jackson and Rosberg have described the "fundamental predicament of statehood in Africa" thus: "Its existence [is] almost exclusively as an exploitable treasure trove devoid of moral value" (1987: 527). They also note that Gunnar Myrdal's term "soft state" can be applied appropriately to "many governments in Black Africa which must operate amidst corruption and disorder" (1982: 9). Myrdal himself used the term to describe all underdeveloped countries: "The underdeveloped countries are all, though in varying degrees, 'soft states.' ... The term 'soft state' is understood to comprise all the various types of social indiscipline which manifest themselves by: deficiencies in legislation and in particular law observances and enforcement, a widespread disobedience by public officials on various levels to rules and directives handed down to them, and often their collusion with powerful persons and groups of persons whose conduct they should regulate. Within the concept of the 'soft state' belongs also corruption" (1970: 208).

The point here is not to say whether corruption and inefficiency are or are not "facts of life" in "underdeveloped" countries. The point is to highlight a particular representation of "underdeveloped" countries. Corruption and inefficiency are attributes that become elements in the definition of "underdeveloped" countries' governments but not "developed" countries' governments. What is interesting and significant is that lengthy discussions of corruption in American politics — Tammany Hall and big-city politics, Watergate, Iran-contra, and so on — are contained within the domestic boundaries of the United States. In the foreign policy domain they cease to be issues; they do not constitute the identity of the United States in international relations. With a "third world" state such as the Philippines, corruption does not remain an internal, domestic issue, but rather becomes a defining feature of the country.

10. This act itself cannot be regarded as establishing purely economic relationships. For example, the "parity" clause, which gave Americans the same rights as Filipinos to exploit the islands' agricultural and mineral resources and to own and operate public utilities, violated the Philippine Constitution, which required that Filipinos own 60 percent of any business engaged in the development of the country's natural resources. Under pressure from the United States, the Philippine legislature approved a constitutional amendment to change this stipulation. Another provision of the act was that the Philippine government was required to obtain the consent of the

U.S. president for any changes in the par value of the peso or any restrictions on transactions in foreign exchange.

11. Jackson and Rosberg (1986) suggest that independence traditionally was contingent on the capacity to govern, but that in the post–World War II era of decolonization the juridical right of self-determination became separated from the empirical capacity for self-government. Decolonization marked a "revolutionary change in the basis of statehood—most dramatically in Tropical Africa." This resulted in the emergence of states that possessed "negative" sovereignty, that is, general legitimacy within the international community and specific freedom from acts and threats of foreign intervention, but lacking in the capacity for self-government, which is an attribute of "positive" sovereignty. Also see Jackson and Rosberg 1982 and 1987.

12. The contrast between the naturalized realm of social being occupied by the United States and the politicized realm occupied by the Philippines (and other "third world" countries) parallels and draws upon Ashley's (1987) discussion of the realm of doxa on the one hand and the realm of orthodoxy and heterodoxy on the other hand. In the realm of doxa, practice "is never seen to be in need of legitimation. For it is never set in visible contrast to alternative practices whose legitimacy might be seriously entertained" (Ashley 1987: 17). In contrast is the realm of orthodoxy and heterodoxy, where "practice is not a matter of living naturally, for how one shall live and conduct oneself, and the consequences of that conduct, are politicized by the explicit play of competing interpretations" (ibid.). Also see Bourdieu 1985: 159–83.

13. See Campbell 1992 for an excellent critical reinterpretation of U.S. foreign policy practices. Also see Doty 1993.

5. RESISTANCE IN COLONIAL KENYA

1. See earlier note on the term *Mau Mau*. Also see Rosberg and Nottingham 1966, chapter 9.

2. See Mockaitis 1990 and Paget 1967.

3. Olenguruone was also significant in the development of the political role of oaths in the postwar period. It was the first time that an oath was employed not only to reinforce mutual confidence and trust but also to raise the level of political commitment (Rosberg and Nottingham 1966: 248). Origins of anticolonial resistance at Olenguruone go back to the 1930s, when the squatter system began to be economically disadvantageous to the European farmers. From the beginning of European settlement in Kenya, European farmers had encouraged African families to come and settle on their farms in order to obtain the labor needed to develop their holdings. Arrangements generally amounted to a loose tenancy agreement by which

the African laborer brought his family and stock and occupied a portion of the European's farm. In some cases there was some payment of rent. This system was backed by government ordinances: the Resident Natives (Squatters) Ordinance of 1918, later replaced by the Resident Native Labourers Ordinance of 1925. This arrangement permitted the Africans to have their system of land tenure and also served to reduce population pressures in the reserves. By 1930, however, the African population and stock on the farms were growing at an alarming rate. At the same time, a severe agricultural depression meant that the European farmer no longer needed African labor. How would the European farmers get rid of the squatters they no longer needed? And where would the Africans go? Many of them by this time knew no other life than that of the European farm. This problem was particularly intense among the Kikuyu, who constituted a large portion of the Africans living outside the reserves as squatters. To add to the problem, it was often the case that land that had formerly belonged to the Kikuyu clan from which squatters came had been alienated to Europeans and was no longer available for ex-squatters. A revised Resident Labourers Ordinance passed in 1937 made it clear that squatters on European farms were no longer tenants and had rights only as long as they were working for the farmer. It gave the European-run district councils the power to limit acreage permitted for cultivation, to eliminate squatter stock, and to increase the number of work days from 180 to 270 per year with no compensating wage increase. New agreements had to be signed under this ordinance with each laborer. Those who refused the new terms were to be evicted with their families, but the secretary of state for the colonies refused to permit implementation of the ordinance until alternative land had been found for the squatters who were to be evicted.

In February 1939 some 52,500 acres of land were made available in various parts of Maasailand for ex-squatter settlement. Part of this area was known as Olenguruone, which covered an area of 34,700 acres at an altitude of 8,000 feet with an annual rainfall of seventy inches. Several of the ex-squatters who settled at Olenguruone believed that this land was meant to replace the land alienated to Europeans and thus constituted their clan land. The European settlers and the administration were not comfortable with the Olenguruone settlement because penetration of Kikuyu into Maasailand undermined the policy of maintaining rigid tribal boundaries. The colonial administration was determined to control and regulate the Kikuyu living at Olenguruone. When settlement rules were translated into Kikuyu, the ex-squatters were shocked to learn that they were referred to as tenants (*ahoi*) and refused to sign the agreement or leave the settlement. The Olenguruone Kikuyu developed a strong sense of community that formed the basis for united action. A group of leaders emerged. To cement resistance, most Kikuyu settlers were given the KCA oath. The government attempted to implement crop rotation and prohibit grass burning and the growing of maize. The Kikuyu ignored this. The government issued an ultimatum threatening eviction unless the agricultural rules were implemented. The Olenguruone settlers responded by initiating a widespread movement of protest that coincided with the outburst of squatter resistance on the neighboring farms and was to have far-reaching consequences. They initiated a new oath of unity, which subsequently formed the basis for the "Mau Mau" oath, that represented a commitment to defy the government. The whole population of Olenguruone had taken the oath by 1946. Their struggle to use their land as they chose continued until 1950, when the last Kikuyu settlers were evicted and transported to the Yatta area. By this time their fight against the government had become a symbol of anticolonial resistance. On their way to Yatta they had passed through several of the most populated centers of central Kenya. As they traveled they sang songs of resistance, raising the name of Olenguruone to a symbol of national resistance and sacrifice.

4. The phrase "strategy without a strategist" is meant to convey the sense of Foucault's understanding of power relations as "both intentional and nonsubjective": "If in fact they are intelligible, this is not because they are the effect of another instance that 'explains' them, but rather because they are imbued, through and through, with calculation: there is no power that is exercised without a series of aims and objectives. But this does not mean that it results from the choice or decision of an individual subject.... The logic is perfectly clear, the aims decipherable, and yet it is often the case that no one is there to have invented them" (Foucault 1980b: 94–95).

5. At a theoretical level, Chatterjee (1986: 22) suggests that most academic discussions of nationalisms suppress alternative possibilities and the contradictions that nationalism leaves unresolved. At a more concrete level, Furedi (1989) argues that Mau Mau was a truly radical nationalist movement that broke with middle-class nationalism. Because it was a mass movement not susceptible to cooptation, the colonial administration had no choice but to destroy it. The repercussions of suppressed possibilities are being felt today in Kenya and throughout the former colonial world.

6. Kenyatta's role in the Mau Mau rebellion is somewhat ambiguous. At the time, colonial authorities attributed to him a central role, as Carothers's remark indicates, and he was arrested in Operation Jock Scott shortly after the declaration of a state of emergency (Edgerton 1989: 67). Still, it has been suggested that Kenyatta was much less radical than the core of Mau Mau's leadership. Indeed, in August 1952, before the emergency was declared, Kenyatta had publicly denounced Mau Mau (ibid.: 62–63). Discussion of Kenyatta's role can be found in Furedi 1989, Edgerton 1989, and Rosberg and Nottingham 1966.

7. The "Other" had begun to speak not only in Kenya. As Corfield notes, "the Nigerian Government was also faced with a virulent Press which was barely kept in check by action in the courts of law" (1960: 192).

8. Mitchell envisioned that multiracialism as a policy would create a new kind of nation in Africa based upon economic growth as a key in solving the political and social problems in Kenya. Economic growth in turn entailed further large-scale immigration of white settlers and gradual development of African participation. Links with the British government would be required "for generations to come." See Rosberg and Nottingham 1966: 198–207. As Mboya (1956: 32–33) points out, multiracialism maintained the status-quo power structure, was based upon the continuance of racial divisions, and therefore was seen by many Africans as "an impediment to the establishment of democratic rights."

9. The title of Leakey's autobiography is itself revealing: *White African.*

10. As Foucault suggests throughout his work, the idea of enclosure and separation is a widely replicable practice that can take many forms. Villagization in Kenya was based on the experiences of villagization in Malaya. One should also note the similarity to the idea of "strategic hamlets" in Vietnam.

11. Foucault's discussion of the repressive hypothesis is mainly to be found in *The History of Sexuality,* volume 1. For a good elaboration on this see Dreyfus and Rabinow 1983.

12. Askwith's assertion is belied by several facts. Kennedy (1987: 28–29) notes that a 1907 report for Ukamba Province reports that "there is great prosperity among the native population, trade increases yearly and large tracts of country are coming under cultivation for native crops." Maughan-Brown (1985: 84) notes that during the first twenty years of this century Kikuyu squatters not only were able to maintain their position as independent producers but also competed successfully with European settlers. Swainson points out that in 1913 products of black African origin furnished about three-quarters of the country's export earnings: "It was hard to perpetuate the myth of racial supremacy in the face of the true statistics on African agriculture" (1980: 7).

13. See Norris 1987 and Curtis 1962.

6. FOREIGN AID, DEMOCRACY, AND HUMAN RIGHTS

1. This statement is from page 150. I might add that the meticulous procedures Foucault refers to also impose meanings and identities. I believe this is also implied by Foucualt.

2. Lumsdaine (1993: 4) notes that foreign aid has been the largest financial flow to most of the South in the past forty years, far exceeding direct investment.

3. See Lumsdaine 1993, chapters 1 and 2; Shafer 1988, chapter 4; and Packenham 1973.

4. For a discussion of welfare institutions as modalities of social control, see Melossi 1990 and Cohen and Scull 1983.

5. Lumsdaine (1993: 33) makes such a suggestion.

6. This bill authorized funds for the full gamut of nine foreign assistance programs, including military assistance, economic assistance, development loans and grants, and technical assistance. Military assistance to Vietnam was not included in this bill.

7. Procacci makes a contrast between "pauperism" and poverty: "If the tableau of poverty is recognized as defining an urgent political problem, what does 'pauperism' signify in this discourse? What does the category designate and what are its purposes? Pauperism is that kind of indigence which becomes by its extension and intensity a sort of scourge, a permanent nuisance to society. Pauperism is thus poverty intensified to the level of social danger: the spectre of the mob; a collective, essentially urban phenomenon. It is a magma in which are fused all the dangers which beset the social order, shifting along unpredictable, untraceable channels of transmission and aggregation" (1991: 158).

8. Section 502B was the culmination of congressional efforts to put human rights on the foreign policy agenda. Beginning in 1973 Representative Donald Fraser of Minnesota chaired a series of human rights hearings in the House Subcommittee on International Organizations that criticized the administration's disinterest and caught the attention of members of Congress on human rights problems throughout the world (Weissbrodt, March 4, 1977). As a result, a very tentative, one-sentence human rights provision was made in the Foreign Assistance Act of 1973. In 1974 Congress added Section 502B, which stated that "except in extraordinary circumstance, the President shall substantially reduce or terminate security assistance to any government which engages in a consistent pattern of gross violations of internationally recognized human rights" (Breslin, March 4, 1977: 17). Section 502B, the first attempt by Congress to require the State Department to analyze the human rights practices of foreign governments, resulted in some eighty hearings and reports on the subject (Loescher 1977). Secretary of State Henry Kissinger withheld the reports at the last minute, telling Congress that the State Department had found no objective way to distinguish among governments that were violating human rights and had concluded that neither U.S. security nor human rights would be served by the "impaired relations which would follow release of the reports" (Breslin, March 4, 1977: 17).

9. Studies have found little statistical evidence of a relationship between either security or economic assistance and the human rights practices of recipient countries. See Donnelly 1993: 104 and Carleton and Stohl 1985.

10. Donnelly (1993: 182 n. 2) notes that the United States failed to ratify the International Human Rights Covenants, as well as most other international human rights treaties—the International Covenant on Economic, Social, and Cultural Rights, for example. In 1992 the United States did ratify the International Covenant on Civil and Political Rights, more than twenty-five years after it was adopted.

11. In 1977 Congress required that the secretary of state prepare and transmit to Congress, for each fiscal year, a report on the human rights practices of other countries. The report, titled *Country Reports on Human Rights Practices,* now includes information about almost all countries in the world except the United States (Cingranelli 1993: 176).

12. President Reagan's speech to the British Parliament, June 9, 1982. Printed in the *Congressional Record,* vol. 128, part 10, 97th Congress, 2d session.

13. Over 99 percent of the annual NED budget comes from congressional appropriations (Council on Hemispheric Affairs paper: 27). The NED blurs the lines between public and private: it is publicly funded yet privately operated with virtually no congressional oversight.

14. President Clinton elevated the offices responsible for promoting democracy at both the State and Defense Departments and at the National Security Council (*Far Eastern Economic Review,* July 1, 1993: 18). According to Lynn Davis, undersecretary of state, democracy and human rights are top priorities for post–cold war U.S. security assistance policies (*Noticias,* March–April 1994). Even the notorious School of the Americas has added a requirement that U.S. officers conduct human rights classes (*Newsweek,* August 9, 1993).

15. See Miller 1993.

16. See Lawrence Harrison's "Voodoo Politics" (1993).

7. REPETITION AND VARIATION: ACADEMIC DISCOURSES ON NORTH-SOUTH RELATIONS

1. For example, see Luke 1991, Leys 1982, Escobar 1984.

2. Ashley and Walker suggest that the assertion of sovereignty is "always a work of imagination, the assertion announces a question that is tinged with desire: How to fill the void. How to compensate for the lack" (1990: 382). While these texts do indeed work to undermine any sense of sovereignty being a permanent and immutable principle, they simultaneously seek to fill the void of foundational meaning to sovereignty created by "quasi states."

3. Ashley (1995: 32–33), in analyzing Hobbes, suggests that analogies between figures of modern man and the modern sovereign state are far from incidental and are indispensable to modern practices of statecraft. This is borne out not only by Ashley's examination of Hobbes's texts but also by

the previous chapters in this volume; the representations that characterized particular kinds of human beings became the basis for characterizing particular geographic entities, later states.

4. Implicitly, the international community has promoted empirical statehood in the former Yugoslavia. Its failure to lift the arms embargo or to intervene in a more direct and meaningful way has enabled Serbia to use its power capabilities to forcibly take over large portions of Bosnia and in the process to engage in practices such as ethnic cleansing. Surely this, at least silent, enforcement of empirical statehood by the international community sustains a kind of corruption every bit as dangerous as that in some African countries. One might also point to the international community's practical, if not stated, support for Indonesian policy in East Timor as an example of support for empirical statehood that has resulted in the perpetuation of policies of genocide.

5. Krasner (1981) and Murphy (1983) use the phrase "what the third world wants" in book titles.

6. A syntagmatic relationship refers to the relationship a sign entertains with the other signs that surround it—the relationship between the words in a sentence or the sentences in a paragraph, for example.

8. CONCLUSION

1. For exceptions, see Campbell 1992, Weber 1990 and 1992, Klein 1990, Der Derian 1987, and various works of Richard Ashley and R. B. J. Wallace.

2. Campbell makes a similar point, referring to the "academic xenophobia" that is often evident in mainstream international relations efforts to "patrol the intellectual borders which frame the study of world politics" (1992: 246).

3. Goldberg (1993: 148) suggests that race has been a constitutive feature of modernity itself and that racialized distinctions are embedded in reason itself.

Bibliography

BOOKS, JOURNALS, MAGAZINES, NEWSPAPERS

Acheson, Dean. 1950. Address at the University of California at Berkeley, March 16, 1950. Published in *Department of State Bulletin*. March 27.

Adams, Charles Kendall. 1899. Colonies and Other Dependencies. *The Forum*. March.

Agoncilla, Felipe. 1899. Memorial to the Senate of the United States Accompanying Letter to the Secretary of State of January 30, 1899. In Maximo Kalaw, *The Case for the Filipinos*. Century, 1916.

Ajami, Fouad. 1982. "Human Rights and World Order." In *Toward a Just World Order*, ed. Richard Falk, Samuel S. Kim, and Sual K. Mendlovitz. Vol. 1. Boulder, Colo.: Westview.

Alatas, Syed Hussein. 1977. *The Myth of the Lazy Native*. London: Frank Cass.

Anderson, General Thomas M. 1900. Our Rule in the Philippines. *North American Review* 170.

Ashley, Richard K. 1988. Untying the Sovereign State: A Double Reading of the Anarchy Problematique. *Millennium: Journal of International Studies* 17, no. 2: 227–62.

———. 1989. Effecting Global Purpose: Notes on a Problematic of International Organization. In *Global Changes and Theoretical Challenges: Approaches to World Politics in the 1990s*, ed. E. O. Czempiel and J. N. Rosenau. Lexington, Mass.: Lexington Books.

———. 1995. Statecraft as Mancraft. Manuscript in progress.

Ashley, Richard K., and R. B. J. Walker. 1990. Reading Dissidence/Writing the Discipline: Crisis and the Question of Sovereignty in International Studies. *International Studies Quarterly* 34, no. 3: 367–416.

Askwith, Tom. 1958. *Kenya's Progress*. Nairobi: Eagle Press.

Augelli, Enrico, and Craig Murphy. 1988. *America's Quest for Supremacy in the Third World*. London: Pinter.

Austin, J. L. 1975. *How to Do Things with Words*. Cambridge, Mass.: Harvard University Press.

Balibar, Etienne. 1991. "Is There a 'Neo-Racism'?" In Etienne Balibar and Immanuel Wallerstein, *Race, Nation, Class-Ambiguous Identities*. New York: Verso.

Barrett, John. 1899a. America in the Pacific and Far East. *Harpers*. June–November.

———. 1899b. The Value of the Philippines. *Munsey's Magazine*. August 21.

Barthes, Roland. 1974. *S/Z*. Trans. Richard Miller. New York: Hill and Wang.

———. 1987. "Textual Analysis of Poe's 'Valdemar.'" In *Untying the Text,* ed. Robert Young. London: Routledge and Kegan Paul.

Bello, Walden. 1988. "Counterinsurgency's Proving Ground: Low-Intensity Warfare in the Philippines." In *Low Intensity Warfare — Counterinsurgency, Proinsurgency, and Antiterrorism in the Eighties,* ed. Michel T. Klare and Peter Kornbluh. New York: Pantheon.

Bennett, George. 1963. "Imperial Paternalism: The Representation of African Interest in the Kenya Legislative Council." In *Essays in Imperial Government,* ed. Kenneth Robinson and Frederick Madden. Oxford: Basil Blackwell.

Bernstein, David. 1953. Buildup and Letdown in the Philippines. *The Reporter,* April 28.

Bhabha, Homi K. 1983. The Other Question. *Screen* 24, no. 6.

———. 1984. Of Mimicry and Man: The Ambivalence of Colonial Discourse. *October* 28.

———. 1990. Dissemination: Time, Narrative, and the Margins of the Modern Nation. In *Nation and Narration,* ed. Homi K. Bhabha. London: Routledge.

Blaufarb, Douglas S. 1977. *The Counterinsurgency Era: U.S. Doctrine and Performance 1950 to the Present.* New York: Free Press.

Bonner, Raymond. 1987. *Waltzing with a Dictator.* New York: Vintage.

Bourdieu, Pierre. 1985. *Outline of a Theory of Practice.* Cambridge: Cambridge University Press.

Brands, H. W. 1992. *Bound to Empire: The United States and the Philippines.* New York: Oxford University Press.

Brett, E. A. 1973. *Colonial Capitalism and Underdevelopment in East Africa.* New York: NOK.

Bromhead, W. S. 1921. "Kenya Colony: Its Present Prospects and Future Development." *United Empire* 12.

Buell, Raymond Leslie. 1928. *The Native Problem in Africa.* New York: Macmillan.

Bull, Hedley. 1977. *The Anarchical Society.* Macmillan.

Bull, Hedley, and Adam Watson, eds. 1984. *The Expansion of International Society.* Oxford: Oxford University Press.

Butler, Judith. 1990. *Gender Trouble: Feminism and the Subversion of Identity.* New York: Routledge.

Campbell, David. 1992. *Writing Security: United States Foreign Policy and the Politics of Identity.* Minneapolis: University of Minnesota Press.

Carleton, David, and Michael Stohl. 1985. The Foreign Policy of Human Rights. *Human Rights Quarterly,* May 7, 205–29.

Carnegie, Andrew. 1899. Americanism versus Imperialism. *North American Review,* no. 506 (January).

Carothers, J. C. 1955. *The Psychology of Mau Mau.* Nairobi: Government Printer.

Carter, Fay. 1971. "Sir Philip Mitchel." In *Kenya Historical Biographies,* ed. Kenneth King and Ahmed Salim. Nairobi: East Africa Publishing House.

Cell, John W., ed. 1976. *By Kenya Possessed: The Correspondence of Norman Leys and J. H. Oldham 1918–1926.* Chicago: University of Chicago Press.

Chatterjee, Partha. 1986. *Nationalist Thought and the Colonial World: A Derivative Discourse.* Delhi: Oxford University Press.

Cingranelli, David Louis. 1993. *Ethics, American Foreign Policy, and the Third World*. New York: St. Martin's.

Clegg, Stewart R. 1989. *Frameworks of Power*. New York: Sage.

Cohen, Stanley, and Andrew Scull, eds. 1983. *Social Control and the State*. Oxford: Martin Robertson.

Constantino, Renato. 1966. "The Filipinos in the Philippines and Other Essays." In *The Philippines Reader: A History of Colonialism, Neocolonialism, Dictatorship, and Resistance,* ed. Daniel B. Schirmer and Stephen Rosskamm Shalom. Boston: South End Press.

Cox, Robert W. 1983. Gramsci, Hegemony and International Relations: An Essay in Method. *Millennium* 12: 162–75.

Culler, Jonathan. 1982. *Theory and Criticism after Structuralism*. Ithaca, N.Y.: Cornell University Press.

Curtin, Philip D. 1964. *The Image of Africa*. Madison: University of Wisconsin Press.

Curtis, Michael, ed. 1962. *The Great Political Theories*. Vol. 2. New York: Avon.

Daily Telegraph (London). December 12, 1898.

Denby, Charles. 1898. Shall We Keep the Philippines? *The Forum*. November.

———. 1899. What Shall We Do with the Philippines? *The Forum*. March.

Der Derian, James. 1987. *On Diplomacy: A Genealogy of Western Estrangement*. Oxford: Basil Blackwell.

Derrida, Jacques. 1978. "Structure, Sign, and Play in the Discourse of the Human Sciences." In *Writing and Difference,* trans. Alan Bass. Chicago: University of Chicago Press.

———. 1982 (1968). "Differance." In *Margins of Philosophy,* trans. Alan Bass. Chicago: University of Chicago Press.

Dessler, David. 1989. What's at Stake in the Agent-Structure Debate? *International Organization* 43, no. 3.

Donnelly, Jack. 1993. *International Human Rights*. Boulder, Colo.: Westview.

Doty, Roxanne Lynn. 1993. Foreign Policy as Social Construction: A Post-Positivist Analysis of U.S. Counterinsurgency Policy in the Philippines. *International Studies Quarterly* 37, no. 3: 297–320.

Douglas, William O. 1953. *North from Malaya: Adventure on Five Fronts*. New York: Doubleday.

Do Unto Others: Clinton's Human Rights Thrust Abroad Takes Shape. 1993. *Far Eastern Economic Review*. July.

Dreyfus, Hubert L., and Paul Rabinow. 1983. *Michel Foucault: Beyond Structuralism and Hermeneutics*. Chicago: University of Chicago Press.

Drinnon, Richard. 1980. *Facing West: The Metaphysics of Indian-Hating and Empire-Building*. Minneapolis: University of Minnesota Press.

East African Standard. July 3, 1919; July 16, 1919; August 7, 1919; August 13, 1919.

Edgerton, Robert B. 1989. *Mau Mau: An African Crucible*. New York: Free Press.

Eliot, Charles. 1905. *The East Africa Protectorate*. Frank Cass.

Escobar, Arturo. 1984. Discourse and Power in Development: Michel Foucault and the Relevance of His Work to the Third World. *Alternatives* 10: 377–400.

Fifield, Russell H. 1951. The Hukbalahap Today. *Far Eastern Survey* 20, no. 2 (January 24).

Foreman, John. 1899. *The Philippine Islands*. New York: Scribner's.

Foucault, Michel. 1972. *The Archaeology of Knowledge*. Trans. A. M. Sheridan Smith. New York: Pantheon.

———. 1977. "Nietzsche, Genealogy, History." In *Language, Counter-Memory, Practice*. Trans. Donald F. Bouchard and Sherry Simon. Ithaca, N.Y.: Cornell University Press.

———. 1979. *Discipline and Punish: The Birth of the Prison*. New York: Vintage.

———. 1980a. Georges Canguilhem: Philosopher of Error. *Ideology and Consciousness* 7: 53–54.

———. 1980b. *The History of Sexuality*. Vol. I: *An Introduction*. New York: Vintage.

———. 1980c. "Truth and Power." In *Power/Knowledge: Selected Interviews and Other Writings 1972–1977*, ed. Colin Gordon. New York: Pantheon.

———. 1982. "The Subject and Power." Afterword to Hubert L. Dreyfus and Paul Rabinow, *Michel Foucault: Beyond Structuralism and Hermeneutics*. Chicago: University of Chicago Press.

———. 1987. "The Order of Discourse." In *Untying the Text: A Post-Structuralist Reader,* ed. Robert Young. London and New York: Routledge and Kegan Paul.

———. 1988. *Madness and Civilization: A History of Insanity in the Age of Reason.* Translated by Richard Howard. New York: Vintage.

Furedi, Frank. 1989. *The Mau Mau War in Perspective.* Athens: Ohio University Press.

George, Jim. 1989. International Relations and the Search for Thinking Space: Another View of the Third Debate. *International Studies Quarterly* 33, no. 3.

George, Jim, and David Campbell. 1990. Patterns of Dissent and the Celebration of Difference: Critical Social Theory and International Relations. *International Studies Quarterly* 34, no. 3.

Gill, Stephen R., and David Law. 1988. Global Hegemony and the Structural Power of Capital. *International Studies Quarterly* 33, no. 4: 475–500.

Gilman, Sander. 1985. *Difference and Pathology: Stereotypes of Sexuality, Race, and Madness.* Ithaca, N.Y.: Cornell University Press.

Goldberg, David Theo. 1993. *Racist Culture: Philosophy and the Politics of Meaning.* Oxford: Blackwell.

Gordon, Colin. 1991. "Governmental Rationality: An Introduction." In *The Foucault Effect: Studies in Governmentality,* ed. Graham Burchell, Colin Gordon, and Peter Miller. Chicago: University of Chicago Press.

Gramsci, Antonio. 1971. *Selections from the Prison Notebooks.* Edited and translated by Quinton Hoare and Geoffrey Nowell Smith. New York: International.

Gregory, J. W. 1896. *The Great Rift Valley: Being the Narrative of a Journey to Mount Kenya and Lake Baringo.* London: John Murray.

Gregory, Robert G. 1962. *Sidney Webb and East Africa Labour's Experiment of Native Paramountcy.* Berkeley: University of California Press.

Halle, Louis. 1985. *The United States Acquires the Philippines: Consensus vs. Reality.* Lanham, Md.: University Press of America.

Hammond, Dorothy, and Alta Jablow. 1977. *The Myth of Africa.* New York: Library of Social Science.

Harkin, Tom. 1978. "Human Rights and Foreign Aid: Forging an Unbreakable Link." In *Human Rights and U.S. Foreign Policy: Principles and*

Applications, ed. Peter G. Brown and Douglas MacLean. Lexington, Mass.: Lexington Books.

Harrison, Lawrence E. 1993. Voodoo Politics. *Atlantic Monthly* 271, no. 6 (June).

Hetherington, Penelope. 1978. *British Paternalism and Africa, 1920–1940.* London: Frank Cass.

Hinden, Rita. 1949. *Empire and After: A Study in British Imperial Attitudes.* London: Essential Books.

Horseman, Reginald. 1981. *Race and Manifest Destiny: The Origins of American Racial Anglo-Saxonism.* Cambridge, Mass.: Harvard University Press.

Hunt, Michael H. 1987. *Ideology and U.S. Foreign Policy.* New Haven, Conn.: Yale University Press.

Huntington, Samuel P. 1993. The Clash of Civilizations. *Foreign Affairs.* Summer.

Huxley, Elspeth. 1954. The Cause and Cure of Mau Mau. *New Commonwealth* 27, no. 2 (January 18).

———. 1956. "1955 — Re-Assessment." In *Race and Politics in Kenya.* London: Faber and Faber.

Ikenberry, G. John, and Charles Kupchan. 1990. Socialization and Hegemonic Power. *International Organization* 44, no. 3.

Ingham, Kenneth. 1962. *A History of East Africa.* New York: Praeger.

Jackson, Robert H. 1987. Quasi-States, Dual Regimes, and Neoclassical Theory: International Jurisprudence and the Third World. *International Organization* 41, no. 4: 519–49.

———. 1990. *Quasi-States: Sovereignty, International Relations and the Third World.* Cambridge: Cambridge University Press.

———. 1993. "The Weight of Ideas in Decolonization: Normative Change in International Relations." In *Ideas and Foreign Policy: Beliefs, Institutions, and Political Change,* ed. Judith Goldstein and Robert O. Keohane. Ithaca, N.Y.: Cornell University Press.

Jackson, Robert H., and Carl G. Rosberg. 1982. Why Africa's Weak States Persist: The Empirical and the Juridical in Statehood. *World Politics* 35, no. 1.

———. 1986. Sovereignty and Underdevelopment: Juridical Statehood in the African Crisis. *Journal of Modern African Studies* 24, no. 1: 1–31.

———. 1987. Quasi-States, Dual Regimes, and Neoclassical Theory: International Jurisprudence and the Third World. *International Organization* 41, no. 4: 519–49.

Jara, René, and Nicholas Spadaccini. 1989. Allegorizing the New World. In *1492–1992: Re/Discovering Colonial Writing*, ed. René Jara and Nicholas Spadaccini. Minneapolis: University of Minnesota Press.

Jeffords, Susan. 1989. *The Remasculinization of America: Gender and the Vietnam War.* Bloomington: Indiana University Press.

Jordan, David Starr. 1901. *Imperial Democracy.* New York: Appleton.

Kalaw, Maximo M. 1916. *The Case for the Filipinos.* New York: Century.

Kariuki, J. M. 1963. *Mau Mau Detainee: The Account by a Kenya African of His Experience in Detention Camps, 1953–1960.* London: Oxford University Press.

Karnow, Stanley. 1989. *In Our Image: America's Empire in the Philippines.* New York: Random House.

Katzenstein, Peter. 1985. Back cover of Stephen Krasner, *Structural Conflict: The Third World against Global Liberalism.* Berkeley: University of California Press.

Kennedy, Dane. 1987. *Islands of White. Settler Society and Culture in Kenya and Southern Rhodesia, 1890–1939.* Durham, N.C.: Duke University Press.

Kennon, Colonel L. W. V. 1901. The Katipunan of the Philippines. *North American Review* 173.

Kenya Daily Mail, October 10 and 20, 1952.

Kerkvliet, Benedict J. 1977. *The Huk Rebellion: A Study of Peasant Revolt in the Philippines.* Berkeley: University of California Press.

Kidd, Benjamin. 1898. *Control of the Tropics.* New York: Scribner's.

Klare, Michael T., and Peter Kornbluh, eds. 1988. *Low Intensity Warfare: Counterinsurgency, Proinsurgency, and Antiterrorism in the Eighties.* New York: Pantheon.

Klein, Bradley. 1990. How the West Was One: Representational Politics of NATO. *International Studies Quarterly* 34, no. 3 (September): 311–26.

Kolko, Gabriel. 1988. *Confronting the Third World: U.S. Foreign Policy 1945–1980*. New York: Pantheon.

Krasner, Stephen D. 1981. Transforming International Regimes: What the Third World Wants and Why. *International Studies Quarterly* 25, no. 1: 119–48.

———. 1985. *Structural Conflict: The Third World against Global Liberalism*. Berkeley: University of California Press.

Laclau, Ernesto. 1990. "The Impossibility of Society." In Ernesto Laclau, *New Reflections on the Revolution of Our Time*. London: Verso.

Laclau, Ernesto, and Chantal Mouffe. 1985. *Hegemony and Socialist Strategy: Towards a Radical Democratic Politics*. London: Verso.

———. 1990. "Post-Marxism without Apologies." In Ernesto Laclau, *New Reflections on the Revolution of Our Time*. London: Verso.

Lakoff, George, and Mark Johnson. 1980. *Metaphors We Live By*. Chicago and London: University of Chicago Press.

Leakey, Louis B. 1954. *Defeating Mau Mau*. London: Methuen.

Lee, J. M. 1967. *Colonial Development and Good Government*. Oxford: Clarendon.

Legum, Colin. 1965. *Pan-Africanism*. London: Pall Mall.

Leigh, Ione. 1954. *In the Shadow of Mau Mau*. London: Allen.

Leys, Colin. 1982. Samuel Huntington and the End of Modernization Theory. In *Introduction to the Sociology of "Developing Societies,"* ed. Hamza Alavi and Teodor Shanin. New York: Monthly Review Press.

Louis, Wm. Roger. 1984. The Era of the Mandates System and the Non-European World. In *The Expansion of International Society*, ed. Hedley Bull and Adam Watson. Oxford: Clarendon.

Lugard, Sir Frederick. 1922. *The Dual Mandate in British Tropical Africa*. London: Cass.

Luke, Timothy W. 1991. The Discourse of Development: A Genealogy of "Developing Nations" and the Discipline of Modernity. *Current Perspectives in Social Theory* 2: 271–93.

Lumsdaine, David Halloran. 1993. *Moral Vision in International Politics: The Foreign Aid Regime 1949–1989*. Princeton, N.J.: Princeton University Press.

MacArthur, General Douglas. 1951. Address to the Congress, April 19. In *The Shaping of American Diplomacy: Readings and Documents in American Foreign Relations 1750–1955*, ed. William Appleman Williams. Chicago: Rand McNally, 1956.

Maughan-Brown, David. 1980. Myth and Mau Mau." *Theoria* 55 (October).

———. 1985. *Land, Freedom and Fiction: History and Ideology in Kenya.* London: Zed.

Maxon, R. M. 1980. *John Ainsworth and the Making of Kenya.* Washington, D.C.: University Press of America.

Mboya, Tom. 1956. *The Kenya Question: An African Answer.* London: Fabian Colonial Bureau.

———. 1963. *Freedom and After.* Boston: Little, Brown.

McGregor Ross, W. 1927. *Kenya from Within.* London: Allen and Unwin.

McKinley, William. *Speeches and Addresses of William McKinley from March 1, 1897, to May 30, 1900.* New York: Doubleday and McClure.

Melossi, Dario. 1990. *The State of Social Control.* Oxford: Polity.

Miller, Judith. 1993. The Challenge of Radical Islam. *Foreign Affairs* 72, no. 2 (Spring).

Milliken, Jennifer L., and David J. Sylvan. 1991. "Soft Bodies, Hard Targets, and Chic Theories: U.S. Bombing Policy in Indochina." Presented at the 15th World Congress of the International Political Science Association, July 21–25, Buenos Aires.

Mitchell, Sir Philip. 1954. *African Afterthoughts.* London: Hutchinson.

Mockaitis, Thomas R. 1990. *British Counterinsurgency, 1919–1960.* London: Macmillan.

Morrison, Toni. 1992. *Playing in the Dark.* Cambridge, Mass.: Harvard University Press.

Mosley, Paul. 1983. *The Settler Economies: Studies in the Economic History of Kenya and Southern Rhodesia 1900–1963.* Cambridge: Cambridge University Press.

Mudimbe, V. Y. 1988. *The Invention of Africa.* Bloomington: Indiana University Press.

Murphy, Craig N. 1983. What the Third World Wants: An Interpretation of the Development and Meaning of the New International Economic Order Ideology. *International Studies Quarterly* 27, no. 1: 55–76.

Myrdal, Gunnar. 1970. *The Challenge of World Poverty: A World Anti-Poverty Program in Outline.* New York: Vintage.

Native Labour in Africa. 1920. *New Statesman: A Weekly Review of Politics and Literature* 15 (April 15).

New York Times, October 29, 1989.

Noer, Thomas J. 1985. *Cold War and Black Liberation: The United States and White Rule in Africa, 1948–1968.* Columbia: University of Missouri Press.

Norris, Christopher. 1987. *Derrida.* Cambridge, Mass.: Harvard University Press.

Noticias 10, no. 2. 1994. Published by the Valley Religious Task Force on Central America.

Odinga, Oginga. 1967. *Not Yet Uhuru.* London: Heinemann.

Oldham, J. H. 1921. Christian Missions and African Labour. *International Review of Missions* 10.

Onuf, Nicholas, and Frank F. Klink. 1989. Anarchy, Authority, Rule. *International Studies Quarterly* 33, no. 2: 149–74.

Packenham, Robert A. 1973. *Liberal America and the Third World.* Princeton, N.J.: Princeton University Press.

Paget, Julian. 1967. *Counter-Insurgency Operations: Techniques of Guerrilla Warfare.* New York: Walker.

Pasquino, Pasquale. 1991. "Theatrum Politicum: The Genealogy of Capital — Police and the State of Prosperity." In *The Foucault Effect: Studies in Governmentality,* ed. Graham Burchell, Colin Gordon, and Peter Miller. Chicago: University of Chicago Press.

Perham, Margery. 1956a. Foreword to Tom Mboya, *The Kenya Question: An African Answer.* London: Fabian Colonial Bureau.

———. 1956b. "1955 — Re-Assessment." In *Race and Politics in Kenya.* London: Faber and Faber.

———. 1963. Introduction to J. M. Karuiki, *Mau Mau Detainee: The Account by a Kenya African of this Experience in Detention Camps, 1953–1960.* London: Oxford University Press.

Pietz, William. 1988. The "Post-Colonialism" of Cold War Discourse. *Social Text* 19/20 (Fall).

Procacci, Giovanna. 1991. "Social Economy and the Government of Poverty." In *The Foucault Effect: Studies in Governmentality*, ed. Graham Burchell, Colin Gordon, and Peter Miller. Chicago: University of Chicago Press.

Ravenholt, Albert. 1951. The Philippines: Where Did We Fail? *Foreign Affairs*, April.

Reid, Whitelaw. 1900. *Problems of Expansion as Considered in Papers and Addresses*. New York: Century.

Rosberg, Carl G., and John Nottingham. 1963. *The Myth of "Mau Mau": Nationalism in Kenya*. New York: Praeger.

———. 1966. *The Myth of Mau Mau: Nationalism in Kenya*. New York: Praeger.

Rosenstiel, Annette. 1954. An Anthropological Approach to the Mau Mau Problem. *Political Science Quarterly* 68 (Spring).

Rostow, Walt Whitman. 1960. *The Stages of Economic Growth: A Non-Communist Manifesto*. Cambridge: Cambridge University Press.

Ruark, Robert. 1955. *Something of Value*. London: Hamish Hamilton.

"Running a 'School for Dictators,' " *Newsweek*, August 9, 1993.

Said, Edward. 1979. *Orientalism*. New York: Vintage.

———. 1993. *Culture and Imperialism*. New York: Knopf.

Schirmer, Daniel B., and Stephen Rosskamm Shalom. 1987. *The Philippines Reader: A History of Colonialism, Neocolonialism, Dictatorship, and Resistance*. Boston: South End Press.

Schurz, Carl. 1899. "American Imperialism." In *Republic or Empire: The Philippine Question*, ed. William Jennings Bryan. Chicago: Independence.

Searle, John. 1969. *Speech Acts*. Cambridge: Cambridge University Press.

Shafer, D. Michael. 1988. *Deadly Paradigms: The Failure of U.S. Counterinsurgency Policy*. Princeton, N.J.: Princeton University Press.

Shapiro, Michael J. 1988. *The Politics of Representation: Writing Practices in Biography, Photography, and Policy Analysis*. Madison: University of Wisconsin Press.

Snow, Donald M. 1993. *Distant Thunder: Third World Conflict and the New International Order*. New York: St. Martin's.

Spivak, G. 1976. Preface to *Of Grammatology*. Baltimore: Johns Hopkins University Press.

Spurr, David. 1993. *The Rhetoric of Empire: Colonial Discourse in Journalism, Travel Writing, and Imperial Administration*. Durham, N.C.: Duke University Press.

Staley, Eugene. 1961. *The Future of Underdeveloped Countries: Political Implications of Economic Development*. New York: Praeger.

Stavrianos, L. S. 1981. *Global Rift: The Third World Comes of Age*. New York: Morrow.

Stephan, Nancy Leys. 1990. "Race and Gender: The Role of Analogy in Science." In *Anatomy of Racism*, ed. David Goldberg. Minneapolis: University of Minnesota Press.

Stoneham, Charles T. 1955. *Out of Barbarism*. London: Museum Press.

Storey, Moorfield. 1901. Speech at Brookline, October 26, 1900. In *Our New Departure*. Boston: George H. Ellis.

Strang, David. 1991. Anomaly and Commonplace in European Expansion: Realist and Institutional Accounts. *International Organization* 45 (Spring): 143–62.

Swainson, Nicola. 1980. *The Development of Corporate Capitalism in Kenya 1918–1977*. Berkeley: University of California Press.

Swift, Morrison I. 1899. *Imperialism and Liberty*. Los Angeles: Ronbroke.

Tignor, Robert L. 1976. *The Colonial Transformation of Kenya: The Kamba, Kikuyu and Maasi from 1900 to 1939*. Princeton, N.J.: Princeton University Press.

Times (London), October 8 and December 12, 1898; July 9, 1920; October 29 and 30, 1952.

Todorov, Tzvetan. 1984. *The Conquest of America*. Translated by Richard Howard. New York: Harper.

Torgovnick, Marianna. 1990. *Gone Primitive: Savage Intellects, Modern Lives*. Chicago: University of Chicago Press.

Truman, Harry. 1946. *Department of State Bulletin*, July 14.

Tucker, Robert W. 1977. *The Inequality of Nations.* New York: Basic Books.

Twain, Mark. 1901. To the Person Sitting in Darkness. *North American Review,* no. 521 (February).

U.S. News and World Report, June 27, 1950.

Van Zwanenburg, R. M. A. 1975. *Colonial Capitalism and Labour in Kenya 1919–1939.* Kampala: East African Literature Bureau.

Walker, R. B. J. 1989. History and Structure in the Theory of International Relations. *Millennium* 18, no. 2.

————. 1993. *Inside/Outside: International Relations as Political Theory.* Cambridge: Cambridge University Press.

Wallerstein, Immanuel. 1979. *The Capitalist World Economy.* London: Cambridge University Press.

Weber, Cynthia. 1990. Representing Debt: Peruvian Presidents Balaunder's and Garcia's Reading/Writing of Peruvian Debt. *International Studies Quarterly* 34, no. 3.

————. 1992. Writing Sovereign Identities: Wilson Administration Intervention in the Mexican Revolution. *Alternatives* 17, no. 3.

Welbourn, F. B. 1961. Comment on Corfield. *Race* 2, no. 2 (May).

Welch, Richard E. Jr. 1971. *George Frisbie Hoar and the Half-Breed Republicans.* Cambridge, Mass.: Harvard University Press.

————. 1979. *Response to Imperialism: The United States and the Philippine-American War, 1899–1902.* Chapel Hill: University of North Carolina Press.

————. 1984. "America's Philippine Policy in the Quirino Years (1948–1953): A Study in Patron-Client Diplomacy." In *Reappraising an Empire: New Perspectives on Philippine-American History,* ed. Peter W. Stanley. Cambridge, Mass.: Harvard University Press.

Wendt, Alexander. 1987. The Agent-Structure Problem. *International Organization* 41, no. 3.

————. 1992. Anarchy Is What States Make of It: The Social Construction of Power Politics. *International Organization* 46, no. 2: 391–425.

White, Luise. 1988. "Separating the Men from the Boys: Colonial Constructions of Gender, Sexuality, and Terrorism in Central Kenya, 1939–

1959." Paper delivered at the Wenner-Gren Foundation for Anthropological Research International Symposium, Mijas, Spain.

Wilcox, Marion. 1900. The Filipino's Vain Hope of Independence. *North American Review* 171.

Wittgenstein, L. 1953. *Philosophical Investigations.* Trans. G. E. M. Anscombe. New York: Macmillan.

Wolf, Eric R. 1982. *Europe and the People without History.* Los Angeles: University of California Press.

Worcester, Dean C. 1921. *Philippines Past and Present.* New York: Macmillan.

Wyatt, E. G. 1953. "Mau Mau and the African Mind." *Contemporary Review,* October.

Wylie, Diana. 1977. Confrontation over Kenya: The Colonial Office and Its Critics 1918–1940. *Journal of African History* 18: 427–47.

Young, Robert. 1990. *White Mythologies: Writing History and the West.* London: Routledge.

BRITISH GOVERNMENT DOCUMENTS

Bishops' Memorandum, November 1, 1919. Cmd. 873.

Conference of British Missionary Societies to Milner. June 18, 1920. CO533/248/30445 (Cell, p. 149–50).

Corfield, F. D., chief native commissioner. 1960. Report on Native Affairs for Kenya. *Historical Survey of the Origins and Growth of Mau Mau.* London: HMSO. Command Paper 1030.

Despatch to the Officer Administering the Government of the Kenya Colony and Protectorate Relating to Native Labour, September 1921. Government White Paper. Cmd. 1509.

Great Britain Parliamentary Debates. House of Commons, April 20, 1920; October 16 and 21 and November 7, 1952.

Great Britain Parliamentary Debates. House of Lords, July 14, 1920.

Labour Circular No. 1. October 23, 1919. Cmd. 873.

Labour Circular No. 2, February 17, 1920. Cmd. 873.

Labour Circular No. 3, July 14, 1920. Cmd. 873.

Masters and Servants Ordinance and Amendments. 1910. Appendix 1 to Cmd. 873.

Native Authority Ordinance and Amendments. Cmd. 1509.

Ormsby-Gore, W. 1925. Report of the East Africa Commission. London: His Majesty's Stationery Office. Cmd. 2387.

Palmer, Sir Leslie. 1952. *Hansards Parliamentary Debates.* House of Commons, November 7.

UNITED STATES GOVERNMENT DOCUMENTS

American Embassy, Airgramm to Department of State, June 21, 1966.

Central Intelligence Agency Report. November 20, 1953.

Congressional Record. 55th Congress, 3d session, 1898–99.

Congressional Record. 56th Congress, 1st session, 1899–1900.

Congressional Record. 57th Congress, 2d session, 1900–1.

Congressional Record. 73rd Congress, 2d session, March 21, 1934.

Congressional Record. 79th Congress, 2d session, July 2 and 5, 1946.

Congressional Record. 89th Congress, 2d session, July 12, 1966 (15327–45); July 13, 1966 (15404–76); July 14, 1966 (15709–48); July 26, 1966 (17057–76).

Congressional Record. 94th Congress, 2d session, Senate, April 12, 1976 (10418–20).

Congressional Record. 95th Congress, 1st session, October 19, 1977 (34092–115).

Council on Hemispheric Affairs. 1990. Paper 27: "National Endowment for Democracy."

Craig, Glenn. 1950. Attachment to the Military Group Joint MDAP Survey Mission to Southeast Asia. *Army Interim Report on Philippine Islands.* September 25, RG330, Box 74, Folder 000.5–333 Philippines. National Archives.

Current Intelligence Weekly. November 20, 1953. CIA: Office of Current Intelligence, OCI no. 1026.

Forbes, J. T. 1950. *Report to Chairman of Joint MDAP Survey Mission on the Philippines.* September 29, RG330, Box 74, Folder 000.5–333 Philippines. National Archives.

Foreign Assistance and Related Agencies Appropriations for 1978, part 3, 605–45. H181–78. July 1977.

Foreign Relations of the United States. 1950. Vol. 6. Department of State Publication. Washington, D.C.: Government Printing Office.

Foreign Relations of the United States. 1951. Vol. 6, parts 1 and 2. Department of State Publication. Washington, D.C.: Government Printing Office.

Foreign Relations of the United States. 1952–54. Vol. 12, part 1. Department of State Publication. Washington, D.C.: Government Printing Office.

Hoar, George. *Congressional Record*. 55th Congress, 3d session, 1898–99.

Holbrooke, Richard. 1977. Testimony before the Subcommittee on International Organizations of the Committee on International Relations, U.S. House of Representatives, Foreign Affairs and National Defense Division, July 25.

House Report 95–417. 1978. *Foreign Assistance and Related Programs Appropriations Bill*. June 15, 1977.

Human Rights and United States Policy: Argentina, Haiti, Indonesia, Iran, Peru, and the Philippines. December 31, 1976. CIS# H462–52.

MacArthur, General Douglas. *Congressional Record,* July 5, 1946.

Massachusetts Institute of Technology, Report No. 17, 1968. *The Role of Popular Participation in Development*. Report of the Conference on the Implementation of Title IX of the Foreign Assistance Act, June 24–August 2, 1968. Cambridge, Mass.: MIT Press.

McDonough, Gordon L., congressman from California. Appendix to *Congressional Record*. 79th Congress, 2d session, July 2, 1946.

National Security Council. 1950. *A Report to the National Security Council by the Executive Secretary on "The Position of the United States with Respect to the Philippines."* November 6. NSC84/1.

Nelson, David. *Congressional Record*. 55th Congress, 3d session, 1898–99.

Office of Intelligence Research (OIR). 1950. *The Hukbalahap*. Report #5209. July. Department of State.

Office of Intelligence Research (OIR). 1952. *A Survey of the Philippines. Background Information for the USIE Country Plan for the Philippines*. April 15. Department of State.

Philippine Commission. 1900. *Report of the Philippine Commission.* Vol. 1 and 2. Also printed as Senate Document 138, 56th Congress, 1st session. Washington, D.C.: Government Printing Office.

Reagan, Ronald. 1992. Speech to British Parliament, June 9. *Congressional Record.* 97th Congress, 2d session (13234).

Renewed Concern for Democracy and Human Rights: Special Bicentennial Program. 1976. Report on the 10th meeting of members of Congress and the European Parliamentarians. September.

Review of the World Situation 1949–1950. Hearings held in executive session before the Committee on Foreign Relations, U.S. Senate, 81st Congress, 1st and 2d sessions. Historical Series. Washington, D.C.: Government Printing Office.

Shifting Balance of Power in Asia: Implications for Future U.S. Policy. Hearings before the Subcommittee on International Relations, House of Representatives, 94th Congress, November 18 and December 10, 1975; January 28, March 8, April 7, and May 18, 1976. Y4.In8/16:As4/2.

The Status of Human Rights in Selected Countries and the U.S. Response. 1977. Prepared for the Subcommittee on International Organizations of the Committee on International Relations, U.S. House of Representatives, by the Foreign Affairs and National Defense Division. July 25. Y4.In8/16:H88/21.

Turner, Augustus. *Congressional Record.* 55th Congress, 3d session, 1898–99.

Van Fleet Mission to the Far East. April 26–August 7, 1954. Report of the mission.

Villamin, Vicente. "The New Philippine Republic." Appendix to *Congressional Record.* 79th Congress, 2d session, July 2, 1946.

White, Henry. 1898. Correspondence with U.S. Secretary of State John Hay. December 14.

Index

Roxanne Lynn Doty is an assistant professor of political science at Arizona State University. She is the author of several journal articles, including "Foreign Policy as Social Construction: A Post-Positivist Analysis of the U.S. Counterinsurgency Policy in the Philippines" (*International Studies Quarterly*, September 1993) and "The Bounds of 'Race' in International Relations" (*Millennium Journal of International Studies*, Winter 1993). She is currently working on a project on state responses to global migration.